Human Resource Management
in the Multinational Company

Human Resource Management in the Multinational Company

R. L. DESATNICK & M. L. BENNETT
Edited by Raymond Maddison

Gower Press

Published by .
GOWER PRESS, Teakfield Limited,
Westmead, Farnborough, Hants, England

ISBN 0 566 02003 3

Typeset in IBM Press Roman and Univers by
Preface Limited, Salisbury, Wiltshire.
Printed in Great Britain by
by Biddles Ltd, Guildford, Surrey

Contents

Preface

The explosive growth of the multinational company has led to much concern world-wide, and justifiably, in view of the economic dominance by those companies of millions of human beings.

The foreign output of multinational companies is expanding at the rate of 10 per cent per year: more than twice the growth rate of the world GNP, and 40 per cent faster than world exports. Well-informed observers predict that by the year 2000 the largest 200—300 multinational companies, being concentrated in technologically advanced industries, will account for half the world's output. Yet more than half the world's population lives at or below subsistence level. Has science and technology made its proper contribution to world development? Certainly the multi-national will have to contribute to redressing this imbalance. Social responsibility must become a major objective of the multinationals: 'outcome' as well as 'output' must feature in business planning.

There are many valid reasons why organizations become multinational and the crossing of national boundaries can occur in different ways. It may involve the movement of people, products, services or capital. It frequently involves the acquistion of, or merger with, a foreign company. It often involves the sale of technical and/or managerial know-how. It could simply be the result of diversification, to avoid total reliance on a single product line.

Commercially, there will be a good reason for going multinational. Perhaps the domestic market for the goods or services is saturated, or cheaper labour offers higher profit margins abroad, or foreign countries offer export subsidies, or scarce raw materials are easier to obtain: there may be opportunities for horizontal or vertical integration, a ready market for goods and services, or encouragement from foreign governments by way of tax relief.

Statistical data is scarce, but one fact is clear: that too often going multinational leads to business failure. A recent study of 407 European acquisitions made by 84 US, French, UK, and German companies showed that results were unsatisfactory in more than 50 per cent of cases, as measured by executives, in terms of preacquisition goals.

The authors submit that the primary causes of failure in multinational ventures stem from a lack of understanding of the essential differences in managing human resources, at all levels, in foreign environments. Certain management philosophies and techniques have proved successful in the domestic environment: their application in a foreign environment too often leads to frustration, failure and underachievement. These 'human' considerations are as important as the financial and marketing criteria upon which so many decisions to undertake multinational ventures depend.

The present book analyses the critical differences between operating in the domestic and a foreign environment, and details their implications for managerial success or failure. It is built on the case study of a large American multinational company, which initially failed to meet these challenges, then recognized its failure, and subsequently met with a high degree of success. An attempt is made to diagnose, on a broad global basis, the following essential human resources considerations:

Cultural and linguistic differences.
Social differences.
Educational differences.
Technological differences.
Climatic differences.
Union/workforce attitudes.
Political/governmental attitudes.
Differences in management practices.

The likely effect of each factor on the success of business operations is studied.

Managers often fail to recognize, however, that despite these differences, there is an underlying universality of human needs, significant in all business environments. That universality is also carefully defined, for it must be recognized and provided for, just as much as local differences must be recognized and taken into account.

This book is based primarily on the authors' own experiences; their discussions with executives of other companies; their observations while working for four years for a multinational company in more than twenty-five countries: this experience is backed by extensive research in the current literature. The authors' experiences have allowed them to delineate the qualities needed by domestic executives for successful adaptation for a foreign environment.

While the emphasis is upon the improvement of productivity and human satisfaction through *adaptation* to the foreign environment, the *key* to success is shown to be the local manager, and his crucial relationship (as part-owner or manager) with the parent company. The corporate boss may be thousands of miles away from the day-to-day operations of the foreign subsidiary, agent, factory, customer or representative. Hence, the proper selection of the local manager, and his training and development, is critical. Where the local manager is not selected but acquired, perhaps through a takeover, suggestions are made on how to educate him in the new corporate and management style.

The needs of employees sent abroad are analysed. Appropriate strategies for manpower planning and forecasting, career development, total compensation and repatriation are suggested, based on careful research, trial and error, and the current practices of successful multinational companies.

Much attention is paid to the development of local human resources, which is particularly important because of the wave of nationalism now prevalent. Guidelines are provided for the transfer of managerial expertise, and on adapting modern management methods and techniques to the local environment.

Because international management development is now a major preoccupation of multinational organizations, a separate chapter is devoted to this important subject. Finally, an attempt is made to identify and analyse those trends in human resource management which are of particular significance to the multinational company in its bid for profits and growth from foreign sources.

It is hoped that the enlightened multinational company will realize that its profit objectives will not be attained unless it becomes the moving force in integrating its goals with those of the individual and the particular society in which he lives.

Note For simplicity's sake the authors have used 'man' and 'he' throughout the book to stand for 'man or woman' and 'he or she'.

RLD
MLB

DEDICATION

Just a note of warm, sincere appreciation:

1   *Dr I. GEORGE BLAKE,* Professor Emeritus in History, Franklin College, Franklin, Indiana, without whose constant encouragement and confidence I would never have completed a college education, and hence this book would not have been written.

R. L. Desatnick

2   *MR DENIS CULLINAN,* former Personnel Director of Norton Abrasives Ltd, who gave me my first opportunity to work in professional human resource management. His guidance, professionalism and dedication made my career possible.

M. L. Bennett

PART ONE
THE NEED

1

The multinational environment

The growth of the multinational company and its future in world society has become the subject of serious discussion everywhere. Clearly, the multinational company can no longer, as in the past, pursue in isolation its goals of expanding markets, lower production costs and increasing profitability. It has become such a significant factor in the social system that unless it accepts its social responsibilities, and discharges them effectively, it may well find itself an appendage of government. The danger exists and must be recognized.

While this book concentrates on the more narrowly defined aspects of human resource management in the multinational environment (which are to improve human satisfaction while increasing productivity and profitability), the principles that emerge are relevant to the building of systems of total integration between technology and society and are important as a basis for global planning.

The local operating company, whether in Europe, the Middle East, the Far East, Latin America or Africa, can legitimately be seen as a microcosm of a greater entity: the nation, the region or the world. If the operating environment, on a local basis, is understood, that understanding is translatable to other socioeconomic systems, international in scope. The opportunities are abundant; yet, somehow, management persists in provincial thinking, insisting for example that 'our' management practices are both directly applicable and far superior. This is true regardless of the environment, and regardless of whether the multinational is by origin American, French, German, Italian, British, Dutch or Japanese.

Advanced industrialized countries contain many second-generation industries which have progressed beyond the era of mass production and are now in a post-industrial era. The problems of mass technology have been solved, but its leaders are still virtually blind to the importance of the human factor in their planning to capture new markets, start up production operations, and make large capital commitments to new ventures. It is the importance of this human factor that is the subject of this book Its appreciation is the key to commercial success.

The biggest obstacles to success are *internal* rather than *external*: they lie within the multinational itself. It is *not* primarily the obstacles of local government bodies, or labour unions *per se*, or a lack of expatriate management sophistication. It is rather a distrust of foreigners, resistance to 'foreign' ideas and business techniques, poor communications and a mutual lack of understanding. It is not the responsibility of the host country to attempt to bridge these gaps in understanding and communication, but it is the *first* responsibility of the foreign businessman

While some firms have finally abandoned the ethnocentric idea that only their own executives can successfully manage foreign subsidiaries, many still persist in this attitude, despite one disastrous failure after another. Nevertheless, the more progressive companies have also recognized that staffing subsidiary companies only with local nationals can also be a disadvantage: it deprives the firm of globally-minded top managers.

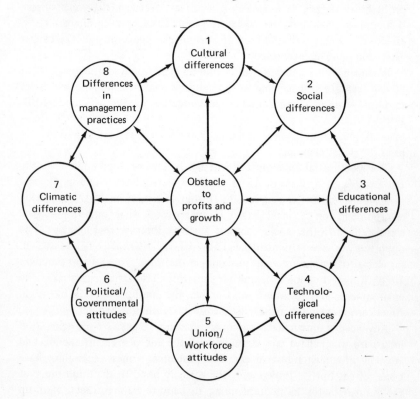

Figure 1 : 1

The parent company must, of course, exercise some on-the-spot protection and control of its investment: it should be less a matter of concern whether that control is exercised by a foreign or local national. What is of primary concern is the attitude of the parent corporation towards its foreign subsidiary: that attitude is demonstrated by the behaviour of the foreign service employee on indefinite or temporary transfer to a foreign location, or by 'visiting firemen'; the task force, for example, sent to 'straighten out' foreign subsidiaries in difficulties.

The world is presently faced with a leadership crisis; governments are toppling, businesses and institutions have an acute shortage of professional managers. Executive search activity is growing by leaps and bounds all over the world, even in those countries where executive mobility has up to now been virtually unknown. The intelligent multinational company no longer pays lip service to global management development, but is indeed providing the resources, both material and human, to make it happen.

Yet, despite all this concern, too many foreign executives fail: it is estimated that 30–50 per cent of all US expatriates, for example, sent on overseas assignments return before the scheduled completion of their assignments. Why? The reasons for failure are graphically depicted in Figure 1 : 1. These differences create barriers to effective two-way communication and understanding. They arouse mutual suspicions, distrust, and eventually hostility. Although they are treated here separately for diagnosis and analysis, they are in practice of course closely interrelated.

1.1 Cultural/Social differences

A number of factors need consideration here. For example, the language barrier is formidable. Yet it is surprising how many expatriate employees make no effort to learn the language of the host country to which they are indefinitely or temporarily assigned. Thus there can be no communication with the lower levels of management and workers – most of whom do not speak the language of the foreign parent company.

In many cultures throughout the world, authority is inherited in business and government. Key positions are filled, in these traditional cultures, from certain families: hence authority is vested in the person himself, rather than in the position he holds. Regardless of the work assigned to them, such individuals expect the same respect as they receive socially in their local communities. Thus it can be difficult to ask young university graduates to undergo dirty or manual training: they would consider it degrading. This is true in most of Latin America and in certain parts of the Far East. What one society values as family loyalty, another condemns as nepotism. When a company is acquired, numerous relatives, family members and friends may be found employed in sensitive positions. These employment patterns need to be analysed: often they can then be used advantageously to influence attitudes and cultural change.

Every 'foreign' community naturally feels its own way of life and cultural values are the best. Overseas managers who disparage the local way of life can expect little cooperation and a poor performance from employees. The experience of western managers from highly industrialized countries strongly indicates that basic cultural influences will often make local nationals behave differently when placed in comparable positions. Local managers often come from family-dominated companies and hence lack both experience and the perspective to carry broad managerial responsibilities. Again, in the less developed countries (and in many developed countries), cultural traditions lead to a lack of positive initiative, and inability or at least a reluctance to communicate with subordinates, an aversion to hard, dirty work and long hours. There may also be a lack of imagination and creativity, and a strict adherence to almost sacred traditions, work practices and systems — however ineffective these may appear to western eyes. In some countries, when a young man gets his engineering degree, he expects immediately to have a large office, staff, secretaries, and all the trappings of authority, even though he has had no managerial, supervisory or business training.

Even when local nationals speak the same language as their parent corporate owners, differences in cultural background can lead to a failure properly to interpret and apply head office directives. Most local nationals are proud and often afraid to seek clarification, even when they do not understand what is wanted and so, for example, a management report will be incorrectly completed. Again, the concept of delegation or teamwork is virtually unknown in a number of cultures.

Management as a distinct progression is only about 20 years old in the United States: in many countries it is still not considered a prestigious occupation. Its role in the culture has not been defined clearly, if at all. Young people of merit will go into government or military service; they will study engineering, law or medicine. The local cultural pattern does not recognize the status of the professional manager, unless he is an owner-entrepreneur. This affects the quality of people willing to accept management positions or trainee-type assignments.

Western management often makes the effort to introduce and maintain high levels of morale and commitment to organization goals among local employees. If they do not understand the relationship between overt behaviour and cultural patterns, they tend to view employee deviations from management expectations as deliberate mistakes, negligence, or sabotage, and hence seek to bring about corrective behaviour through the use of their managerial authority. This is then regarded as an attempt by arrogant foreigners to reduce the human dignity of the members of the local culture. The result is mutual frustration and more antagonism. Local employees need a great deal more reassurance than criticism: it must not be assumed that a local work force will automatically commit itself to the foreign management's goals, which often conflict with traditional habits, attitudes, and work values.

Social factors can provoke further difficulties for foreign managers. The social system in any country reflects the society's attitudes towards status, prestige, position and wealth. In many countries there is still a social structure without a middle class. The concept of social status is reflected in business or industry in a variety of ways. For example, the top man often receives 100–200 per cent more total remuneration than any of the subordinates reporting directly to him. In such social systems, closely related to the cultural structure, authoritarian behaviour is the rule. Subordinates may tend to view consultation and participation in management decisions as demonstrating ignorance or weakness in the general manager. They expect dictatorial behaviour. Middle managers would rather be managing directors of small companies than high-level functional managers of very large corporations. Yet these same subordinates will gladly pass responsibility for decision-making to a higher authority, and will often be reluctant to accept promotion because of their social deficiencies for the new position.

In many parts of the world, bribery or the tipping of officials is a common practice: a tangible appreciation for services rendered is expected. Again, many government officials will refuse to do business with someone if he has not come from a family with a high social standing in the community.

Western management must recognize that foreign attitudes towards delegation, decision-making, discipline, and acceptance of responsibility have deep implications for organization structure top management workloads and overall efficiency of the management 'team'. This is particularly true in the many places where the concept of teamwork is virtually nonexistent.

Working relationships, particularly in small to medium-sized, family-owned companies, are largely personalized: managers tend to adopt a paternalistic attitude towards employees. This is still fully accepted in many parts of the world. Employees, particularly in developing countries, are thus viewed as incapable of making a decision for themselves: indeed, they are, because they have never been given the chance to make decisions.

The position of women in the society can be important. In parts of Africa, the Far East and Latin America, women have an inferior status. Even in Argentina, a relatively advanced country, a woman cannot travel abroad with her children without written permission from her husband, certified by the government, for each trip abroad. Such attitudes clearly affect the status of women, and hinder their being placed in certain positions of responsibility or authority. Again, women are not universally employed. In some countries, they can only work before they are married. Equal pay for equal work is virtually unknown. In both work and social/psychological structures, such attitudes pose problems of recruitment, promotion, remuneration, working conditions (segregation of the sexes may be necessary), changes in the organization of work, supervision and discipline.

Managers may find that they have very broad responsibilities in countries with relatively undeveloped social institutions, or where a primarily agricultural economy is still becoming industrialized. In Japan, for example, even today, management is expected to provide housing, shopping facilities, recreation and personal and medical care for all workers. The foreign manager must understand the social system in which he is to work: only then can he realize the full significance of what he may or may not do and act accordingly. Social protocol is equally important. For example, a man does not shake hands with a Moslem woman.

Factors of kinship, tribal ties, racial, religious and personal differences affect working relationships in many countries. These factors can complicate recruitment, promotion, transfer, discipline and discharge; they can lead to favouritism within the company – often to the detriment of the enterprise. Western concepts of equal opportunity, promotion based on ability or performance, may be neither understood nor accepted.

Some social and cultural habits survive from colonial times when a sense of loyalty to the employer was in no way generated. Work disciplines, such as regular hours, concern for quality, productivity and honesty are not within the value system of certain indigenous people – both workers and managers. So, pilfering, dragging of feet, inadequate care of machinery and equipment, absenteeism and bribery are still common. In many parts of Latin America and the Far East, the concept of 'conflict of interest' is virtually unknown. Employees and managers feel no guilt about using company assets and company time to further their own personal interests, even to the extent of starting small spareparts businesses, supplied from company warehouses.

Recruitment is normally not a major problem, given adequate time and proper advance planning. The main difficulty lies in developing in recruits the necessary internal industrial disciplines: thoroughness of approach, precision in performance, exactness in timing and ambition in achieve-ment, when the society does not value such concepts and writes them off as inhumane and robbing the worker of dignity.

Workers cannot be expected to have, at work, attitudes they never encounter in their private lives. Thus, a worker's home in certain parts of the Far East, Latin America and the Middle East, is unclean, not kept up and generally disorderly. This is not always the worker's fault, but it is unreasonable to expect such people automatically to keep a factory, machineroom, toolroom or office clean, neat and orderly. Time must be taken patiently to teach and explain these virtues, unappreciated in their own culture. In one Latin American country, office clerks come early, stay late, and are eager for overtime: the air-conditioned office is far more pleasant and agreeable than their own homes.

However, in both developing and developed countries local nationals will accept a foreign manager if he has demonstrated competence in his discipline in his own society. Hence, foreign experts can succeed in any culture in getting their teaching and guidance accepted and adopted. This, of course, presupposes an in-depth knowlege of their jobs, the accept-ability of their personalities, and a conscious need on the part of the local participants. Suggested management practices must, however, be adapted to suit local conditions, taking into account factors likely to affect their application. The best approach is to help the local participants to solve their problems, meeting them on their own level of expressed need, whether or not that need seems to the adviser to be the most pressing problem. Most countries are disposed and willing, even eager, to accept advice as long as it is within the framework of their needs and their culture: they can also be receptive to change if change offers an improvement, they, by their standards, think desirable. The prospect of higher financial returns may not, abroad, always seem desirable. In some cultures, higher returns will only involve the manager in more obligations to relatives, friends or religious organizations. In parts of Africa, for example, he may have to make funds available for a long-term loan to a friend who desires to get married and must literally buy his wife.

Acceptance of the need for behavioural change will only follow changes in the self-images and perceptions of employees. Until they are made aware and accept that a problem of this nature exists, they cannot assist in its solution. It must be made clear to the employee, in terms he understands, exactly what is expected of him and why. He has to be shown that there are alternative behaviour patterns he is capable of adopting and which will provide what he will regard as reward satis-factions. Many foreign managers fail to recognize the deep sensitivity and pride of local nationals: these people have normal desires and anxieties, even though they may not always be expressed. Foreigners often talk down to them, yell at them, ridicule them, and ignore requests for help. Such attitudes make failure certain.

Employees in foreign subsidiaries often show little concern about long-range problems their actions may create for the firm. They feel that the foreign parent company has little concern for their future welfare, so they reciprocate accordingly. This kind of feeling is accentuated when foreign nationals avoid local contacts, remaining in their own ghettos and clubs: hostility and resentment is increased between 'two nations'.

Foreign companies feel disappointed by the lack of appreciation of the benefits and high wages they provide: they do not realize that non-economic factors (desire for status, prestige) are often more important to the local employee than high wages.

It is important, therefore, to understand the objectives and goals of the local workforce, as members of a distinct society, as informal groups of workers and as individuals. It is necessary to satisfy local expectations and needs by relating these needs to improved operating efficiency. It must be determined whether the local workforce has the requisite knowledge, skills, attitudes, training and experience to perform the work in accordance with the levels expected: if not, this training must be provided within their culturally acceptable traditions.

There are a number of companies with overseas affiliates which concern themselves not only with the physical adjustment of families moving to a foreign location, but even more importantly with cultural adjustments. It is well worth while paving the way for the entry into a foreign culture of an executive and his family. Social acceptability may be the most important criterion for success in a foreign environment. Two of these companies in the USA are: International Relocation Corporation, Sandy Spring, Maryland; and Overseas Briefing Associates, New York.

Cultural benchmarks must be established: they must take into account local traditional values, social structures, individual and group goals, approved methods of goal-seeking, and acceptable behaviour patterns. Some communities will put much store by customs or traditions which will not exist at all in other communities. Some societies have, for example, strong traditions about food: these may be linked to religion, and are therefore a particularly sensitive area. Any such local traditions must be taken into account when, for example, setting up an employee cafeteria. In most parts of the world, a canteen is necessary for competitive purposes or mandatory by law. It can become either a major source of employee dissatisfaction, or a major asset in winning employee loyalty. Money is well spent in providing a well-balanced quality meal according to local customs: be it black beans and rice in Brazil, or meat and wine in France.

The element of fatalism in some religions has elsewhere to be taken into account. There is no drive to consume. There may be strong opposition to birth control. Remuneration may not be a strong motivating force. Yet, in some places like Brazil, a few cruzeiros more per day may induce an employee to change his job. It is necessary to know where and why money is important or relatively unimportant. Perhaps a lack of consumer goods and services will mean that there is nothing on which to spend more money: in some countries, significant pay increases have led to rises in absenteeism. In predominantly agricultural communities, frequent and prolonged absenteeism are perennial problems: many workers have small plots of land, and must work them during planting and harvest times. There is no way of inducing them to come to work, if that would mean sacrificing their crops of vegetables or tobacco.

Finally, the communication barriers which arise from cultural/social factors must never be forgotton. A study of these, in France, Britain, Israel and the US, came to some startling conclusions, reported by M. Z. Brooke and H. L. Remmers in *The Multinational company in Europe* (Harlow, Longman, 1972). The study measured the level of oral communications as a function of the cultural environment, the managerial structure, and the type of business. The investigators showed an average daily interaction per person as follows:

USA	5.0
UK	5.3
France	0.75
Israel	1.6

When there is a low level of oral interaction, there is a high level of written communication, and a complex bureaucracy. In France, this is influenced by the Church, the government, the military and the educational system. The conclusion pertinent to multinational managers is that natural differences in communication patterns are a basic, most important cultural characteristic to be overcome in doing business in foreign countries.

1.2   Educational differences

The extent of the availability of higher education in a country is the major determinant of its economic growth. In those countries with a high rate of illiteracy and relatively limited facilities for higher education, poverty, starvation, and a general lack of industrial development are most prevalent. (See Figure 1 : 2.) The predominantly illiterate society poses great problems for new multinational ventures, particularly those with sophis-

THE FOOD GAP

Food production in developing countries has increased, but population growth has cancelled gain.

(1961–1965 = 100: Communist countries excluded)

TOTAL FOOD PRODUCTION

PER CAPITA FOOD PRODUCTION

140
130
120
110
100
90
80

56 58 60 62 64 66 68 70 72 74

Source: Agency for International Development

WHAT PEOPLE SPEND FOR FOOD

Percentage of disposable income; latest available figures:

Germany	17.7	Zaire	62.0
Britain	22.1	India	65–70*
France	21.7	Bangladesh	60*
US	16.9	Pakistan	40–45*
Japan	23.0	S. Korea	33*
USSR	38.0	Thailand	40–45*
Algeria	54.0	S. Vietnam	40–50*
Tunisia	66.0	Indonesia	50*
		Madagascar	56.0

*Estimated

Source: US Dept. of Agriculture

POPULATION EXPLOSION

(Billions)

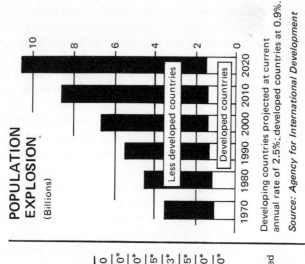

Less developed countries

Developed countries

1970 1980 1990 2000 2010 2020

10
8
6
4
2
0

Developing countries projected at current annual rate of 2.5%; developed countries at 0.9%.

Source: Agency for International Development

Figure 1 : 2

ticated technical processes. Such problems as communications, training, etc., are all so much greater when people cannot read or write.

When the traditional educational system is itself a function of an underdeveloped society, and that society equates wisdom with the teachings of old men, education is apt to stagnate. The new teacher echoes the views of his teacher, and so on, often through an oral as opposed to a written form. A docile acceptance of the teacher's views or mere rote memorization stifles creativity and logical inquiry. This type of conditioning will retard the pace at which industry can adapt natural resources, products and processes to local needs and conditions. This is true even in agriculture: farmers must become literate before agrarian reform can advance. This is a major reason why collective farming and mechanization have failed in many developing countries. As a result, and as can be seen in parts of Africa, there are no markets for modern tractors or harvesting machinery.

Education alone can create the conditions for social and economic development; it prepares the way for changes in attitudes, values and beliefs, so that people appreciate the need to improve their condition and will make the efforts necessary to do so. When that has happened, societies can then progress to the development of human resources necessary for industrialization. Thus the role of the enlightened teacher is perhaps the most important profession in a developing country.

The social changes needed may involve a change in attitude towards work. If manual work is regarded as undignified, only fit for lower castes or immigrant labour, people will refuse to do manual work. These attitudes can be changed: this has been proved by African and Asian engineers, for example, working in the USA or Europe. Only continuing education and training programmes, linked to management development schemes, will however ensure that these new attitudes, once adopted, are maintained.

Of course, differences in national educational systems are pronounced even as between one industrialized country and another. For example the French school system tends to foster Cartesian philosophy in students which demands a systematic and quantitative approach to any problem. The American system, by contrast, tends to focus more on the utility of the end result. Some French executives therefore regard their American counterparts as superficial in their diagnosis of problems, while Americans may tend to regard the French approach as bureaucratic and inefficient.

Strong social stratification still exists in Western Europe. This results in educational inequalities and therefore social immobility, and inequality of opportunity. In a number of European countries, Italy and Spain, for example, free public education is inadequate and ends at a much lower grade level than in the United States. When companies receive economic inducements to locate in underdeveloped areas, it is found that the workers' education is not up to the minimum standards demanded by modern production technology. There will also probably be a serious shortage of people suitable for supervisory and management positions.

The social status of a foreman is low in many European countries. This is partly the result of the educational system which perpetuates the social class structure. The effect extends into the area of middle management and, hence, people are inadequately prepared, educationally, to assume the full responsibilities of their positions. The foreman's job is unattractive even to those who have left secondary schools. The lesson for companies entering into new European ventures is to intensify foreman training, increase the pay, prestige and status of the job, and give foremen more managerial responsibility.

The educational system, including type, quality and availability of advanced education, particularly in management, determines, to a large degree, the social and cultural patterns of behaviour. This translates itself into a recognition of the need for special training and development to prepare local nationals for future supervisory and managerial positions.

1.3   Technological differences

The introduction of new technology, particularly in developing countries, is often viewed with favour by the host country. In fact, technologically advanced countries are seduced into locating new facilities in preindustrial countries. Technology appears to promise desirable improvement in living standards, to provide more jobs, and generally to benefit the economy of the host country. However, the host country itself may fail to recognize the full implications of the new technology on its way of life. Soon, they cry 'rape', after having been the seducer. The horrifying discovery is made that the new technology, originally welcomed, conflicts with the traditional cultural and behavioural patterns.

Imagine a small village whose inhabitants have always worked locally. For some of them then to take jobs at a factory in a neighbouring town represents a significant change in the lifestyle of the community.

Transportation to the factory is in itself disruptive in terms of social relations and status. Technological differences are closely related to, and definitely affect, social and cultural values, as well as the educational and economic system of the country.

The development of advanced technology, for example, requires a longer period of formal education. A change in just this one cultural trait, affects, for example, the age at which people marry, have children, and reach peak income potential. The changes may be opposed: for little benefit accrues to a preindustrial society which tries to bridge a 20-year technological gap without first accepting the need for, and concentrating on, changes in habits and attitudes of the local population. The lesson is the same for new industries: preconditioning is a prerequisite to success.

The simplest involvement in the new technology requires accuracy in work, intensive concentration, and some regimentation in working hours – all of which need special care and effort. New relationships are thus defined for the men who must accept and learn to use them. Local employees thus need to be taught to recognize that modern business practices and new management policies are necessary for optimum return on the investment made by the foreign country which has committed capital and resources.

Training employees in preindustrial areas efficiently to use modern technology is far more involved than training new employees in an industrialized nation: the most difficult task is to induce the local workers to accept the efficient organization of effort implicit in the practices of modern industrial management. The local society seldom realizes that it is being offered an entirely new way of life, one often in sharp contrast to local traditions. The local employee will strive hard to convince the foreign manager of the unreasonableness of the new regulations.

The results are a lack of industrial discipline, government interference, severe criticism of management and low operating efficiency: these attitudes are characterized by foreign managers as uncooperative. To avoid such conflicts, and anticipate them, the overseas manager must quickly learn local behavioural and cultural patterns. This involves understanding the process of change within the employees' context, not his own. What are the approved prestige patterns, the approved social goals and the methods for achieving them, the systems of authority and the rules of moral behaviour? All these questions must be answered from the viewpoint of government, management and workers in the host country. In at least one Far East country great resentment is caused by the foreign supervisor who pats the employee on the back or the shoulder: this is described as being 'pushed around' by an arrogant foreigner.

Managers in Western cultures grow up in the midst of technology: they learn mechanical principles from toys in childhood. They learn conceptual practices and elementary budgeting from their parents; they understand the relationship of costs, profits, income, hard work and success. They learn to plan, evaluate and achieve goals. Such experiences are nonexistent in developing countries, particularly those with high rates of illiteracy, and it is well to remember just how high that rate can be: in Egypt, for example, by no means the most backward country, it is some 60 per cent. Managers who grow up within the environment of developing countries do not appreciate that their success is determined by the success of their subordinates: they are not accustomed to rigorous self-appraisal, self-discipline and goal-orientation.

In a traditional culture, planning consists only of such preparation as is necessary to maintain conformity to custom. In such a country there is no selection of economic goals, no attempts to improve efficiency and no cost accountability. In the employee's mind, his personal relationship with his supervisor, not his commitment to organizational goals, determines his welfare. Even local managers tend to avoid responsibility, and they bring all matters, major and minor, to their expatriate manager for solution. They have to be taught to accept the delegation of authority. The local manager himself is often unwilling or unable to give responsibility for results to subordinates: to do that makes him feel insecure. It is essential, therefore, to have job descriptions and goals for each key position, and each lower-level job. Employees can learn the specific functions of their jobs, but they have to be taught; if they do not understand, they will not ask.

The multinational corporation has a great responsibility, not only to transmit the technology needed in developing countries, but also to teach the local nationals the how and the why, and to secure their acceptance of a new way of life which is necessary for their own long-term economic welfare. It is a challenging task, and it is not surprising that two-thirds of the capital investment made by mulitnational companies is made in other industrialized countries: there the problems of training, government relations and productivity are much easier to solve.

To establish new technology in a developing country, and ensure a proper return, means massive capital investment, and automated processes involving relatively few workers. Many foreign governments, however, favour jobs being provided for as many people as possible: they resist the latest technology and prefer less advanced machinery and equipment, which involve more labour. This increases costs, and makes it difficult to produce for export in competitive world markets. Some governments will only grant import licences for machinery and equipment which involve a high labour content.

Rapid population growth, pronounced in Latin America and the Far East, brings serious social and political consequences. It accelerates the forces for change. Unless these population increases are matched by rapid economic development, the *per capita* output declines, social unrest develops, and the stage is set for revolution. Western businessmen must accept their responsibilities and find new creative ways of transferring technology, or they will lose large potential markets for their services and products. International business enterprises play a dominant role in the total development of nation states. Social responsibility must be one important element in any plans for the introduction of new technology.

1.4 Union/Workforce attitudes

Labour/management relations differ significantly between the well-established industrialized nations and the developing nations.

Developed countries

In the industrialized countries, collective bargaining is well established: trade unions represent the vast majority of factory workers and negotiate the collective agreements between employees and employers. Such agreements specify terms and conditions of the employment contract and are negotiated in a variety of forms at local, industrial and national levels. They normally include established procedures for settling employee grievances which arise from disputes over wages, hours, and working conditions, and cover all employees within the bargaining unit, as well as providing for resolution of individual worker complaints. The agreements cover employees in the factory, the field, and in many cases the office. Direct government intervention in the settlement of labour disputes, *per se*, is minimal. Trade unions have become a powerful, political force in the industrialized nations, and have been instrumental in obtaining legislation to establish minimum industrial standards covering a wide range of employment practices: cost-of-living adjustments, worker safety, employment conditions, job security, hiring practices, discharge, transfers, promotions, and employee representation in the management of the individual company itself. The norms were established, after years of conflict, when employers accepted the rights of trade unions to organize, bargain for employees, and strike in support of their demands.

The task of employee representation has become increasingly more complex for unions because of new technology, new laws and regulations, and new demands by workers for relief from the monotony of industrial life, for a direct voice in all that affects their working life: hiring staff, selection processes for supervisors, time and motion study, transfers, promotions, career planning, and those decisions historically the preserve of management, for example the location of a new plant.

Labour unions in industrialized countries now employ economists, lawyers, industrial engineers, and other consultants from a variety of disciplines. The repercussions on public life and society resulting from technology and the demand for corporate and union social responsibility have altered the traditional bargaining process. Public opinion has become a major factor in the employer/employee relationship. The economic weapon of the official strike on a national scale in a given industry is now unattractive to all parties, because in capital-intensive, high-technology industries, the costs in both lost profits and lost wages tend to reach astronomical figures, and no one wins. Accordingly, the future will see a decline in strike activity, particularly because of the growth of arbitration and conciliation. Already this occurs where vital public and health services are affected.

It is likely also that industry-wide bargaining will give way to plant and company bargaining. It is, however, unlikely that trade unions will, in the foreseeable future, be successful in conducting negotiations at the corporate headquarters level of multinationals, for all affiliated subsidiaries, on a worldwide basis. In the West the trend is for negotiations to take place on a local company level, with a prior agreement neither to strike nor lockout employees, and to submit those areas where agreement cannot be reached to arbitration by a disinterested third party, jointly selected and approved by both unions and management.

Notwithstanding this favourable trend in the collective bargaining process, management has now to contend with a new kind of worker, with different values, and different attitudes towards his work from those of his predecessor a generation ago. The worker in the West, born after 1945, is not only better educated than his father, but attaches more importance to his own development as a human being. He is less obedient, less conformist, and more questioning about what he finds in society. This is good in the sense that each human being has the right and indeed the obligation to develop his capacities to their fullest potential. But management was not, and still is not, prepared to cope with these changes. The new workers fully expect to enjoy continuing increases in material prosperity; they expect and receive government assistance in adversity; they do not have to cope with the spectre of unemployment as did their fathers. Many workers today question the purpose and operation of industry itself. They reject traditional management authority; they are reluctant to enter industry if any more attractive employment is available.

The implications for management are that unless the top executives adjust their thinking to accommodate these changing attitudes, alienation and friction will increase; it will be difficult to recruit for industrial work, and virtually impossible to sustain economic growth. This is not only true at the worker level, it is significant also at the level of lower and middle management. The role of authority and the exercise of power are being questioned. The quality of leadership from the top to the lowest supervisory levels, as determined by the personal qualities of the leader himself, merit the closest attention of top management. The leader must recognize and respect the wishes of his followers, while keeping clearly in mind the purpose of the company and the goals of his position. He must find ways and means of satisfying both. Management must maintain the initiative through finding agreement on common purpose and common interest with the workers.

In brief, the challenge to authority is a revolution which cannot be arrested or reversed. It is accompanied by a strong desire for a higher quality of life and changing human expectations. It crosses all cultural frontiers and natural boundaries; it appears simultaneously in such diverse nations as the UK and Japan, the USA and Switzerland. It questions not only the authority of corporate management, but also the authority of the trade union, the university, the government, and the Church.

The younger generation no longer sees achievement as the final purpose of life. They are asking and demanding the right to determine the conditions of their work, their hours of attendance; for periodic leave-of-absence and sabbaticals to further their education and change their careers; for transferability of pensions, monthly salaries instead of piece rates, quick lucrative promotion, and high mobility. Germany, for example, provides opportunities, with pay, for any employee who wishes to further his education, and thus probably change his career and his employer. Even in Japan, labour is becoming scarce, and workers are demanding a new social status.

Technological change, while undoubtedly providing a higher standard of living and increasing the abundance of material goods, tends to confine and restrict employees to dull and monotonous jobs, and even threatens job security. In at least 15 nations already, the law makes it virtually impossible to reduce the workforce or to discharge an employee, regardless of his low productivity. The social impact of the pursuit of high productivity is now in debate. It is clear that management must have well-defined and publicized industrial relations policies, which must be constantly reviewed at the corporate policy level, and implemented through intensive training at first-line supervisory level. Management must make every effort to work closely with trade unions and workers' councils and committees, to deal effectively with employee needs and desires in all aspects affecting their work and job conditions.

Finally, companies that wish to avoid future problems arising from the challenge to authority must take the few simple but practical steps to bring about controlled worker participation and involvement. This is especially important because, as already mentioned, employers' freedon to dismiss or censure employees because of incompetence (poor quality work, low productivity, lack of initiative) is all the time being eroded.

It is useful to experiment by organizing small, autonomous work groups in a factory, wherever it is possible so to reorganize the work. The ideal group will be 10 or fewer employees. This helps individuals to retain their independence and individuality. Scandinavian and German models have shown that productivity and quality will improve, not suffer. Allow the group to establish its own, simply stated objectives for quality and productivity, guided by management in terms of its needs and expectations. All group members must be made fully acquainted with all aspects of the work, its relationship to other work groups, and the company's overall objectives. Each group member should repeat the group's goals and thoughts in his own words to avoid misunderstanding. The group and each individual within the group must accept the group's goals.

The group must have a leader. He should be appointed by management, but endorsed and trusted by the group. Often the selection of the union representative as group leader has, in the past, proved to be most effective. It is the group leader's job to allocate operational tasks, to encourage workers to try new methods and creative approaches to their work. The leader must also encourage and develop appropriate problem-solving procedures, both technical and human. Group responsibility must be developed. All communications within the group, and in particular the instant feedback of results achieved, must be through the group leader. Knowledge of success and speedy rewards (not necessarily financial) are important to make the system work. All communications must be friendly and informal.

The task of the group must go beyond the mere solution of specific technical problems and the achievement of routine targets. It must develop itself as a group, and each of its members as individuals. The social skills and degree of interaction achieved are at least as important as the production goals because it is in this area that permanent beneficial change takes place for the individual, the group and the company. Constant improvement will then become a way of life.

Management may find it necessary to reorganize to achieve these human goals, but the results will more than justify the additional time, effort and initial cost involved. The Swedish automobile and the Japanese domestic appliance industries, while working from entirely different cultural bases, have developed a high degree of homogeneity of intention, and brought a sense of dignity to the factory worker.

Industrialized multinational companies cannot afford strikes, nor can the economies of the many nations in which they operate: a strike involving ten thousand workers which lasts for a few weeks may cost the company more than the annual capital expenditure budget for the factory. The human capital in the company must by design and experimentation be husbanded and improved through more humane and acceptable work environments.

Developing countries

In developing countries, labour dissatisfaction and protest have arisen primarily from the sudden and harsh impact of an imported technology inconsistent with local cultural standards. Unfortunately, this has usually been met with an equally harsh response from the new capitalist employers, who use their traditional methods of selection, training and placement: there have been too few systematic, well-developed approaches in these areas. Discipline has been reinforced by oppressive measures. Safety precautions have generally been disregarded and life has been considered cheap, particularly in countries where labour has been cheap and plentiful. Human rights and the dignity of the worker have been given little consideration unless pressure groups have forced the hand of the new employers.

Initially, these malpractices in human resource management were allowed because they reflected practice in the family, tribe, or school system: those days are rapidly passing. Accumulated dissatisfactions are now given various expressions: high absenteeism and staff turnover, work stoppages, sabotage, sitdown strikes. Such incidents have led to government intervention and, eventually, the formation of trade unions. There is great similarity between the reactions of people in developing countries and the early labour history of industrialized countries.

1.5   Political/Governmental attitudes

Political/governmental relations will play an increasing role in the future of multinational companies: the human resource considerations involved in these relationships will thus also become more important. For example, if the managing director of the local subsidiary is well connected at the highest levels of government and skilled in negotiations with government officials, the problems affecting mergers, acquisitions, joint ventures, taxation, nationalization, sale of products or services to government officials, will be minimized. Indeed, the opportunity to continue operating in some countries will be directly related to the relationship between the local managing director and senior government officials..

An increasingly powerful role for government is recognized; yet this does not rule out the continuing powerful role of business. Private enterprise still generates approximately three-quarters of the GNP in Western Europe and Asia: leading businessmen are drawn into government advisory boards and are thus involved in national economic planning. The true relationship must be that of partners. Most foreign governments take very seriously their role of modernizing agents: they have unlimited ways and means of ensuring that private organizations help them to achieve their goals. The intelligent businessman recognizes this, and will be willing to play his part.

The businessman operating in a foreign environment must fully understand the government structure, the live political issues and the current government's policies. Many leaders, for example, have been elected because they have promised broad, sweeping social reforms, which involve improvements in the quality of life as well as the material standards of workers. Multinational companies and host governments frequently fail to understand each other's goals, attitudes, constraints and modes of operation. This leads to failure on the company's part properly to appraise the investment climate, and subsequent development which may radically change this climate.

It is not necessarily the law itself which creates problems, because that is often vague: it is the interpretation of the law by unsympathetic administrators which causes difficulties over import controls, exports, prices, profits, income, currency repatriation, work permits and taxes. Current administrative practice often leads to excessive delays, higher business costs, discrimination against multinational enterprises, and ill will: they lead to bribery to get something done. Such difficulties must always be analysed to determine if they are the result of incompetent administration, or new governmental attitudes and policies, or just sheer harassment. The political climate must always be accurately gauged and carefully monitored to avoid financial disaster.

A foreign subsidiary may be vulnerable for a variety of reasons. It directly affects economic growth and national pride. It creates a drain on foreign exchange, and possibly hinders indigenous development. Many developing nations see multinationals as a latter-day form of colonial exploitation. Others, making serious efforts to develop local industries, are shutting out the foreign employer by legislation designed to protect native enterprises.

But unsympathetic government policies are not always publicly defined, and even less frequently are the administrative and interpretative difficulties on official record. It they have not already faced such issues, multinationals can expect soon to be asked questions such as: *'How many new jobs will be created?'* This is particularly common in developing countries with high unemployment: it is also now being asked in Western

Europe. Where trade unions are influential with the government, the issue becomes one of creating new jobs in nonindustrialized areas. Thus *the question of plant location* is also critical to a host government attempting to upgrade underdeveloped areas. It is an issue that may also be a question of personal concern to politicians, as in France, Spain, India or Japan. There is already too much industrial congestion and pollution in and around the major industrial cities of the world, and additional proposed industrial complexes may become delicate political issues.

Heavily industrialized nations in Europe are anxious continually to update their technology, and jump literally years ahead by importing industries with advanced technology, such as nuclear energy and computer manufacture. Japan is also actively seeking advanced technology. On the other hand, some nations, in the early stages of industrial development, rather seek technological resources more appropriate to their immediate needs: that is, equipment demanding low operating skills and simple maintenance, and thus suitable to the educational level of their people; equipment that would be considered obsolete in industrialized nations.

What will be *the net foreign exchange gain* to the host country may well be the most important question. It affects the actual investment by the multinational company. Many countries have exchange controls, restrictions on dividend remittances, and on the terms of technical assistance agreements. *The form of the investment* may be as important as the investment itself. For example, there is a growing preference by foreign countries for joint venture arrangements which may result in the foreign enterprise ultimately holding only a minority interest.

Many countries now vigorously pursue a policy of *top jobs for local nationals*. This is expressed, for example, as Indianization or Africanization. It is, simply stated, a form of nationalism. There is increasing pressure, particularly in Latin America, for *local manufacture*. The company which, historically, has only sought distribution outlets for its products and/or services is now treated with suspicion. Foreign governments now want various advance guarantees, encompassing not only eventual local manufacture, but also in such matters as wages, taxes, prices, and the permanency and stability of operations.

These developments emphasize that going abroad with a business involves issues going far beyond questions of expanding markets and lower production costs: it is a matter of participating in the development of another society. Future foreign business ventures will involve more specific commitments, but the climate for foreign investment will remain favourable, provided the foreign investor pays close attention to the diverse human, cultural and social factors involved. This will minimize government interference and encourage support for the new venture.

When operating abroad things are different and so are people.

Politicians, legislators, civil servants, ministers and judges are vastly different from the foreign businessman in background, values, expectations, attitudes, mores and interpersonal attitudes. These differences magnify the misunderstandings and communication problems that language difficulties create. The foreign businessman must know who in the local environment can serve him best as a negotiator; what short and long-term business strategies will most appeal to governments. Such problems are more acute in Asia, Africa, the Middle East, and parts of Latin America, than Western Europe. A foreign business must demonstrate its contribution to the national interests of the host country, and minimize conflict with the government, recognizing that most foreign governments are much involved in their national economies. A company cannot keep a low profile in a country where its operations have a significant impact on the economy. However, while all nations are increasingly involving themselves in the affairs of multinational companies, that is partly because they need private enterprise and foreign investment to achieve growth, stability and full employment. Thus relationships will continue, but on a something-for-something basis.

A word of caution. A number of developing countries have only recently achieved political independence: the new government overnight, tends to make rash promises of quick economic independence, with jobs and security for everyone. The tide of nationalism runs high, and new social patterns are introduced by ambitious governments to encourage property and labour mobility. Some governments fail to recognize the need for highly trained technical and managerial personnel to make the smooth transition to an industrialized economy. These promises, raising the expectations of the people, create conditions of unrest and political instability. Holders of public offices are all too often incompetent political appointees, more interested in personal power and self-aggrandizement than in carefully planning the mobilization of the nation's resources. Their incompetence causes the gap between the 'haves' and the 'have nots' to widen. Bureaucracy flourishes, decrees and regulations proliferate, and a combination of political instability and public apathy breeds corruption.

Private enterprise may fall into the trap of seeing such a situation as an opportunity to court government favours, perhaps by the appointment of unqualified politicians to important positions in the company, as advisers or local directors. In the short term this can be highly profitable — through new government contracts, the removal of import restrictions and tax advantages. but such a policy reinforces and institutionalizes corruption as a way of life within the company — even among its own managers. Ultimately, this ruins the social fabric and integrity of the enterprise, destroys the morale of the employees, and adversely affects both productivity and quality.

Serious thought therefore must be given to just how far a foreign employer can go in its relations with a government without detrimental long-term effects on the business.

1.6 Climatic differences

There is a high degree of correlation between the climate of a given country and its rate of industrial development. The Asian Productivity Organization recently sponsored a symposium on training. It concluded that climatic factors affect receptivity, and Western working hours were not likely to suit the trainee who is in general an introvert and not willing to participate in group discussions: non-participation makes the trainee very quickly bored and unreceptive to the teaching.

Climatic extremes are of major significance in developing countries. A drought in Africa, Pakistan or India can result in hundreds of thousands of people starving to death; and even in the normal course of events, thousands die each week of malnutrition. Many economies are dependent of a few basic agricultural products for their livelihood. The diet of a nation is a major element in its mental, psychological, social and physiological development.

The failure rate of expatriates in developing countries runs as high as 50–70 per cent, in terms of those who do not complete their assignments. The dryness and heat of the Arab desert, the Asian monsoons, the extremes of heat and humidity so common in many parts of Asia, combined with boredom, are anathema to the third-country national, or the US expatriate.

The hours worked, the number of weeks worked, and the productivity per man-hour are drastically affected by temperature variations even within one country; it is virtually impossible to achieve in the heat of the Amazon basin the same high level of productivity as in São Paulo or Rio. Offices may be air-conditioned; factories are not. Extreme heat and humidity are enervating: people move and think more slowly, and appear to have less initiative and ambition.

The health, life span and general wellbeing of people in hot, humid climates is significantly affected by diet. The majority of workers in developing countries cannot obtain a well-balanced meal by Western standards. Dietary deficiencies make it naïve and rashly optimistic to expect a worker in Calcutta or Bombay to produce as much as his German counterpart, even given the same technology.

In the Far East, as even a tourist will observe, many people are ill-fed, ill-clothed and sickly: this inevitably affects industrial performance. Extreme climate and poor diet play a significant part in the slow pace of industrial development. When all these matters are borne in mind, it is easy to understand why two-thirds of the world's investment in the transfer of technology and managerial expertise still takes place in the developed countries: they offer conditions most likely to ensure commercial success. Perhaps it is time, however, to re-evaluate investment criteria and place a higher emphasis on social obligations, rather than solely on profit.

1.7   Differences in management practices

There are vast differences in management philosophy, style and degree of sophistication even within the highly developed industrialized nations. These differences are the direct result of the cultural and social systems which have developed in each nation. The US expatriate, for example, who is assigned a managerial post, even in some Western European country, should not be surprised to find:

Lack of business planning.
Lack of business strategy.
No marketing sophistication (including lack of information about competition, price policy and price strategy).
Poor cost accounting and financial management, analyses and controls.
Poorly defined or nonexistent staffline relationships, and organization confusion.
No production and inventory controls, high receivables and borrowing.
Lack of managerial delegation, participation or involvement in major company decisions.
Personnel managers functioning as record-keepers, clerks, social benefit administrators, but not involved in policy matters, or professional human resource management.
Absence of manpower planning, forecasting, training and development.
Too many levels of management.
Too broad a span of control.
No job descriptions or performance standards.
Inadequate or nonexistent management information systems.
No management-by-objectives.
Inadequate budgetary controls and follow up.
Poor and nonexistent communications throughout the organization.
Lack of measurements skills, priorities skills.

Many US multinational corporations of course fall down on some of these things, but their absence is more noticeable in many medium- and large-sized local companies in much of Western Europe.

Professional management, with all its scientific tools, methods and approaches, is still a relatively new discipline in Europe. In most family-owned companies, almost every item in the above list is conspicuous by its absence. This presents problems to the multinational company interested in acquiring a European subsidiary. In Europe, as a result of the social and educational structure, there is still widely prevalent a paternalistic and autocratic style of management. This, in itself, precludes the use of many modern management tools. Europeans tend also to adopt a bureaucratic style in business administration. Where management training and development is accepted, a bureaucratic system inhibits the development of top executive talent, even though good, young engineers are fed into the system. Moreover, the workload of the European managing director may be enormous, because of his failure or inability to delegate, his lack of trust and confidence in his subordinates, and his insistence on making personally every major decision and too many minor ones.

This situation is changing, but the complete metamorphosis may take up to another generation: one of the challenges for the multinational companies is to expedite this change. Successful techniques for dealing with these differences in managerial approach, and the transference of managerial expertise, will be fully discussed in Chapter 4 (page 49). This affords another example of the necessity for the expatriate manager to make a careful assessment of the local situation before applying managerial principles and techniques which have been successful in his home country.

In developing countries, the absence of a tradition of sound management practice (according to Western standards) is even more pronounced. The dominant cultural, social, educational, and climatic patterns have virtually precluded the rise of professional management: the jobs of teaching and putting into practice the management skills listed above is therefore far more difficult and complex. To begin with, managers in developing countries are virtually nonexistent. Industry may not even be getting off the ground at all. Management education at university level (if it exists) is inadequate and narrow. Industrial engineering, for example, is a concept unknown in many countries.

The company will have to initiate and develop its own programmes from scratch. This raises difficulties when one of the first questions put by a host country will be: 'How soon will our people be prepared for and placed into the top management positions?' Management will be faced with a long period of careful preplanning (including a study of local culture patterns) before the venture is begun. Elementary management instruction will be necessary. Audiovisual aids, simple, practical, problem-solving exercises must be developed, to teach local people the most basic and simple management practices. The programme must be structured to take account of their point of view: it must demonstrate how they personally will benefit from learning.

Despite all the difficulties, a lot can be done. The case study of a multinational company which successfully met these challenges in both developed and developing countries is presented in Chapter 3 (page 37). It is very important to remember that participation, delegation and involvement are concepts which are not accepted in many cultures. A manager may often be rejected and thought to be stupid because he does not maintain his social distance or appear aloof from the workers. Participative management has been tried and has failed because people have not yet been ready, willing or able to accept a new style of management in direct contradiction to their attitudes, values and beliefs about the role of a manager.

Even when the local people are eager for, and receptive to, management know-how, they are often not prepared to accept the consequent changes in attitudes and life styles that are called for. They may not be ready for textbook knowledge, although they can relate to the experiences of an expert, and understand the problems he has encountered and solved. Some local managers tend to view professional management as a panacea for all problems: their initial expectations may be very unrealistic. They have to be shown how to develop slowly, learning to work together in the solution of their own problems by team effort. Of course, the sooner they begin to apply management techniques and see the results obtained, the greater will be their enthusiasm to learn and apply more.

2
Employee needs

It is, of course, always important to recognize specific problems that may affect employees, but equally there are important factors that will affect them generally. The recognition and satisfaction of these general demands can contribute significantly to a company's profits and growth. In the authors' experience it would certainly seem that the factors which motivate employees, of all races, are similar, wherever they are working. It is Dr Frederick Herzberg who has divided these common needs of all employees into the following helpful categories:

Hygiene needs	*Motivation needs*
Good bosses	Achievement
Communications	Recognition of achievement
(i.e. interpersonal relations)	Involvement
Working conditions	Participation
Remuneration	Advancement
Policy and administration	
Job security	

2.1 Hygiene needs

Employees who are well treated will reciprocate: they will do a fair day's work for a fair day's pay. While this will not in itself necessarily lead to a significant improvement in a company's performance, it will at least help to ensure that a company is not damaged by strikes, go-slows and high rates of absenteeism and staff turnover. However, treating employees well means treating them well according to their frames of reference: these frames of reference may not be the same as the employer's. The employees' frames of reference must be understood and appreciated if the right approach is to be made to them.

In developing countries, for example in Africa and Latin America, the hygiene needs of the employees may be so important to them now that employers may have to take little account, at the moment, of motivation factors. However, that is likely to be true only in the short term: as living standards improve, more people will become more concerned about what they do, and motivation factors will become increasingly important.

Good bosses

It always has been and it always will be very important to have a good boss. To be a good boss in a multinational environment calls for just the same personal and professional qualities as are needed at home. This is so important a matter that it is dealt with separately in Chapter 6 (page 141).

Communications

The total area that should be covered by communications, as a hygiene factor, has not always been fully appreciated. It should embrace the whole gamut of an employee's interpersonal relationships at work – and his social life. Employees are often so badly treated that they only want to forget about work when they go home. Work, instead of being the rewarding experience that every good manager knows it should be, becomes for the employee just a continuing frustration.

There is also a need for communications to be two-way. Every employee, for example, ought to have easy and immediate access to the person in the company who can solve his problems, whatever they may be. Rigid organization structures with formalized communication channels make this difficult, and can waste a lot of time. Again, most directives or explanations that go down to employees through some hierarchical scale lose a lot of their meaning on the way down. Communications then cease to be effective and, in the end, employees cease to care. When employees cease to care, problems arise for others.

Working conditions

In developing countries employees are often still seen as just instruments of production. Labour, and indeed life, seems cheap, so there is usually an inadequate concern by employers for the safety of their employees. As a result, too many serious accidents happen at work. Advanced societies usually protect employees by law. Health and safety at work is controlled and there are heavy penalties for employers who ignore regulations. In developing countries, where this has not yet happened, an individual employer who shows concern for the safety of his employees will stand out. Moreover, in demonstrating care for his employees, he will earn their regard for him, and for the company with which they identify him.

Remuneration

The question of what is a fair day's pay for a fair day's work is probably insoluble. Employees will always want higher wages. The employer must remember, however, that it is a fallacy to believe that money will buy employee loyalty. It is also quite wrong to think that incentive schemes will always increase a company's real productivity and profits. In fact, incentive schemes are often more trouble than they are worth. They give rise to innumerable disputes over interpretation and often encourage deception by employees: they cheat and hide mistakes. Production figures become artificially inflated, and, in the end, many companies are shocked to discover huge 'phantom inventories'. Moreover, incentive schemes are expensive to operate because they need a large staff of watchdogs as well as complicating the calculation of wages.

Rather than create a system that is potentially a source of grievance and conflict, it is much better for the company to establish fair, straight-forward rates of pay after fixing reasonable production targets.

Policy and administration

In most companies the personnel department is too negative in its policy. It fails to take the initiative to create the right working conditions for employees: it confines itself to sorting out difficulties after they have arisen. Very few companies have taken the trouble to encourage the personnel department to devise consistent policies over the whole range of employer/employee relations. As a result, there are óften inconsistencies, seen by employees as injustices, in selection, promotion performance reviews — indeed, in every area of the company's personnel policy.

This is quite wrong. It is essential that a clear, comprehensive policy on employer/employee relations be laid down by the company, on the advice of its experts, and then all managers must be trained by the local human resources manager in the consistent interpretation and application of that policy.

Job security

Local labour laws may condition company policy in this area. In many European and Latin American countries the law makes it very expensive for an employer to discharge an employee, except perhaps for serious misconduct. In other countries, however, such as India, although the law gives the employee little if any protection, the loss of his job may mean starvation for the employee, so there are powerful moral pressures on employers to keep staff. Either way, the employer has, in practice, only a restricted freedom to dismiss employees.

It is always essential for the company to take these local conditions into account when formulating its policy. Otherwise the expense, in human or financial terms, will be heavy, and to ignore these factors is to ensure that the company will never become an integrated part of the society within which it hopes to function and flourish.

2.2 Motivation needs

Employees do not only have to be treated well materially: they must be employed in a way that takes account of their aspirations as human beings. A job which does not give the employee the chance to use his potential is a job that will soon have no applicants for it. There is a need for new skills in managing human resources.

Achievement

More and more people are now looking for jobs which will allow them to use to the full their ability and to develop fully their potential. Most people now leave a job because it no longer gives them a sense of satisfaction or achievement. Many young people turn away from a business career just because they do not feel it would give them an opportunity for self-fulfilment. On the other hand, the more people are encouraged to develop, the more, as a rule, they find they can achieve.

This need for employees to feel a sense of achievement makes repetitive jobs on assembly lines (calling for no initiative or thought) very unpopular. That is why employees have been known to cheer when the production line has broken down, not because as employees they were lazy. As far as possible even the most humdrum jobs should be so organized as to give employees a chance to develop some expertise and to take a pride in their work. Even in developing countries this is becoming a necessary condition for job satisfaction. It is important to remember that very often when employees complain about their pay, what they are really expressing is dissatisfaction with the work they have to do.

Recognition of achievement

Every employee must feel that what he achieves is recognized and appreciated. Only then can he feel that his status as an individual human being is confirmed. Most people have a personal pride and this must be satisfied by the employer's recognition of the employee's worth. Even highly paid senior managers will grow restive and discontented if they are not made aware that they are appreciated. This recognition of the employee's work must always be evident. An annual 'thank you' after a whole year is not enough.

Involvement/Participation

Employees are now asking to be more involved in the planning of their work. They want a part in the decision-making. The initiative must, of course, rest with management: the company has to control strategy and lay down guidelines, but all managers and employees must still have their own area, however circumscribed, in which to display some initiative: that implies that they may make mistakes as well as succeed. This is one fact of the growing demand for industrial democracy, which is treated at length in Chapter 11 (pages 306–9).

Advancement

The advance of the individual is synonymous with the growth of the corporation. Progress is essential to both. The enlightened multinational company will have as one of its fundamental objectives and policies, the provision for each employee of opportunities, through his work, for him to develop fully his individual capabilities. Otherwise, the employee will stagnate, and in a stupid job will end up as a stupid person.

Fortunately experience shows that the best reward for achievement, and the best way to show the employee that his achievement is recognised, is to give him the chance to achieve even more. Most employees are eager to accept more responsibility, and will gladly take advantage of any opportunities they are offered to be trained in new skills: to the ultimate benefit of both the employee and the employer. The employee gains in self-confidence and skill: the employer gains from his better performance as a more skilled and contented worker. Thus, the provision of training for promotion and individual development should always be company policy. It makes sense as a policy that relies on the strengths, not the weaknesses, of the labour force.

2.3   Implication for management

The hygiene and motivation factors are universal in their impact on employer/employee relations; but management must always adjust its policies to take them into account, in accordance with local circumstances. The expatriate businessman in the multinational company must, therefore, first of all study the social environment in which he will manage the undertaking. The success of a new business venture in a foreign environment depends as a rule, far less on the introduction of superior technological and managerial skills than on the careful adjustment of management techniques to the local human environment. After all, success in business depends ultimately on people.

This accommodation to local conditions takes time and money: instant large profits cannot be expected. In the long run, however, it is a policy that ensures a secure base for the business. The multinational corporation becomes involved in the local society and becomes identified with the local programmes for the betterment of that society. In the next chapter the successful way in which an American multinational corporation responded to these challenges is analysed to show how, with intelligent anticipation, management skills can be adapted to totally alien business environments.

PART TWO
THE OMEGA STORY

3
The company

OMEGA (The name is fictitious, and data have been deliberately altered. But the events described did actually happen.)

This case history starts approximately four years ago. The company in question is truly international in every respect: full production, sale and servicing of its equipment. It is in the electromechanical industry, and one of the earliest US companies to have operated abroad. It is appropriate to begin by outlining some of the characteristics of the company and the environments in which it operated in late 1970.

The industry is more than a century old. It is labour intensive as opposed to capital intensive. Hence, ease of entry into the market poses a tremendous competitive problem: in practice there is no patent, or proprietary protection.

The product, basically, is still similar to the original one, although many refinements have been added. Originally, it was a highly engineered, custom-built product, but the market has changed, and many parts are now mass-produced. Product safety, quality and reliability are crucial because the public frequently uses the product day and night. Service (quality, dependability and speed) is equally crucial to commercial success. The unit price is high. Throughout the world, there is still a lack of uniform specifications, governmental safety codes, and quality in the sense of size, construction, engineering required, and customer demands.

Customers include governments, government agencies, builders, architects, engineers, designers and developers. They may be large customers with repeat business (although the unit cost is high), but thousands are small customers who offer little repeat business, if any. There are at least four distinct market segments, distinguished by the type of installation and the need it fulfils. There are several large, multinational competitors and hundreds of smaller, local competitors. There is intensive price competition and all-out competition for market share: thus, profit margins are frequently low.

The company in the case study always has been, and still is, the world leader in product innovation and holds approximately 20–25 per cent of the world market. It is much stronger in some countries than in others, and its market share ranges from 5–50 per cent of the total market in any one country. There is, generally, a lack of management sophistication in the industry. This case concerns itself exclusively with the international operations.

3.1   Position of the company in late 1970

The total sales volume for 1970 was approximately $350 million for the international operations alone: net profits were less than $50 000. The company had affiliates, agents, or wholly-owned subsidiaries in approximately 100 locations encircling the globe. It was well-represented in both developing and developed countries, although roughly two-thirds of its business, by volume, was in developed countries. It had approximately 38 000 employees. At the time of this study, early 1971, the US parent corporation exercised a great deal of influence and, indeed, control over its international operations. Many of the key decisions were made at corporate headquarters.

The growth rate of the international operations was about 15 per cent per year; the domestic operations were growing at an annual rate of 5 per cent per year. The company, although still the world leader in market share and product innovation, was gradually falling behind. It had ignored a growing segment of the market and had allowed small competitors to become strong. However, it still maintained a good reputation for quality, delivery, service and maintenance. There was no international product policy as such, and so products often failed to meet specific local needs. There were indeed few policies, even at the corporate level: these were not designed to meet international needs.

Because of the technical leadership enjoyed by the company, formal apprentice programmes existed in most of its large international operations. For many years, there had been a lack of capital investment in executive manpower, in new plant facilities, modern production machinery, and applied research and development for international needs.

There were virtually no management or operating controls. Very little management accounting information was available; very few studies of the market or competitors were carried out; the pricing policy was designed to capture a market share for years of subsequent servicing. The company was slowly going downhill. The business was characterized by a lack of product and market diversification, excessive inventories, high receivables, poor cash management, high interest costs, lack of knowledge of product costs, absence of cost control, no break-even analysis, and finally some signs of deterioration in factory shipments, product quality, service and maintenance.

3.2   Summary of company's human resource management

The company's history of human resource management in its international operations can best be described as one of neglect. The result was inadequate management in a substantial number of key positions. The style of management was paternalistic and autocratic. There was very little initiative and imagination left in the company. Employees and managers, however, were loyal, indeed unusually so for a large international company. Despite this loyalty, they were complacent, and there appeared to be no incentive to improve performance at any level.

The absence of management controls, combined with a nonaggressive, poorly trained sales force, had led to substantial losses in new sales and loss of market share. Salesmen were good technical engineers from the school of 'hard-knocks', but little else. Virtually all promotions came from within the company; most were based on a man's technical and product knowledge. There were relatively few graduates in a number of operating companies. It was felt, quite wrongly, that unless a man had spent 20 years in the business, starting as a lower-level mechanic, he would be unable successfully to run an operating company as managing director. Several large operating companies run by such managing directors repeatedly lost money for several years in succession.

Save in a few of the larger operating companies, there was no management development or training. Management-by-objectives was unknown. There was a general lack of discipline within the company, shown by the absence of refined objectives, organization planning, job descriptions, performance standards, and performance appraisal and review. This had begun to show in low productivity in the field and factory, while costs and expenses increased. In many locations, managers were grossly underpaid in relation to other multinational companies in comparable industries.

Managers in the office, field and factory had no knowledge of their financial performance because financial and budgetary controls were inadequate. There was virtually no staff turnover at management level. No one was rewarded and recognized for outstanding performance; no one was criticized for marginal or poor performance.

Finally, there were no clearly defined corporate or international policies, no strategic business planning, no sophisticated marketing appraisals, no management information and communication. The company was slowly deteriorating. There had been a strong effort made to increase market share, but the new sales were largely unprofitable. International operations were managed from the New York office, with a small handful of people, and an unimaginative managerial team.

For health reasons, the international vice-president stepped down: a long-serving executive replaced him; a non-US citizen, resident in Europe, well-educated, highly intelligent, dynamic and innovative. He had no staff positions, nor anyone specifically assigned to international operations to be responsible for marketing, production, human resources, finance, engineering, product management, legal work and administration. A few of these essential functions were performed on a part-time basis by corporate staff personnel, with limited international experience. The major problems he faced were:

No strategic business, market, or organization planning.
Reduced market share, poor profitability and low productivity at all levels.
Inadequate products for growing market segments.
No price policy.
Inadequate personnel throughout the organization.

The question posed to the reader is: 'If you were appointed vice-president international, exactly what steps would you take, in what order of priority? How would you develop your basic strategy, long-range objectives, and short-term goals? Specific action plans and timing? How would you measure and control results? All of this in a multinational environment, involving 100 locations in both developed and developing countries. Recognize that you have two to three years to provide a successful profit performance.'

3.3 Solution implemented

It was clear that immediate action had to be taken on several fronts. One top priority was to establish a high degree of independence from corporate operations, to have a free hand to turn the international operations around. International headquarters were moved to a major European city. Four regional headquarters operations were set up, dividing the world geographically and working closely with the operating companies:

Europe (already existent) was expanded.
Far East was established in Singapore.

Latin America was established in Buenos Aires.
Transcontinental was established in Paris.

These four regions were staffed permanently through internal promotions, drawing from the best available executives. Some outside recruitment was done.

Certain select policies were defined for the international division: objectives were developed and communicated. For example:

Products would no longer be sold at a loss.

Prices were increased substantially.

More products, designed specifically for international operations, were developed within the local operating companies.

Short-term goals were determined for each operating company in conjunction with the newly appointed regional vice-presidents, in such areas as:

Productivity improvement at all levels: management, field and factory.

Cost improvement and expense reduction.

Heavy investment in new executive manpower, facilities and equipment.

An international staff was formed, and a senior human resource director was among the first executives hired, as one of the priorities. Six positions were subsequently filled: three from within, three by recruitment.

Each staff and line executive prepared a plan of action, with specific short-term goals for his area of responsibility, and briefing material which was circulated to all senior executives (line and staff), reporting directly to the vice-president, international division. A two-day planning meeting was arranged, at which each executive presented his plan of action, indicating how it was to be implemented. Discussion was free and open: a general and coherent sense of direction was established by interrelating goals. It was not sophisticated: just simple and direct. The idea was to get immediate results while building for the future. There was no historical analysis, no participation by the operating companies. Time was too short; inertia had to be removed; challenging goals were mandatory and non-negotiable.

The agreed new policies and objectives were circulated and explained to all operating company managing directors by the most senior line and staff executives. They were shown how to achieve goals and given support, assistance and guidance.

3.4 Role of human resource manager

Because the content and theme of this book is *multinational human resource management*, the remainder of this chapter deals only with that issue. It must be stressed, however, that the results achieved represented a team effort, and without the cooperation, support and assistance of the most senior line and staff executives, including the international vice-president, little could have been accomplished.

The first and most essential business principle to be followed in human resource management, or any other functional business activity, is the clear definition of the problem, in its full magnitude and complexity. All successful changes start at the top; it was therefore logical to begin with problems relating to the most senior executives. The first priority was to establish a worldwide manpower inventory, initially of only the top 350 positions globally. The purpose was to:

Identify potential talent for senior management positions.
Identify individual and collective training and development needs.
Identify and define existing level of management expertise and profession-
alism on a country-by-country basis.
Determine company executive manpower strengths and weaknesses.
Establish a basis for management audit and essential executive recruitment
needs to strengthen operating companies.
Meet, face-to-face, all the senior managers in the largest companies.

An A B C type of analysis showed that some 20 local companies accounted for more than 90 per cent of total sales by volume and profit: these were the first to be visited. Then, over four years, a series of major actions were undertaken, and a professional human resource programme, concentrating primarily on the executive level, was gradually established. The plan was divided into several phases, a number of which took place concurrently.

During the personal visits to operating companies, a management audit was performed. This consisted of face-to-face, two-hour interviews with the managing director, all line and staff executives reporting direct to him, and a few other key executives, below the second level of management, who could substantially influence business results. Only a few basic issues were discussed, such as:

Describe your job responsibilities in order of importance.
Describe the three major problems and opportunities within your areas of
responsibility.

Describe your working relationships (and types of problems on which you collaborate) with executives on the same level, level above and level below.

What types of management meetings are held? How frequently; what subjects are discussed?

What are your three top priorities, goals, objectives? What is your plan for accomplishment?

What are the local company's policies, objectives and goals? How communicated? Process for achievement?

What are the three major problems and opportunities of the total company today? Plans for resolving problems and taking advantage of the opportunities?

Availability of organization charts, manpower plans, position descriptions, performance standards?

Obviously not all points were put to all executives in all companies. The approach varied considerably, adapted to the particular cultural and managerial environment. Being a US multinational company, interviews were conducted in English; if necessary with an interpreter.

3.5 The action steps

Several steps followed these worldwide interviews. First, the manpower inventory was established. Informal executive manpower reviews were held with local company managing directors and regional vice-presidents. Approximately 35 senior executives were hired from outside the company to strengthen regional staff and operating companies.

The vast recruitment problem was solved over four years by using executive search firms and the human resource director's own contacts. For the most senior management positions — staff directors and managing directors — a selection committee was established. It consisted of the new international president, the human resource director, five line and two of the most senior staff executives. To be successful, a candidate had to be unanimously approved.

All executive search activity was gradually centralized by the human resource director. It was necessary to provide executive search firms with organization charts, position descriptions, performance standards and a work plan for the first year. They were told to put forward only one well-qualified candidate, meeting approximately 40–70 per cent of the personnel specifications as written and discussed.

The professional executive search firms help to save time. It is uneconomic to review 20 résumés, interview 10 candidates and parade three or four of the best to the company's top senior managers. In most cases, only one candidate was presented to the top management; only three out of 35 were rejected. Both top management and the search firm had to be educated to work most efficiently and productively in selecting the right man

A number of senior executives demonstrated that they were unable to cope with the pressures and demands for a significantly higher level of performance: they were removed from their positions but, in most cases, assigned constructive work within their capabilities. Very few people suffered reductions in pay; some chose early retirement, but, overall, the morale, motivation and company team work improved.

Both newly hired and long-service managers were given intensive training outside their home countries to expose them to the best managerial operations of the company and to increase their professional knowledge. This was personally monitored by the international human resource director.

Training lasted from six to twelve months, even for highly qualified general managers brought into the company. Tailored to the individual's needs and background as well as to the position to be filled, it involved training in several different operating companies in Europe, selected on the basis of comparability of operations and products, as well as advanced levels of development in a particular functional discipline.

Newly hired managers were given both project assignments and exposure to the product, organization systems, financial aspects of the business, marketing, production, field operations, and other major functions. The training in professional management (management-by-objectives and motivation) was handled primarily by the international director of human resources. After this training, the new man could much more effectively evaluate his new assignement. He was a local national; and his task was to adapt what he had learnt to the cultural patterns of the country in which he was to manage a company.

The director of human resources also developed and conducted specially tailored management seminars and follow-ups, to ensure the success of the new senior executive. These two-day seminars enabled the new executive quickly and fully to appreciate the status, problems and opportunities of his company and each of its managers. The director of human resources conducted these seminars only on request: no pressure was exercised or needed, possibly because of the close relationships developed during the new executive's training when he reported informally to the human resources executive.

Executive incentive compensation plans were established for key line and staff executives. Annual merit and salary reviews were initiated and made mandatory. Guidelines and audit were provided by the international human resource director. Worldwide compensation and benefit surveys were conducted.

Management-by-objectives as a management development process was also initiated and implemented worldwide by the international human resource director. This was also accomplished through individually tailored, two-day participative management seminars. The seminars were attended by the 15–20 most senior line and staff executives of the local company (through the first two or three levels of management), according to the local situation).

Material for the seminars came from interviews used to supplement the manpower inventories. Organization development took the form of interrelating individual goals for the solution of the company's most pressing problems. In many companies, professional management was introduced for the first time, and key managers were taught priorities, skills, teamwork, and how to plan, organize, coordinate, integrate, control, follow up and measure results. Repeat visits at least every three months were necessary, particularly in developing countries; to check progress and provide additional counselling and guidance in implementing this new managerial way of life.

All seminars were conducted by the human resource director: if necessary, simultaneous translation was used. All discussions were in the native language. Major company problems were exposed and gradually resolved through open and frank discussions, establishment of short-term goals and detailed plans for implementation. In the management-by-objectives seminars, the problems common to all companies were highlighted. Special attention was given to delegation – the why and how, including preparation of lower levels of management to accept it. A great deal of training, particularly at the lower levels, was already built into the companies, but no efforts had been made to measure and evaluate the results of training, nor to control training costs and expenses. Some companies had the idea that to recruit more people would solve any problem: there was generally a need to learn about the more effective utilization of human resources and the need to justify additional personnel.

Basic organization principles dealing with span of control, clear definition of positions, performance standards and working relationships were implemented. Gradually, systems of total remuneration, including job evaluation and incentive rewards, were developed. From these visits and seminars, executives with high potential were identified and provided with developmental and promotional opportunities, locally and abroad. This training was also personally supervised by the director of human resources international. These events expanded the role of the human resource director, who began to function as a business planning consultant, involved in all major aspects of the business. Overall, people were highly receptive to this new emphasis in human resource management at the professional level. Many executives asked the questions: 'Why was this not done 20 or 30 years ago?' and 'How soon can you come back?'

Personnel policies were developed, dealing with all aspects of professional human resource management. Particular attention was paid to the foreign-service employees, over whom there was a history of inconsistency in policy. Every aspect of their employment, duration of assignment, terms and conditions of transfer allowances, statement of results expected, the mandate to hire and train the best local nationals to replace themselves, was regularized. Executive search assignments were personally handled by the international director of human resources, and the number of foreign-service employees was gradually cut by half.

Top management were enthusiastic about the improvement in morale and results, and requested a worldwide survey of human resource policies and practices. This was completed and formed the basis for the establishment of additional personnel policies, and guidelines for their implementation in small- medium- and large-sized companies. It was a complete, coordinated company-wide approach to professional human resource management.

A performance appraisal system was introduced after pilot schemes in a few operating companies. This came after the implementation of management-by-objectives, because many executives were not at first ready for man-manager discussions: performance standards and job descriptions were lacking, and differences in management style were rife.

The entire programme represented a major change in attitudes in a now $600 million international organization, which was still clinging, to some extent, to nineteenth-century management concepts and practices. The rate of managerial obsolescence had been high: it could slowly have killed the company, had it not been arrested. However, the need for more effective human asset management was finally realized, and then the necessary support for effective policies was forthcoming. In addition to measurable increases in human satisfaction, sales rose from $350 million in 1971 to $650 million in 1974, and net profits from $50 000 to $35 million: the number of employees decreased by 4000.

3.6   Conclusion

Most managers eventually realized that their conventional skills were not the main ingredients for success. Too often they concentrated their managerial expertise on physical and material resources, neglecting people whose motivational needs must be accommodated in advance planning just as meticulously as the maintenance needs of conveyor systems.

It is a major responsibility of the human resource executive to make all managers fully aware of their stewardship and accountability for the human resources entrusted to their care. These resources are at least as important as plant or equipment assets. Undoubtedly managerial attitudes and behaviour can be changed. But such changes necessitate a new awareness of sound professional human resources policies. This can be learned but it must be taught. The human resources executive must provide this teaching, along with the simple, workable, practical procedures and routines.

These procedures must embrace all legitimate human concerns of top management, including the development of a climate in the company which encourages and rewards initiative. The techniques range from determining manpower requirements (analysing present and future organization requirements) to recruiting and interviewing techniques, counselling, performance appraisal, goal setting, attitude surveys, and control of absenteeism and staff turnover.

They must also include provision for soliciting and rewarding employee suggestions for cost improvements and for sales and supervisory training and management development. In every country, without exception, it is the local manager who, by his own actions and example, earns the acceptance, understanding, loyalty and support of his work people through professional human resources management.

A business effectiveness catalyst

Thus the director of human resources emerges as an internal consultant — a business effectiveness agent for purposeful and progressive changes in attitudes and behaviour. This role demands that he be a good listener, an encourager of new ideas, a problem solver and an innovator. He helps to foster a creative environment by assisting managers clearly to define and solve human problems. He counsels on the establishment of priorities and literally follows through the process of change and implementation.

The need for a director of human resources as a senior consultant to line management in the successful discharge of 'human' responsibilities is now rapidly becoming a recognized fact. Gone are the days of the old-style personnel manager who concerned himself primarily with the cafeteria, wage administration, union relations and clerical activities. His new task is to take the lead in building flexible, innovative, problem-solving teamwork among responsible managers and superivisors at all levels within the organization.

The next chapter will concentrate more specifically on how this transfer of managerial expertise took place in the OMEGA company giving detailed examples of what was done and how results were measured.

4
Transferring managerial expertise

For any manager who has had a foreign assignment, the transfer of managerial expertise has, no doubt, caused him acute frustration. In many instances, senior managers of foreign companies, shortly after acquisition, have been fired or downgraded because of alleged incompetence. In this chapter, the ways and means of transferring managerial expertise to a foreign environment will be explored. Each of the techniques described has been used successfully to the advantage of both the individuals concerned and to their companies.

The evaluation process must necessarily start with a 'management audit'. A typical example is described in Figure 6 : 1 (see page 151). It does not, however, detail the various considerations necessary for full and complete recognition of cultural, social and managerial differences. This might best be explained as follows. In any multinational survey of management practices, it is very difficult to maintain an unbiased approach. For example, if a foreign executive is not very fluent in our language, this may be misinterpreted as a lack of managerial ability. Conversely, a foreign executive who is highly fluent in our language may be regarded as a first-class executive — his results notwithstanding.

The international human resource executive must develop a sympathetic understanding of foreign personal characteristics: these may be a tendency to talk little, to use 'closed' expressions, to be unwilling to participate in discussions, or to seem withdrawn. An understanding of alien patterns of organization and social structures is also vital to an understanding of managerial practices. This is a real challenge in conducting a management audit. It involves a self-reference criteria correction routine. To assess a business situation in one culture from the background of another culture is misleading and dangerous.

It is helpful to meet executives in other companies when trying to assess a local situation. A disinterested view of differences in managerial styles can thus be gained. The evaluation process itself must be analyzed.

Facts and assessments must be differentiated, and the particular ethno-centric outlook which has conditioned the assessments appreciated. Then, local assumptions not based on universally accepted management principles, but derived from local conditioning will be identified.

If everything possible has been done to eliminate cultural bias, but it is clear that management principles and practices have been ignored, or misapplied, then the question is: 'How do we get them to change?' After experimenting with various accepted techniques, it seems that a management development approach through the techniques of management-by-objectives can best improve management behaviour and thus business results. After all, indigenous people are anxious to learn and do want to improve their managerial abilities – that is, as long as the consultant approaches the problem with an appreciation of their point of view.

The most acceptable point of reference is the problem, or problems, which local management has already confessed to be particularly bothersome. This is the logical point of departure. If a series of problems are identified through individual interviews, then the challenge is to get all local, senior management thinking and working together as a team towards the solution of what emerges as their common problems.

Accordingly, in the case of the OMEGA company individual seminars were specifically tailored to meet the expressed need of local operating company managers.

4.1   The introduction of management-by-objectives

A representative seminar was developed after personal interviews with the top 10 or 15 line and staff executives of the foreign subsidiary. A typical seminar agenda was developed and mailed, together with other information, to the managing director, for circulation and comment six to eight weeks in advance of the seminar. The following basic approach was used:

COMPANY A (in developing country)

16 May and 17 May 1973

Theme

Developing managers to improve business results and provide for future growth.

Seminar objectives

Provide for the identification and resolution of the major problems affecting the present and future profitability of Company A.

Determine how best to take advantage of the company's opportunities — present and future.

Develop present management team through the introduction of professional management methods and techniques, to improve management skills and business results, while at the same time providing opportunities for individual growth and advancement.

Determine ways and means of improving individual business effectiveness and personal contribution to company goals through participation and exchange of ideas.

Identify and measure key result areas which provide greatest opportunity for improved profitability.

These objectives were based on Company A's needs, determined after a management assessment of individual interviews. Many of these objectives were common to developing and some developed countries.

Typical meeting agenda

16 May

0900–0915	Opening remarks. *Managing director*
0915–1030	What is professional management in Omega company? *International director of human resources*
	Qualities necessary for effective management today.
1030–1045	Coffee break.
1045–1245	Small group discussions to identify three most important problems and opportunities of Company A to be solved locally using own resources.

These small group discussions were based on a summary of the homework assignment sent in advance to the managing director and the 10–15 individual line and staff participants.

The homework assignment asked each individual to prepare a position description for himself (formats and examples are to be found in the Appendix to this chapter, pages 69–81), and in one or two sentences to describe the contribution of his position to company growth and profitability. In other words: 'Why does his job exist?' In addition, to list the three most important problems and opportunities — solely for his own position. Then, the three most important goals he had *personally* to accomplish within the next 12 months to improve business results. How were these results to be measured? Finally, what, in his opinion, were the three most important overall company problems to be resolved in the next 12 months. Selection was to be made based on magnitude of impact (i.e. possible effect: good or bad), on profits, innovation, productivity, cost improvement, competition and human resource management.

These responses were the final determinant of the approach to be used in any given company. For example, if 15 people identified a total of 19 problems, it was clear that there was an absence of teamwork, group cohesion and unity, and possibly communication problems.

The local managing director and international director of human resources did not participate in these small group discussions. They served as roving consultants, to clarify each group assignment, and to ensure that the group got started in the right direction and did not get too far off track.

1245—1400   Group luncheon (seating arranged in advance).
1400—1530   Summary presentation by group leaders.

Each group was asked initially to select a chairman who would report the group's conclusions and the rationale through which they reached these conclusions. They also chose a recording secretary.

When all groups had reconvened, each group leader presented the consensus of major company problems and opportunities. All participants were encouraged to challenge the findings and the logic behind them. In the vast majority of the countries, this technique did lead to open and frank discussion. The only exceptions in 25 management seminars were two countries in the Far East who were totally unaccustomed to group dynamics and participation. A different approach was evolved for these countries.

In many countries, both developed and developing, such seminars represented an entirely new experience, inasmuch as most major and many minor decisions had been considered hitherto to be sole prerogative of the managing director. Nonetheless, the meetings were highly successful and very much appreciated by all participants.

1530—1545   Tea break.

1545—1630   Synthesis of group discussions. *International Director of Human Resources*

This was a key point of the two-day meetings and, as a general rule, the group discussions and subsequent general meeting exchanges resulted in narrowing down a long list of company problems and opportunities to the four to six most important ones, which became the priorities for concentration.

1630—1900   Management-by-objectives in Company A.

Here, again, the approach to managing by and with objectives was designed to suit the local situation by the human resource director. By now, adequate information had been acquired to give what was needed in the form which was needed, according to the participant's perceptions and state of readiness to absorb and apply. The approach varied from the most simple basics to a serious discussion of philosophy and relationship to the budget in the more sophisticated, highly developed countries. Even then, subsequent follow-up meetings were required to ensure understanding implementation and that problems were actually solved.

Typically, interrelation of goals was a relatively new concept; the various functional heads had previously acted as separate companies, with little interdepartmental cooperation, and a virtual absence of delegation to the lower levels.

As a result, the advance homework assignment to be completed between the first and second day of the seminar was redesigned, to encourage each participant to focus on the major priorities of the company on an overall basis, whether problems or opportunities. Once the groups had arrived at a consensus on these issues, the next step was to get them to focus their individual efforts toward a collective solution of company problems. At the same time, they were given an opportunity for practical applications of MBO.

The next assignment was for each individual participant, on his own, and within the framework of his position responsibilities, to develop one goal wherein he could make a *personal* contribution to the solution of one of the major problems identified on the first day. Alternatively, he could develop one goal, to take advantage of the opportunities identified for profit improvement and growth. For the goal identified, the individual was required to state:

Exactly how he would achieve it.
The action steps, including beginning and ending dates for each step.
Who, in his organization, would do the work.
How progress and results would be measured and controlled.
Information and any additional resources required to do the job.
Who in the organization, outside of his department, could help or hinder
   him from achieving his goal.
The final net result to the business, stated quantitatively and qualitatively.

17 May

0900—0915   Opening remarks. *Managing director*

This normally included a commentary on the previous day's session, his reaction to the quality of the discussions and his agreement with the major issues identified by the participants. Again he stressed the need for open and frank discussion of the company's problems and the necessity to improve teamwork to move the company forward.

0915—1045   Individual presentations of goals.

Each participant was given 10 minutes to present his short-term goal. Others in the group were invited to comment on the goal in terms of its realism, practicality, achievability, quantification, importance of magnitude, and in general, the degree to which it fulfilled the stipulations of the homework assignment.

1045—1245   Continuation of individual presentations along with
                  continual summary and commentary by international
                  director of human resources.
1245—1400   Lunch.
1400—1530   Conclusion of individual presentations and review by
                  human resource director.

In a majority of the 25 seminars, in both developed and developing countries, a commonality of problems and opportunities manifested itself. The major areas for improvement in over 75 per cent of the 25 companies based on local interviews, seminars and identification of such by 300 senior management participants were as follows:

Profits.

Productivity.

Market share.

Training and development at all levels.

Position descriptions.

Performance standards.

Management-by-objectives.

Delegation.

Communications.

At first, it was not realized how important it would be to plan sufficient (and frequent) follow-ups, particularly in developing countries. While the local nationals performed well at the seminars, if a follow-up meeting and visit were not held within three months, momentum was lost and little accomplished. This was primarily because the concepts of priorities and delegation were unfamiliar: managers in developing countries were not accustomed to meeting deadlines, with a strong follow-up and precise measurement of results.

The international director of human resources therefore drafted material which, translated into the local language, was used as a basis for subsequent follow-up meetings. Some of the more important of these documents which produced favourable results are included in the Appendix to this chapter (pages 93–112).

4.2 Justification for addition of new personnel

Particularly in the developing countries, and to a lesser degree in the developed countries, senior management tended to believe that any company problem could be solved if only they had more staff. It seldom occurred to them that perhaps fewer but more qualified people could provide the answer to their problems. The organization of work, delegation and full utilization of existing personnel had to be learned, and it had to be taught.

In a number of Latin American and Far Eastern countries, where rapid growth was anticipated and problems in meeting factory schedules were being experienced, the number of open requisitions, if filled, would have wiped out a great deal of the anticipated profits, as well as creating organizational confusion. Hence, the director of human resources prepared the following paper and used it as a discussion tool in subsequent seminars:

JUSTIFICATION FOR ADDITION OF NEW PERSONNEL TO THE PAYROLL

The requesting manager must first prepare a position description and the work to be done by the new employee. The manager must also specify, in writing, with precision, the following information:

A work plan and results to be accomplished in the first year by the new employee; and effect (positive) increase in profits, or reduction in total costs, e.g. overtime hours.

Who is doing the work now, if it is being done at all?

Is the work being done on an overtime basis; if so, what is the total additional annual cost?

Are mistakes being made; if so, when is the negative impact on profits quantified on an annual basis, e.g. extra costs incurred?

What would be the effect on business results/profits, costs, if the work to be completed, which is not now being performed, is left undone or is inadequately performed?

What would be the negative effect, measured quantitatively, if no new person is hired to do the work?

Age and experience of person to be hired, and how soon can he be effective in his new job?

How will he be trained to bring him up to optimum performance as soon as possible?

Any marginal performers in the work group who should be replaced, trained, to increase efficiency, productivity, etc.

Is there any other way to solve the problem:

reorganization of workload?

redistribution of the work, etc.?

Is the position expected to be a permanent addition, or just a temporary solution or response to an unusually heavy peak load?

Our experience has been that most managers will not go to the trouble to complete the foregoing; they will find a creative way to solve the problem. On the other hand, if a manager completes all the related data, his case and explanation will be self-evident.

The local personnel manager was responsible to the managing director for implementation.

4.3 The task-force approach

Another problem revealed by the seminars was the lack of teamwork, at all levels, in both developed and developing countries. This sprang from the traditional attitudes described in 1.1 (pages 5–11).

When a major problem demanded close cooperation by several departments, a lack of teamwork usually led to an unsatisfactory or partial solution. Managers were shown how teamwork could solve a problem which all had agreed was crucial: delays in shipments from the local factory. The technique used was to set up a task force. The approach and the outcome are described in the Appendix to this chapter (see pages 87–92).

4.4 On training standards and measurement

The OMEGA company and its subsidiaries had always believed in training, particularly at junior levels. Training, however, was not seen as an investment in human resources: no attempt had been made to control or measure the return on this investment. Accordingly, the following paper was prepared by the director of human resources, translated and circulated, to form the basis for policy guidelines and follow up management-by-objectives seminars:

ON TRAINING STANDARDS AND MEASUREMENT

1. In conducting approximately 30 management seminars to date, at least 22 companies have specified training and development at all levels as one of their three greatest problems. According to these companies, the lack of qualified personnel at all levels has had adverse effect on:

Productivity, efficiency, company image, new sales and service sales and, hence, present and future profitability and growth. The evidence tends to support these preliminary findings.

2.   With the increased emphasis on training at all levels within operating companies, as reflected in recently approved budget appropriations, we must ensure that all monies spent provide a proper return to the business.

3.   In order to accomplish this, it is necessary to control and measure this activity with the same precision as we do when making an investment in a new piece of capital equipment or machinery.

4.   My observations indicate that the training programmes conducted to date have not produced optimum benefit to the operating companies for the following reasons:

While the technical content of training efforts *appears* to meet the needs of the company, there is little, if any, effort made accurately and precisely to measure the results of this training.

It has been adequately demonstrated that if we do not measure our training activities, we cannot control them, set standards for improvement or remedy defects. Hence, we never know the real impact of training expenditures on profitability or costs.

We sometimes begin our efforts by training groups of people *without specific, advance knowledge of*:

    (*a*)   Skills, knowledge and experience requirements of the job itself. This is more often true in clerical and management positions than in hourly-paid positions.

    (*b*)   Adequate, precise, measurable knowledge of the problems we are trying to correct, etc. We are lacking in feedback mechanisms which really measure the full magnitude of the problem, in all its dimensions.

    (*c*)   The internal problems which give rise to inefficiency and lack of control *vs.* external problems (e.g. material delays from outside supplies, building not ready, etc.), but we do not plan in advance what percentage of improvement we can realistically expect by the expenditure of time, effort and money on training of personnel. This applies to all activities of the company, at all levels, whether management, supervision, clerical or hourly-paid employees.

No one individual is totally responsible and accountable for the results of the training; and there is a lack of coordination in all training programmes with a common base of skill and knowledge requirements.

5.   In order to correct these problems, the following minimum criteria

for a successful training effort should be incorporated into our advance planning:

Adequate manpower planning and forecasting.

Advance recruitment based on realistic sales, production and FOD (Field Operations Department) forecasts, including sales and service completions.

Proper orientation programme for new employees.

Training plans and activities according to knowledge, skill and experience requirements of the position(s) to be filled, and the *specific* problems to be solved.

6.   All training, whether for newly hired employees, preparatory training in advance of a promotion, or training to upgrade existing levels of skills and abilities, should follow a careful, preplanned approach as follows:

(a)   Always start out with a small pilot project for accurate measurement and control and follow-up. If it is not successful, the failure will be a small one and relatively easy to remedy with a minimum expenditure of costs, time and effort.

(b)   Make every effort to use experimental and control groups, that is to say, take two groups of individuals performing roughly comparable work: give the training to one (experimental group), but not to the other (control group). This permits ease of measurement and comparison of results, whether it be training for improved sales, construction efficiency, works efficiency, service or maintenance, or quality improvement.

(c)   Carefully and accurately define the problems to be solved in quantitative terms. Set realistic performance standards; determine also, in quantitative terms, the degree to which improvement is expected to take place according to a preplanned schedule with specific action steps, including *beginning and ending* dates for each step.

(d)   Place one person in charge of the project, giving him full responsibility and authority to get the job done.

(e)   Make a plan for the training activity, which should include the following:

(1)   Project study and plan which will include a study of the job to be done and a careful definition of the problem to be solved, with all its ramifications and all its dimensions, as well as magnitude of impact on business results stated in quantitative terms, if it is not solved.

(2) Develop, in advance, and in writing:

Training objectives.

Form and content of training.

Who will be actually physically responsible for the training?

What assistance will be needed?

Cooperation from other departments line and staff.

Information requirements.

Feedback of information on changes in performances, measurable results.

Form, content and timing of training reports, including progress results relative to the accomplishment of predetermined objectives.

Teaching, learning materials, brochures, methods manuals, audiovisual aids.

Total costs of the training in time and money.

Plan for introducing the training programme in writing and in person to all concerned with the training, e.g. trainees, supervisors, managers. Solicit in advance, comments and critique from those whom the training is supposed to benefit. Their comments must include:

Clear statement of problems to be solved, with precise measurements of existing problems, together with proper analyses of real causes of problems.

Beginning and ending date for each phase of the training and how progress will be recorded and measured.

Who is responsible for each phase of the program.

Provision for feedback from participants, trainees, supervisors and managers.

Plan to remedy or correct defects of the programme as observed by:

Failure to obtain desired results.

Comments of participants.

Comments of supervisors.

Comments of customers.

Comments from those internal operations affected by the output of the department in which the problem has been clearly identified.

Field test and audit the effectiveness of the training
at frequent intervals to:
Maintain higher standard of performance.
Detect additional problems.
Further modify, improve and extend training
to other areas.

Regardless of the nature of the training or the reasons for undertaking a training programme, these suggested criteria, methods and procedures will accomplish the intended results if properly applied.

The most essential ingredient for success is to have a formal, *written detailed plan, prepared in advance* by the individual responsible for the training and/or the problem(s) to be solved through training. This plan must receive the advance support, approval and cooperation from all personnel in the company who are directly or indirectly affected by the results of the training.

It has been proven repeatedly that properly trained and motivated people, at all levels, can accomplish a great deal more than they are presently contributing. A mere addition of people will often further complicate the problem, instead of contributing to its solution.

Finally, with the expansion of many of our businesses, particularly in Latin America, we must recognize that the addition of any new person to the company represents a substantial investment.

One result of this approach was the identification and selection of training costs, and the development of guidelines for controlling expenditure in training.

4.5   A further result of the management seminars

Between the first seminar and the second follow-up seminar, individual participants were requested to refine their short-term goals and submit them to the managing director for approval. These goals became the basis for a subsequent management-by-objectives follow-up by the international director of human resources.

Typical examples of the quality of work done by local nationals are presented in the Appendix to this chapter (see pages 82–7).

Companies which had sustained losses for several years became profitable through this more precise method of managing and controlling their operations.

4.6   On Delegation

For the kind of reasons noted in 1.4 (see pages 17–21) delegation to lower levels of management had been virtually nonexistent in a number of companies. The following paper, written by the international director of human resources, was distributed and incorporated into subsequent management-by-objectives follow-up seminars:

ON DELEGATION

It is obvious to me that unless major tasks are broken down into smaller projects and delegated to middle- and, in some cases, lower-management personnel, the project will not succeed. Therefore, this delegation must be properly defined, in writing, and include timing.

Preparing managers to accept delegation

1.   When presented with a problem ask for possible solutions, including advantages and disadvantages of each. 'Force' the man to think through the problem and come up with a solution. If you make his decisions for him, he cannot be accountable for results and he never really learns to accept responsibility and develop initiative. It is a poor use of your own managerial time to make decisions which could and should be made at lower levels of management.

2.   Ask each man reporting to you to list the 8–10 major responsibilities of his job, in order, by priority of importance, as he sees them. Then you do the same yourself for each individual. This done, meet and compare notes. The results may come as a revelation.

3.   Ask the man which of his responsibilities (as mutually agreed to form the first session), are being performed in a fully satisfactory manner. Make him justify his answers by telling you his frame of reference and standard of measurement. Idea is to develop his framework for performance standards and the necessity to quantify, whenever possible to do so.

4.   Ask the man to establish one short-term goal in a critical area, which requires improvement, or a new project to be undertaken. Get the man to agree that improvement is both necessary and possible. [Use the management-by-objectives approach, as outlined and discussed in 4.1.]

5. If necessary, establish his first quantitative goal for him, but obtain his agreement that the job can be done by him.

6. Make sure that his first goal is realistic, practical, achievable, measurable and represents a real challenge for successful completion . . . . . a real contribution to the company.

7. Let the man know, in advance, your expectations and your personal preferences, if any, on how he should approach the project. Make sure he understands his work, his priorities and his goals, by getting him to tell you them in his own words and putting everything in writing — his complete plan on how he will achieve his goal, including timing.

8. Let the man know you have confidence in him; do not closely supervise his activities. Permit him the latitude of a few mistakes.

9. Follow up regularly, but informally, through progress review and report meetings scheduled in advance; know how well the man is doing. Insist on his strict adherence to time schedules. Always establish dates and schedules.

10. Be available, at all times, for coaching and guidance.

11. Quickly compliment and praise (publicly) *significant* progress and results achievement. If you must criticize, do so in private, with specific examples of under-achievement. Tell the man exactly how and why he failed to meet your expectations.

12. Have informal progress review, at least twice a month; this is particularly important in the beginning. Listen more than you speak. Find out how well you are doing as a manager in terms of availability, help, guidance, removal of obstacles, etc.

13. Keep your promises to the man to provide him with information, additional resources, support and assistance.

14. Do not attempt to use formal performance appraisal of MBO results for the first year, particularly as a basis for salary action or inaction.

15. Stress the management development aspects of this approach to the man. Let him know you are interested in his future progress.

This paper became another vital step in the transfer of managerial expertise to local nationals, in both developed and developing countries: it took time to change habits, but delegation did become an integral part of the management process. It was less difficult to implement in developing countries than in developed countries.

Teaching the art of delegation and getting it practised was difficult: problems of marginal and unacceptable performace were highlighted.

Without performance standards the company in the past had virtually had no self-induced turnover: any level of performance had been acceptable. It became apparent that some old, faithful employees could not measure up to the new standards demanded of managers: something had to be done. It was the company's fault more than that of the individual manager. He had never been given the opportunity to perform: 'He got that way under our supervision'. So, what had to be done?

Standards of performance had to be determined for the individual, preferably with his concurrence. In particular, the degree of tolerance had to be precisely ascertained.

The individual had explained to him, in writing as well as orally, exactly what he was expected to achieve in each of his position responsibilities.

An attempt was made to get him to agree exactly what would be a reasonable standard of performance.

At three- and six-month intervals, his direct superior held a 'How am I doing' discussion with him.

If and when it became clear that the man was inadequate for his job, it was discussed with him and he was given specific examples of his failure to meet predetermined, realistic goals.

The man was then removed from his position, but placed as a face-saver somewhere he was still capable of making a distinct contribution to the business. Generally there was no reduction in pay. His title was changed to consultant, project specialist or manager of special assignments.

Performance standards for his new position were established with the individual affected.

In relatively few cases, the man had to be released: then, generous severance allowances and/or early retirement were granted.

A poor performer, in a key management position, drags the whole company down. Any inadequate performance tends to set the standard for the whole company and inhibits overall improvement. Often a job change is welcomed by the individual; he generally realizes he is not up to standard, and over a period of time may even become physically ill.

4.7   Meeting evaluation

After each seminar, participants were asked to give their views on the meeting, just as openly and frankly as they participated in the discussions. The forms were handed in anonymously. The following is a sample of the evaluation format used:

MEETING EVALUATION QUESTIONNAIRE: DEVELOPING MANAGERS TO IMPROVE BUSINESS RESULTS AND PROVIDE FOR FUTURE GROWTH

Management conference

Signature not necessary

1. Please indicate your overall impression(s) of the meeting (check all appropriate boxes):

.... Excellent	.... Too long	.... Too directed
.... Good	.... Too short	.... Too participative
.... Fair	.... Just right	.... The right mix
.... Poor	.... Other	.... Other

Comments ....

2. Reactions to presentations:
...............Excellent ....Good ....Bad ....Indifferent
Would you repeat this next year? ....Yes ....No
What aspects of this approach do you like? Why?
What aspects of this approach do you dislike? Why
Comments ....

3. Reaction to discussion groups:
(*a*) Were they worthwhile? ....Yes ....No
Comments ....
Did they accomplish the following objectives (Yes/No)?
.... Identify business fundamentals.
.... Stress generic practical application.
.... Permit opportunity to share experiences.
.... Stimulate possible applications in your operations.
.... Clarify policy consideration.
Commentary on foregoing ....
Length of sessions: .... Too long
.... Too short
.... Just right
Comments..
(*b*) Did you feel you had sufficient opportunity to participate?
.... Yes .... No

Any other ways to stimulate and encourage participation?
Comments ....
(c) Which presentation was of *most* interest to you in terms of its value
for practical implementation?
....
(d) Which presentation was of *least* interest to you in terms of its value
for practical implementation?
....

4. Identify three practical ideas obtained from the Seminar that were of
most benefit and interest to you:
(1)........................... (2)........................... (3)...........................
What is the best way to follow up these ideas to be sure they are
implemented?
....

5. Which subjects should have been included, but were not?
....
Which subjects should have been excluded?
....

6. What is the most important thing we can do to improve future
meetings?
....

7. What, in your opinion, should a meeting like this accomplish?
....
To what degree was this accomplished at this meeting?
....

8. Adequacy of time to meet with an exchange of ideas with other
participants?
.... Not enough time
.... Too much time
.... Right amount of time
Comments ....

9. Any general comments you would like to make about the meeting?
....

10. What should the international division staff do to contribute to the
improved effectiveness of the operating companies?
....

Most participants, from these forms, seemed grateful for the opportunity to learn more about professional management. Of particular interest were the comments which helped to improve the follow-up meetings. The most frequent reactions were:

Teamwork in small groups was highly appreciated.
It is good to work out as a group the objectives of the company.
More detailed help in analysing the daily work of management (priorities, skills and delegation) would have been helpful.
The need for integrated objectives was recognized.
More guidance was wanted on how to improve teamwork in a company.
Homework was appreciated as a basis for discussion.
Meeting was too short fully to understand and apply all the new ideas. Follow-up is necessary.
Unusually good participation indicated high motivation.
'I came ready to criticize such a waste of time; I found out what a really poor manager I was.'
'This should have been done 20 years ago.'
'How to measure results' was the most useful.
The next session should be held two months before the business plan review, to improve that planning.
'The different points of view over the same subject were amazing to me.'
'It was the first time anybody listened to me.'
Management members should meet at least once a month as a group.

The comments were obviously sincere, and indicate just how the local companies had been denied guidance on management development and professional management techniques. The situation rapidly improved as these seminars developed. Other special seminars were held if requested: indeed seminars were only ever conducted by request, and their value was so soon recognized that there was virtually no need to 'sell' this service after the first few seminars.

Special seminars dealt with problems of quality and delivery, line/staff relationships, financial performance standards, application of industrial engineering principles, analysis and remedy for business plan failure, motivation and comunication, and forecasting.

Ultimately, performance appraisal and review was introduced. Performance appraisal should never be formally introduced until a full year or more after the introduction of management-by-objectives. It may not succeed everywhere. However, most people want to know how well they are doing as well as what they can do further to improve performance. Performance measurement covers individual appraisal, group appraisal, and the feedback of assessment to those appraised. Performance appraisal is an attempt to think clearly about what each person does, how well he does it, and what his future prospects are when viewed against the background of his total work situation, including the direction and opportunities which his manager has provided.

Whether a manager intends it or not, his every word, suggestion, criticism and look tells an employee how his performance is being judged. Each builds him up or tears him down. Performance appraisal is the most sensitive part of the manager's job. Either he uses this management tool effectively to build loyalty, teamwork, cooperation and understanding or he abuses it and fails to achieve both highest job satisfaction and highest job productivity. All employees have a right to be told where they stand, for better or for worse. The manner in which it is done is important.

Appraisal is a line responsibility, but specific guidelines are needed from a corporate office, so that ratings, as far as possible, are consistent, particularly where products, processes, technology and markets vary, and a corporation is beginning to experiment with interdivisional promotional transfers.

Feeding back results is the manager's most important responsibility, both to his subordinates and himself. How he does it will determine whether he builds, or destroys morale, increases or decreases productivity and profitability, and helps or hinders individual development. Much is to be gained when a manager is conscientious about appraisal review. Formal appraisals serve a number of purposes: they pinpoint areas where improvement is needed, make clear who is responsible for what, allow a review of priorities, and identify problems so that they can be resolved.

Performance appraisal should commend good work, serve as one base for pay increases and promotions, stimulate individual self-development, teach subordinates — and reveal how well a manager himself is doing and what some of his own developmental needs are. The format and instructions for use will be found in the Appendix to this chapter (see pages 106–111).

Appendix to Chapter 4

This appendix gives examples of the various documents used in conjunction with the programme described in Chapter 4.

POSITION DESCRIPTION
PART I: ALL MANAGEMENT POSITIONS

In each and every management position within OMEGA, there are certain elements of managerial work which must be performed. These include:

1 Planning.
2 Organizing.
3 Integrating and coordinating.
4 Controlling, implementing and follow-up.
5 Measuring results.

1 Planning

Within the framework of regional and company objectives, the manager must determine the short-term goals (to be accomplished within one year) for the function for which he is responsible. These goals should be relatively few in number and must complement, support and directly contribute to the realization of the company's short-term goals and long-term objectives.

Specifically

1 Plans must be formulated, written and circulated to all concerned who must implement specific action steps to obtain desired results.
2 Plans must be stated with quantitative, measurable impact on business results.
3 Plans must spell out the specific actions required, by whom, together with necessary timing.

2 Organizing

Determine total work necessary to achieve the planned goals.
Decide how many and what kinds of people are required.
Hire and train people to do the work.

Determine and communicate the best methods and procedures for getting
the work done.

Describe and define each job, establish priorities and performance
standards for each individual and for each activity.

3   Integrating and coordinating

Make sure that each individual understands his job and its particular
contribution to the improvement of business results. A position
description for each job is necessary.

Delegate responsibility, define authority given to each individual in the
performance of his job.

Coordinate and integrate the efforts of all personnel reporting direct. This
includes integration of their goals. Coordinate with executives on the
same level, on the level above and on the level below.

Determine information required by the individual to do this job.

4   Controlling, implementing and follow-up

Determine key reports required, and the frequency and timing of
information needed to establish simple, but effective systems of control
and follow-up.

Develop an early warning system immediately to detect deviation from
planned results.

Take immediate action to correct deviations, instead of delayed reaction.

Be available to assist, guide, coach, counsel subordinates, and help to
remove obstacles to their effective performance.

Become sufficiently knowledgeable and involved in the business to be able
to verify accuracy of information received and appraise the results
obtained in relation to established goals and approved budgets.

Create and maintain an attitude and atmosphere of excellence, a
productive and harmonious work climate, constantly striving for higher
achievement.

Train and develop subordinates through establishment of high performance standards and delegation.

Lead the group through establishing and maintaining the highest personal
standards of excellence and through proper planning and organizing of
the managers' own work and time.

5   Measuring results

If an activity cannot be measured, it cannot be controlled and, hence, we will never know what is its real contribution to business results, nor will we be able to measure the degree of improvement or deterioration which is taking place. Hence, each and every key result area of the business, as determined by the magnitude of its impact on sales, costs, expenses, productivity and profitability, must be measured. It is the basis for establishing priorities of work.

Clear, specific, quantitative and qualitative performance standards must be devised, developed and communicated to each individual for each activity to determine where improvement can and should be made.
Record, report and discuss individual and collective performance.
Analyze, appraise and interpret results against plan. This may be required daily, weekly, monthly, or quarterly depending on the importance of the activity, the project, or the problem to be resolved. The causes of underachievement must be quickly identified and corrected.

A format and instructions were designed to enable each seminar participant to see his job in a new light: its financial implications, working relationships, accountability, authority, contribution to business results and subsequent short-term goals. It served also as a basis for formal job evaluation and, eventually, performance appraisal and reviews. It stressed each man's personal contribution to business results. It reads as follows:

POSITION DESCRIPTION
PART II: EACH SPECIFIC MANAGEMENT JOB

1 Job title

The job title should clearly indicate the nature of the responsibility.

2 Purpose of the job

Why does this position exist: what does it actually contribute to business results?

3 Scope of the job

(Including financial responsibility) What is this position broadly respons-ible for; specifically which areas of the business does it directly influence and control through financial impact of his function? This includes such items as:

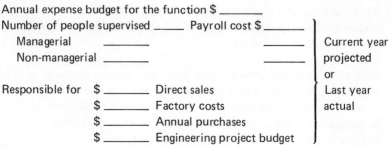

Annual expense budget for the function $ _____
Number of people supervised _____ Payroll cost $ _____
   Managerial   _____   _____   Current year
   Non-managerial _____   _____   projected
                                                 or
Responsible for $ _____ Direct sales   Last year
                 $ _____ Factory costs   actual
                 $ _____ Annual purchases
                 $ _____ Engineering project budget
Etc.

4 Principal responsibilities

Brief statements of the major responsibilities of the position: normally 8—10 is sufficient to identify the actual work content and establish priorities.

5 Authority to act independently

Consider such items as:
   Approve/Recommend policy; short range/long-term.
Must work within policies established by corporate, international, regional, company, including capital expenditure limitations.
Right to hire, fire, transfer, promote, award salary increases.
Make all decisions independently as long as they are within framework of the budget as established by the managing director and approved by the regional vice-president.
Set his own goals and implement plans for achievement.
Must get managers' approval of proposed goals, projects, plans.

6 Working relationships

To whom (which position) does this position report?
Which positions report directly to this position? Describe *only* the major functions of each position or organization unit which reports direct.
With what position does this man work directly and integrate with for accomplishment of his job? How? Why?

Example. Contract control manager works closely with managers of new sales, service sales, engineering, production and Field Operations Department, in order to determine proper lead times to avoid delay in deliveries and satisfy customer requirements with minimum cost and optimum inventory levels.

7 Qualifications required to perform the job satisfactorily (not necessarily the background of the individual currently assigned to the position)

Specific formal education such as:
> Technical college (2 years).
> Engineering Degree.
> Master's or PhD degree.

Specific on-the-job experience required and length of time it takes to obtain it. This refers to knowledge and skills which can only be obtained through experience, such as:
> Technical product knowledge.
> Administrative experience, etc.

Managerial experience.

Other requirements, such as:
> Analytical ability.
> Ability to travel extensively; energy level/physical health.
> Language ability.
> Geographic dispersion of the job may require high degree of adaptability.
> Language skills.
> Human relations skills, e.g., more important in a staff or sales position. This refers to the degree of importance in handling interpersonal relationships.

8   Performance standards

How does one know when the job is being performed satisfactorily?

Specifically describe in quantitative and/or qualitative terms the conditions which will exist for each major responsibility if it is being performed in an acceptable manner.

Example: *Works Manager.* To meet 98 per cent of factory production schedule within or below budgeted costs.

9   What are the major challenges in the job?

Define the major problems to be solved and their potential impact on costs/profits.

Example: Personnel Director. Annual employee turnover (quits) is 75 per cent or 300 quits per year. This costs the company approximately $300 000 per year because of lost productivity, bad quality, late deliveries, hiring, training costs, etc.

10   What actions do you reserve for yourself?

For example: projects, policy-decisions, etc., which are not delegated, but which must remain the *personal contribution* of the job incumbent.

Specific: Managing director. Make the final decision on market strategy in launching a new product.

Because all effective change must start at the top, the first description developed was for the local managing director. This incorporated all key result areas, and served as a basis for the development of performance descriptions for the next two levels of management. In some cases, it was a revelation; it generated much enthusiasm. In some parts of the world, however, it evoked opposition: some people did not want to be pinned down and committed to results. Some people find it is much easier to live with confusion, particularly if they are inadequate or marginal performers. However this approach proved to be 80 per cent successful — that is, it was effectively implemented in eight out of ten companies.

The key to success was to have the right managing director at the local operating company level. It helped that the international director of human resources was directly involved in the recruitment and selection of 16 managing directors, and personally responsible for their training and development: he also had the cooperation and support of the regional vice-presidents. The following position description was devised:

POSITION DESCRIPTION
PART II: MANAGING DIRECTOR

Purpose of the job (Why does this position exist?)

To manage a company in such a manner as to achieve optimum profitability and return on shareholders' capital in both the short-term and long-range.

Scope of the position including financial accountability

The managing director is the chief operating line executive with responsibility for the company. In this capacity, he is responsible for:

Number of	How many	How many	Current year projected or Last year actual
employees	managerial	others	
Payroll $	$	$	
New sales $			
Service sales $			
Profit $			
Company investment — all assets $			

Principal responsibilities and performance standards

Within the framework of corporate, international and regional policies, the managing director is responsible for the development and subsequent realization of business objectives and goals in accord with the approved budget and long-range plan. His principal responsibilities, together with performance standards, are as follows:

1. Develop and recommend a sound organization structure; recruit, train and *develop* capable executives for all key positions.

Performance standards

(a) The degree to which his organization is able to cope effectively with short-term problems, and to which they are able to accomplish all necessary work in time and in a professional manner, to achieve planned results in accord with the approved business plan and budget.

(b) The existence and communication of well-defined performance standards for each key position and each key results area.

(c) The degree of the organization's performance improvement in engineering, new sales and service sales, field operations and production with regard to profits, costs and productivity.

(d) The existence of documented evidence to demonstrate that performance is discussed regularly, areas of under-achievement are quickly highlighted, and appropriate, timely action is taken to eliminate marginal performance.

2. Provide for the necessary engineering work, as required locally, to meet market and customer demands for product reliability and quality at lowest possible cost.

    Performance standards
    (a) Existence of engineering project budgets for product modifications, to meet customer demands and alleviate production bottlenecks, quality problems, etc.
    (b) Engineering lead times available and respect for all contract work by product, including traditionals and models.
    (c) Quality and timeliness of data, drawings, estimates, etc., supplied to other departments.

3. Formulate and implement market strategies for the company, based on thorough market analyses, including competitors': products, quality, market coverage and share, costs, strategies and price policies. Achieve a continuous improvement in market share at acceptable spreads in both new sales and service sales.

    Performance standards. Continuing improvement in:
    (a) Market participation and market share by segment.
    (b) Spread (profitability).
    (c) Reduction of sales costs and expenses.
    (d) Quality of the marketing plan, as measured by the achievement of goals in sales and service and the percentage of accuracy in forecasted *vs.* actual results obtained.
    (e) Profit contribution per salesman.

4. Ensure the continuing improvement in efficiency (productivity), quality, timing of completion, costs and profitability of erection, service and maintenance operations, while providing for growth in number and profitability of service contracts.

    Performance standards. Improvements in:
    (a) Total FOD (Field Operations Department) and service labour efficiency multiple.
    (b) Hours and cost performance.
    (c) Total completions, FOD and service, as well as units and jobs completed for service.
    (d) Spread estimated *vs.* recovered.
    (e) Cost of contracts in process turnover (FOD inventory).
    (f) Callback rate.

(*g*) Immediacy of customer acceptance of completed work and payment of his bills on time.

(*h*) Meeting planned completion dates on schedule.

5. Ensure the production of equipment on schedule, within quality standards at minimum cost with the shortest lead time. Achieve continuing reduction in manufacturing costs while maintaining, or improving, product quality through application of industrial engineering principles to improve employee production. Reduce costs of purchased items and services. Recommend necessary capital expenditure and audit to ensure that desired results are obtained.

   Performance standards. Continuing improvement in:

   (*a*) Cost and expense reduction.

   (*b*) Inventory financing costs, by establishing and maintaining optimum inventory levels.

   (*c*) Manufacturing income contribution, productive hours, PNP (indirect labour) ratio, headcount and productivity per man hour and per machine.

   (*d*) Meeting delivery dates within established lead times at the desired level of quality with error-free shipment.

   (*e*) And lastly, the existence of accurate daily production reports and time standards for all productive work.

6. Read, understand, analyse, interpret and communicate key financial measurements to all departments. Establish financial controls over all significant areas of costs and expenses, to maximize profit through best utilization of company assets — material and human.

   Performance standards. Degree of improvement in:

   (*a*) Receivables turnover (billings, collections, overdues).

   (*b*) Billing coverage (customer payment terms, delays in billing).

   (*c*) Establishing and implementing price adjustment clauses and other contract conditions.

   (*d*) Meeting deadlines for management reports.

   (*e*) Quality, completeness, flow and timing of financial data — external as well as internal reports — to establish more effective budget and cost controls.

7. Ensure the development and application of management information systems and controls to highlight business trends, problems, opportunities and unfavourable variances, which could adversely affect

company profitability, or growth in the short-term or long-range. Take immediate action to correct unfavourable deviations instead of delayed reactions.

Performance standards

(a) The existence of an effective management control system, the end result of which is consistently to supply the required material at the required place within the required time to fulfil all contractual obligations at the minimum total cost to OMEGA.

(b) Evidence of dissemination of all *necessary* management information and reports to all levels of management (staff and line), to enable each to monitor the financial performance of his particular activity, to be able to take immediate action, should results begin to fall short of expectations.

(c) Evidence of proper coordination among sales, engineering, factory, FOD and finance, to fix responsibility and accountability for the specific contribution of each function to the attainment of planned and budgeted results.

8. Ensure the establishment of sound, locally competitive employee and union relations policies and practices, which encourage and promote individual development while improving business effectiveness and profitability.

Performance standards

(a) The existence of well-defined local wage and salary structures, based on comparisons with other comparable local companies.

(b) Existence of formal programmes and plans for orderly, planned recruitment, orientation, training and development, to increase the professional competence of *all* employees within the organization.

(c) Existence and implementation of formal programmes to:
    (1) Reduce overtime.
    (2) Improve the total activity and productivity of each and every employee in the company.
    (3) Improve the ratio of productive and nonproductive employees.
    (4) Reduce total employment costs.
    (5) Improve management employee communications.

9. Represent the company in its dealings with government, customers, suppliers and the local business community, to promote the company image and acceptance of its products, policies and practices.

Performance standards

(a) Determined by the managing director's ability to solve difficult problems quickly with all outside agencies, customers, government, etc., based on his established credibility and continuous interchange through personal contacts.

(b) Ability accurately to assess company position in all external relationships and to take proper, timely decisions to avoid difficulties for the company, which could result in loss of market share, work stoppages, excessive financing costs, adverse legal actions and inability to obtain necessary materials, services and personnel when needed.

10. Become personally involved in the identification and resolution of any *major* problems which could have an adverse effect on company profitability and growth, e.g., a quality problem.

Performance standards

The failure of any manager in the company quickly to bring to a solution a problem which is having negative impact on business results, e.g., union strike action, loss of major negotiation, excessive pressure on service engineering facilities, high employee rate of quits, excessive overdue collections, delay in deliveries, etc.

Authority to act independently

Develop and recommend to regional manager necessary local policies (written guidelines) for the successful operation of the company, considering local factors such as the political, economic, social, cultural and competitive environment in which he operates. This may include, for example, recommendations for:

Product policy.	Growth policy.
Price policy.	Benefits policy.
Employee relations policy.	Market strategy.

Operates the company in close consultation with the regional staff, to obtain advance approval in such major areas as:

Determining long-range objectives for the company.

Formulating short-term goals.

Recommending annual operating budget for the company.

Developing specific action plans based on approved budget.

Determining the right organization to accomplish long-range objectives and short-term goals.

Advance approval of major changes in organization and/or key personnel, e.g., additions, hires, promotions, transfers, discharges.

Operates within the framework of written corporate, international, regional policies, objectives and goals.

Once the annual business plan and operating budget are approved, the managing director is free to take independent action on all matters within his position responsibility, respecting the limitations as cited above.

Working relationships

The managing director normally reports to the regional manager.

Depending on the size, complexity and needs of the company, the managing director may have a number of the following positions reporting directly to himself:

> Financial manager.
> Engineering manager.
> New sales manager.
> Service sales manager. } Zone manager
> FOD manager.
> Production manager.
> Personnel manager.
> Contract control manager.
> Districts manager.

The managing director works closely with:

> His staff, integrating all their individual efforts into an efficient team with interrelated goals.
> The regional staff for consultation, advice and policy matters, for budget approval, for approval of objectives and operating plans.
> He may supervise other companies, agents or representatives.
> Other managing directors where the companies are interdependent, e.g., mutual source of supply or customer relationships within the company, source of export to other countries to non-company clients.

Qualifications required to perform the job satisfactorily

Education desired

Engineering degree, plus graduate work in business administration.

Experience requirements

At least 3 to 5 years general management experience in a medium-sized electromechanical manufacturing company.

At least 5 to 10 years progressively responsible experience in marketing and production, or finance and accounting.

Demonstrated working knowledge of modern management tools, such as organization, delegation, communication, management-by-objectives, financial management analysis, cost control, production, inventory control and management information system.

Record of accomplishment, including evidence of significant improvements in profits, costs and market share.

Personal qualities

Persuasive, tactful and sensitive.
Demonstrated ability to build a strong, effective, loyal management team.
Strong communication skills — written and oral.
Dynamic, high energy level — executive stature.

Special qualifications

Must speak the language of the country to which he is assigned.
Fluency in English: read, write and speak.
Knowledge and experience in local business environment.
Evidence of application of Western management philosophy.
Sufficient knowledge of the business to be able to verify the accuracy and establish timing of essential information required to make good, timely decisions.

Major challenges of the job

The local managing director will have to complete this section because the major problems of the company to be solved will vary considerably from company to company.

What actions do you reserve for yourself?

This must also vary locally: for example, the managing director of a smaller company must necessarily become more involved in the detailed activities of his company. But nevertheless, the managing director should list three or four projects, policy decisions or items which cannot be delegated, but which must be performed by himself. These will represent his *personal contribution* to the company.

Example. Make the final decision on the market strategy to be followed in launching a new product.

To illustrate what can be done at local level by an enthusiastic manager, the following is an example of a position description, prepared personally by a marketing (operations) manager in a developing country.

POSITION DESCRIPTION
OPERATIONS MANAGER, DEVELOPING COUNTRY

1   Job title

In charge of new sales, service sales and field operations. Area coverage: 4 countries.

2   Purpose of the job

Contribute to company profitability and growth by concluding sales and service sales contracts at prices and terms in the best interest of the company.

Survey and analyse current and potential markets for customers' receptivity and interests and marketing strategies. Innovate and launch new products.

Ensure quality in field work and customers' satisfaction with work performed. Apply new techniques and methods to improve efficiency and reduce costs and ensure availability of the people to do the work.

Advertise and create friendly relations with customers, consultants and architects.

3   Scope of the job

Responsible for new sales, service sales and field operations. Financial responsibility for current year projected:

My annual expense budget: $30 000

Number of office people supervised:	82	Annual payroll cost $300 000
Managerial:	4	Annual payroll cost 40 000
Nonmanagerial:	78	Annual payroll cost 260 000

Responsible for $10 000 000 — sales and service sales — 4 countries.

4   Principal responsibilities

(a) Planning all phases of the work to be performed, by setting measurable objectives, defining roles and missions, forecasting, establishing timed programmes for achieving objectives, establishing policies and procedures, implementing price strategy, tactics and budgeting.

(*b*) Organizing the work by dividing it among groups for efficient production, and coordinating and integrating efforts and information for accomplishment of individual and group objectives. Ensuring effective flow of ideas and conductivity upward, laterally and downward.

(*c*) Determining the requirements for, and ensuring the availability of, personnel to perform the work, and developing personnel by providing opportunities in line with capabilities. Investing money in human resources at different levels for future requirements and anticipated expansion.

(*d*) Providing direction, training and knowledge to subordinates, assigning and defining responsibilities, scheduling work, delegating responsibilities and providing assistance when and as needed. Applying a policy of educate and prevent rather than inspect and reject.

(*e*) Measuring performance and assuring effective accomplishment of objectives, as scheduled and within established budgets; giving careful consideration to reducing costs by seeking economies and improving methods.

(*f*) Evaluating employees' performance and ensuring that recognition is based on results. Assuring a safe working environment and practising good human and social relations.

(*g*) Taking corrective action to bring about performance improvement toward objectives.

5 Authority to act independently

Recommend and obtain managing director's approval on planning, policy, price strategies, methods and objectives.

Approve policy, short-term goals and long-term objectives of my subordinates.

Recommend to hire, fire, transfer, promote and award salary increases. Final decision by managing director.

Make all decisions independently, as long as they are within my authority and within established and approved budgets.

6 Working relationships

I report to the managing director.
Following positions report to me:
    Service sales manager.

Field manager.

Sales coordinator, in charge of: sales engineering, major negotiations and special assignments, estimating and abstracting, and sales activities in branch offices.

Sales coordinator.

Branch managers in three countries concerning sales, service sales and field operations activities in their territories.

7   Qualifications required to perform the job satisfactorily

Formal education:

(*a*) BSc engineering degree.

(*b*) MBA — helpful.

Specific on-the-job experience: filling in positions:

(*a*) Draftsman, estimator, field engineer, sales engineer, assistant manager and general manager.

(*b*) Training in sales, service sales and field operations, sales engineering, with specialization in traffic analysis, for recommendations to architects and consultants for major and monumental projects.

(*c*) Assistant sales manager, sales manager, marketing manager and zone operations manager.

(*d*) Training courses in at least two developed countries (construction and service).

Experience acquired in management, administration, and marketing resulted in the successful results, performance and profitability achieved during my five year work period with present OMEGA subsidiary.

Other requirements:

(*a*) Ability to define, analyse, interrelate, measure and solve major problems in the best interest of the company.

(*b*) Ability to measure and recognize results, improve productivity and performance of individuals.

(*c*) Ability to delegate responsibility and encourage participation.

(*d*) Ability to take preventive measures, to meet our fast-growing market in terms of capabilities and talent, and invest money on human resources.

(*e*) Language ability: local language, plus English.

(*f*) Ability to coordinate and integrate efforts to achieve short- and long-term goals. Ability to review, adopt and adjust to suit conditions.

(*g*) Ability to establish good relations and friendship with customers, consultants and architects.

8 Performance standards

Performance should be measured by identifying in the right time significant deviations that may have an impact upon the achievement of objectives.

Meet 95–120 per cent of forecasted sales and service sales and realize profits above what was anticipated.

Meet 100 per cent of contracted commitments on penalty contracts and 95 per cent of other contracts due to the present overload.

Observe quality and product performance of field work (erection and maintenance) to meet company standards and customers' satisfaction.

Have initiative to maintain leadership in the product field.

9 Major challenges in the job and problems to be solved

(a) Increase profits

In sales and service sales from anticipated x% FY 1974 to y% in FY 1975 for new sales; and from anticipated x% in FY 1974 to y% in FY 1975 for service sales. To achieve this goal it will be necessary to:

Set up a pricing strategy based on market analysis, with careful consideration of statistics on competitors' bids, quality and performance.

Accomplish close coordination between all departments, to seek economies and cost reduction by improving production techniques, reconsidering purchasing policies and procedures, improving field performance and methods, obtaining better terms of payment and enforcing faster collections.

Innovate new products and introduce new ideas. Take initiatives to improve quality and maintain company's historic leadership.

(b) Enforce standardization

By selecting and designing a range of *product models*. Thus a line of production will be established at a decreased cost and a price advantage to the customer without sacrificing quality.

A close coordination between sales, production and FOD will be necessary.

Conduct a big campaign in assigned territory to push the new models.

Promotional literature pertinent to the new models will be created, probably with the assistance of outside specialists. Anticipate to have this goal achieved in January 1975.

(c) *Job description review and salary survey*

A job description review will be conducted, to have a defined job responsibility and to utilize people to the best of their ability.

In a fast-growing company as ours, this review, together with our market forecasts and planned expansion in the area, will provide us with a good indication of the number and kind of people we must recruit, train and develop.

Managers must delegate responsibility and give priority to major problems. They should develop subordinates and provide them with direction, broad guidelines and assistance when and as needed.

A salary survey will be conducted among other companies of similar size which operate in comparable industry.

Will assure that evaluation of personnel and personal progress is based on results and performance. Employees who developed themselves should get ahead. Anticipate to have this goal achieved by February.

(d) *Training programme*

Will take preventive measures to meet our fast-growing market, in terms of capabilities and talent, especially in areas of technical activities. For this reason, we must invest money in human resources at different levels, for future requirements and anticipated expansion in the territory.

A field labour programme is now actually in process with successful results. This programme will be strengthened and extended to various levels of technicians and supervisors, to improve individual productivity and overall efficiency.

Training programme will be established for all sales and service sales representatives covering commercial and technical aspects.

Development, direction and training of subordinates and key personnel (4 men in new sales, 4 in FOD, and 2 in service sales). They will be acquainted and familiarized with the weighing and proper handling of problems of importance in order to meet requirements of our expanding operations in the Middle East. Will start this goal in 1974 and have it achieved by end of FY 1975.

10   Actions I reserve for myself

(a) Planning of work to be performed, defining roles and missions, establishing policies and procedures and quality standards.
(b) Organizing the work for efficient production and effective conductivity
(c) Implementing price strategies, tactics and budgeting.
(d) Approving and measuring objectives of my subordinates.
(e) Insuring availability of people to perform the work and setting plans for development and training of people at all levels for future requirements to meet planned expansion.
(f) Measuring and evaluating employees' performance.

Delays in deliveries from the local factory often involved also problems of quality control. A successful technique was to assign a task force to cope with the problem: this forced a local managing director to accept teamwork, and to delegate. The approach was as follows:

THE PRODUCTION TASK FORCE

Composition and method

1   The task force should include senior executives, who contribute to the problem and/or to the solution. These would include managers of sales, engineering, production, human resources, field operations, contract control and finance. The managing director is excluded: he must maintain objectivity, to analyse the problems and the proposed solutions.

2   In defining the problem, for example, the task force should analyse in depth the following (first, each individual for his own functional responsibility):

Sales

(a) Availability of accurate, specific forecasts by model and by unit, as well as market segment.
(b) Commitments by salesmen to customers, according to predetermined lead times.

(c) Status of present commitments.

(d) Adequacy of market coverage by qualified sales personnel.

(e) Analysis of customer complaints with regard to installations, service and quality: e.g., 'trouble reports'.

Engineering

(a) Establish lead times by model and by unit for all engineering work, including drawings, specifications, parts lists.

(b) Engineering cost analyses build-up for all components, in order to establish correct price. This should include price escalation for inflation.

(c) Engineering project management approach for all major contracts, project scheduling systems and controls.

(d) Engineering backlog analysis *vs.* current and projected demands for engineering time.

(e) Engineering department organization as well as right number and quality of personnel trained to do the work.

(f) Engineering data retrieval system.

(g) Measurement of accuracy, quality and timeliness of data submitted in useable form to sales and factory.

(h) Provision for analyses of problems caused by improper or incomplete drawings, specifications and data — part of trouble reporting system from the factory and field.

(i) Existence of value analysis and value engineering section within engineering department to reduce total costs and eliminate, or minimize, factory bottlenecks.

(j) Engineering cost and efficiency improvement programme.

Production

(a) Existence of data on factory capacity, including machine loading, factory loading: analyses of factory layout and material movement.

(b) Anticipated *vs.* actual productivity by component, by cost centre, by operator, by machine.

(c) Productivity per employee — direct and indirect. Existence of standard times and proper methods for all productive operations.

(d) Identification of factory bottlenecks.

(e) Percentage of machine utilization and analysis of reasons for under-utilization.

(f) Analysis of present backlog and present and projected requirements.

(*g*) Causes of parts and materials shortages, e.g., lack of qualified people, poor organization, lack of controls and follow-up, lack of raw materials, poor cash-flow, lack of methods and standards, poor workplace layout, inadequate daily, weekly, monthly production schedules by contract, by machine, by cost centre.

(*h*) Existence and use and follow up of trouble-reporting system.

(*i*) Analyses of total paperwork and flow as an integrated system for factory control, including purchased parts, components, supplies. This also applies to receiving and shipping departments and personnel therein.

(*j*) Inventory control system, raw, in-process and finished components.

(*k*) Effectiveness of scheduling and dispatching, and expediting functions and personnel.

(*l*) Proper organization to do the work, enough of the right people, properly trained to do the work.

(*m*) Existence of quality standards and inspection procedures and adequacy of these standards, procedures, controls, and properly trained personnel to do the work.

(*n*) Actual scrap and wastage experienced and recorded, and analysed to develop plan to eliminate, or at least minimize.

(*o*) Proper tools, dies jigs, fixtures, machinery in good working order to do the work.

Field operations

(*a*) Lead times for erection by unit and by contract.

(*b*) Job planning and project management for major jobs.

(*c*) Adequacy of personnel in number and quality for present and future projected workloads.

(*d*) Problems with time lost because of delays, partial shipments, wrong parts, delivery and unpacking of parts for ease in erection.

(*e*) Scheduling, routing of personnel.

(*f*) Existence of standard data (time, methods) for all erection procedure by unit, by job, e.g., efficiency, productivity, cost measurements.

(*g*) Quality of work as measured by:
Immediate customer acceptance.
Immediate acceptance by service department.
Number and types of complaints reported by day, week, month.

(*h*) Cost improvement programme — timetable and follow-up for improving productivity and efficiency.

(*i*) Major problems experienced which could be corrected through adequate training of supervisors and workers.

Finance

To assist in identifying all costs affecting, or affected by, production operations:

(*a*) Complete cost analyses, timing and frequency of reports to sales, engineering, production and field operations, e.g., distribution cost analysis, including expense controls, to determine how and where money is spent because of poor deliveries. Develop accurate cost data and controls and review as often as necessary with managers responsible for doing the work as it affects the factory.
(*b*) Periodic audit of all functions to improve management and cost controls.
(*c*) Regular follow-up of financial reports, to train managers and supervisors in techniques of financial management analysis, including ratio analysis, methods for budget, cost and expense controls in proper relation to sales and revenues, with emphasis on factory production costs.
(*d*) Proper organization and adequate staffing with fully trained personnel to do the work.

Human resources

(*a*) Determine overall training needs of managers, supervisors and employees, based on problem-identification and performance in relation to planned results: understanding and acceptance of job responsibilities, priorities, performance standards, accountability and establishment of short-term goals by managers, supervisors and for each major activity within each function.
(*b*) Adequacy of own organization, and manpower plans and forecasts as well as training requirements for present and projected needs.
(*c*) Manpower inventories for each function — present and projected — to include quantitative and qualitative data based on measurement of performance.
(*d*) Assist each task force member in applying methodology of management-by-objective to the solution of problems as analysed.

Contract control

(*a*) Function of coordinating work of all departments to meet production schedules.

(*b*) Includes an analysis of all paperwork system, to improve flow, timing, accuracy and dependability, to eliminate confusion, duplication, overlap and unnecessary paperwork.

(*c*) Establishment of proper lead times — agreed to by all functional managers.

(*d*) Establishing proper systems for control, implementation, follow-up and immediate identification of problems, which cause the system to bog down. Recommend immediate corrective action and follow-up with responsible managers to insure action is taken to eliminate the causes of problems.

(*e*) Initiate and implement a system of trouble reports to identify causes of problems.

General overall considerations

All senior managers who affect, or are affected by the output of the factory, must first look to their own departments for:

Problem identification and analysis. Analysis in detail of backlog in his own department: e.g., 'What can I do to help contribute to identifying the causes and providing solution to the problems?'
'Is my department properly organized to do the work?'

(*a*) Clear written, communicated objectives, goals and priorities for my department as a whole.

(*b*) Job description and priorities for each individual and each activity.

(*c*) Experience and education requirements for each job and each man.

(*d*) Training requirements for each man to ensure understanding of his job, his priorities, performance standards and that he is fully qualified to do the work.

(*e*) Manpower plan and forecast for future work load.

(*f*) Advance recruitment and training plans.

(*g*) Measuring results of training and performance to identify areas for improvement.

(*h*) System of feedback immediately to detect deviations from plans and take corrective action.

(*i*) An attitude on part of each manager of accepting his responsibility for success of other managers: e.g., 'How can I contribute to solution'?, as opposed to defensive attitude.

Conclusion

After the task force, individually and collectively, have analysed all major problems along with cost implications:

(*a*) Suggest alternative solutions, agreed to by all task force members, weighing advantages and disadvantages of each to:
   (1) Eliminate backlog of work — all departments.
   (2) Set up an efficient system and detailed written plan for implementation, with commitments from all department heads to each other.
(*b*) Make presentation to managing director, highlighting differences of opinion, if any.

Managing director ensures use of management-by-objectives approach

Definition of problems and causes.
Statements of goals to be achieved and results expected.
Specific action steps for each goal:
   Beginning and ending dates for each step.
   Who will do the work?
   How progress will be controlled and measured.
Anticipation of obstacles.
Additional resources required, information, manpower, tools, etc., plus costs of each and net additions to profit if resources are committed.

Weekly group meetings until system is fully implemented and the problems solved, i.e., delays in deliveries are eliminated and factory is producing and shipping according to schedule with proper levels of quality.

Prior to the next follow-up management-by-objectives seminar, a production task force was formed in accord with the guidelines. They met weekly, a plan was developed by the group. It was highly successful and the production problems were solved. The approach was as follows:

DEVELOPING COUNTRY
APPROACH. PRODUCTION TASK FORCE

(1) Problem areas identified	(2) Reasons for existence of problem	(3) Actions to solve problems	(4) Expected results Problem areas (A), (B), (C)
(A) **Late deliveries of finished products** Purchase of local materials. Purchase/Import materials. Specifications. Shipping.	Inadequate knowledge of suppliers, prices, deliveries. Lack of quality control/purchased materials. No storage/purchased materials. Lacking data on material requirements/quantity, timing. Inadequate controls and organization. Unrealistic forecasts. No definition of lead time. Lack of follow-up. Errors in specifications. No real system in department.	Listing all local purchases. Kardex of suppliers. Price and delivery dates — from local suppliers. Minimum reorder point. Economic lot purchases. Quality control of local purchases. Control routine in receiving. Establish a storage area. Factory to control purchase orders. Procedure to follow-up shipment dates. Coordinate market plan with factory's ability to produce. Make product data sheets and layouts. Review specifications before producing parts. Rent warehouse space. Private trucking firm to supplement own fleet. Reduce number of shipments for one order.	Reduce factory costs and field instruction costs by saving X + Y numbers of hours: This comes from more efficient factory costs. Increasing shipments weekly from X to Y numbers of units. Reduce factory overtime by .... per cent. *Note* For each action as defined in col. (3): A beginning and ending date were estimated. The person or persons responsible for doing the work were identified and accepted the assignment. The costs and expenses of implementation were measured against the potential savings over a 5-year period. People from different functions started to work as a team for the first time and to appreciate the

(1) Problem areas identified	(2) Reasons for existence of problem	(3) Actions to solve problems	(4) Expected results Problem areas (A), (B), (C)
(B) Production systems Manufacturing methods. Rationalization. Machinery – Tooling.	No labour 'order' for each piece produced. Inadequate controls for following labour orders in process. Separate pieces are not separately identified and scheduled. No 'standard' pieces for production. No real production 'system flow'. No in-process quality control. No programming of factory production. Old, inadequate methods. Insufficient number of machines. Inadequate tooling – jigs, dies, fixtures.	Process order prepared for each piece manufactured. Control to be developed to locate an order in process. Small shop area set aside for special, unusual and non-standard pieces. Parts to be standardized according to marketing and engineering definition. Define series for parts production. Define machine loading. Establish QC system. Programme production load according to contracts sold. Certain machines, tools, dies, fixtures to be purchased as capital expenditure.	help-solve-problems outside their own function. The task force actually tripled production and reduced total cost of production by 50 per cent.
(C) Quality and number of personnel.	Stock room, kardex file: Production control. Shipping.	New man to hire.	

FIELD OPERATIONS MANAGER
EXAMPLE OF MANAGEMENT DEVELOPMENT THROUGH
MANAGING BY RESULTS IN FIELD OPERATIONS

Goal or Result to be achieved

Reduce the time required for installation by 40 per cent no later than 30 October, while at the same time improve the quality of installations as measured by:

Reduction in number of customer complaints from .... to ....

Reduction in number of repair visits from .... to ....

Reduction of service time from an average of .... hours per item in service to .... hours.

Action steps	How to be done	By whom	Date
1. Define major problem areas and opportunities for improvement of efficiency in erection.	Analysis of exact time spent on each step by each individual on completed contracts. Analysis of methods. Analysis of tools and materials used. Analysis of maintenance and servicing. Analysis of quality of component parts received.	Field supervisors. Adjuster. Construction superintendent. Administrative manager. Financial manager. Field operations manager. Sales personnel.	Start 1 June 1972. Finish 1 Aug. 1972.
2. Develop new methods and sequence of steps in erection	Revise construction procedures. Revise sequence of installation.	Field operations manager. Field supervisors.	Start 1 Aug. 1972. (Set dates for each step

Action steps	How to be done	By whom	Date
installation and adjustment.	Scheduling and routing personnel. Audit proper use of tools; use right tools.	Construction superintendent. Adjusters. Regional field operations manager. Field engineer.	in training process.) Finish total training by 31 Jan. 1973.
Train and measure performance of all personnel involved in installation, service and maintenance.	Select, develop, train supervisors, engineers, adjusters and erectors and service personnel.		
3. Set specific weekly goals and targets for measuring improvements in efficiency and quality: Show progressive reduction of number of hours for each job, each contract, each unit and each individual. Also each area and each supervisor.	Analyse results weekly. Review progress or lack of progress, to determine where problems exist and to correct same. Analyse and improve on new methods. Analyse and audit proper use of old and new tooling. Analyse to be sure that sequence of steps are maintained and revise to improve efficiency and quality.	Same group as in step 2.	Set weekly improvement goals.
4. Communicate new methods throughout all regions and to all local representatives.	In the beginning, weekly meetings with all involved field operation supervisors, managers and workers. Include same categories of service and maintenance personnel. Issue and distribute minutes to all regions and to senior management.	Same group as in step 2.	1 Aug. and continuing.

5. Maintain control and follow-up results.

Check accuracy of erection forecasts and timing of completions.

Check and reroute scheduling of personnel.

Account for all time spent by each individual.

Issue formal monthly progress reports on individual, supervisory and regional improvements in efficiency and quality and distribute to all field operations personnel and all senior management, to control results and measure progress against projected targets.

Follow-up with special training and new testing procedures where required, to ensure achievement of quality and efficiency goals.

Sales manager.
Financial manager.
and
Same group as in step 2.

Each month a formal comparative progress report:
Show on graph actual *vs.* projected reduction of number of hours.

Developing country
Latin America

MARKETING MANAGER
FISCAL YEAR 1973 *vs.* 1972
EXAMPLE OF MANAGEMENT DEVELOPMENT THROUGH
MANAGING-BY-RESULTS IN SERVICE SALES

Goal or Result to be achieved

Being actual forecast on special market sales equal to
with actual profit over selling price of 27 per cent or
to increase this figure for FY 1973 (over 1972) by 40 per cent or up to
with a spread over selling price of 30 per cent or

$540 000
$145 800
$756 000
$226 800

Action steps	How to be done	By whom	Date
1. Establish the special market business potential	Through a complete survey on records of existing passenger units featuring signal control.	District managers. District sales manager. Sales manager's administrative assistant of the head office. Service salesman.	Start 1 June 1972. Finish 1 Aug. 1972. (Weekly reports on progress to be submitted to the sales manager by the administrative assistant. Coordination by sales manager through regular meeting for review.)

2. **Preparation of a sales folder**

Covering modernizations – for conversions.
From signal control to minimod, and
Car switch and push-button to collective operation.
Explain briefly advantages of conversion, based mainly on economic reasons.
Approximate cost of folder.

Sales manager.
Sales manager's administrative assistant.
District sales manager.
Service salesmen.

Start 1 June 1972.
Finish 1 Sept. 1972.

3. **Selection of prospective customers**

Based on type of building.
Location.
Economic conditions.
Shutdowns.
Repair visits, etc.
Through visits of service salesmen and service supervisors.

District managers.
District sales managers.
Sales manager's administrative assistant.
Service salesmen.
Service supervisors.

Start 1 Aug. 1973.
Finish 1 Oct. 1972.

4. **Preparation of estimates and proposals**

Based on survey prepared by service salesmen, and service supervisors.

District managers.
District sales managers.
Service salesmen.
Service supervisors.
Service sales chief estimator.
Service sales personnel.

Start 1 Oct. 1972.
Finish 15 Nov. 1972.
(Coordination by sales manager's administrative assistant.
Weekly reports on progress to be submitted to the sales manager.)

Action steps	How to be done	By whom	Date
5. **Sales policy**	Written instructions to service salesmen, containing solid arguments to perform the actual selling job to prospective customers.	Sales manager. Sales manager's administrative assistant.	Start 1 Oct. 1972. Finish 30 Oct. 1972.
6. **Proposals to prospective customers and obtaining of orders**	Through information to contract control department, which will co-ordinate actions with field operations and factory.	Sales manager's administrative assistant. Service sales chief estimator. Contract control manager. Field operations manager. Factory manager.	Start 15 Nov. 1972. Finish 30 Sept. 1973.
7. **Coordination for orders obtained**	Through information to contract control department, which will co-ordinate actions with field operations and factory.	Sales manager's administrative assistant. Service sales chief estimator. Contract control manager. Field operations manager. Factory manager.	Start 15 Nov. 1972. Finish 30 Sept. 1973.

FINANCE MANAGER
EXAMPLE OF MANAGEMENT-BY-OBJECTIVES IN FINANCE DEPARTMENT

Goal

To obtain a level of accounts receivable which represents three months of billing by 30 September 1972. Total accounts receivable at year end should be represented by:

	Balance	Month of billing	Actual month of billing
New sales	24 239 000	2.57	3.84
Service	6 517 000	2.0	2.64
Notes	4 292 000	–	–
Intercompany	2 400 000	–	–
Others	1 570 000	–	–
	39 018 000	3.0	3.6

(Figures expressed in units of local currency.)

There will be a reduction of accounts receivables of 7 817 000, which represents a saving in interests expenses — at 10 per cent per annum — of 781 700. In addition there will be a more adequate cash-flow, which will permit to satisfy certain important commitments, such as the prompt payment of Intercompany for Merchandise, TAC and others.

From the analysis which follows, it can be seen that one collection man could be required with an annual cost of 40 000; additional costs for travelling and legal expenses would not exceed 80 000.

Currently we follow instructions which outline the collection policy which includes a system of dunning letters to the client and which allows, under certain circumstances, that construction can be stopped when the receivables are beyond 60 days. The costs of this programme are being taken into consideration in the estimates; therefore, the only extra costs involved are those mentioned in previous paragraphs.

Action steps	How to be done	By whom	Date
1. **New sales and service 'S'**	Analyse reasons for the existence of overdues.	Managing director. Financial manager.	Start 1 May 1972. Finish 30 Sept. 1972.
	Breakdown of overdues.	Sales manager.	Weekly
	Breakdown of overdues according to:		
	Contracts turned over to customer.		
	Contracts whose erection has been stopped.	Credit and collection supervisor.	
	Contracts in process.		Monthly
	For contracts completed, establish plan of action considering legal action.	Salesmen.	Weekly
	Contracts in suspense, obtain client's consent to continue or cancel legally the contract.	FOD personnel.	
	Contracts in process, continued follow-up based on the dunning system, until reaching contract suspension.		

	Pressure and extra effort to obtain overdue balances from government. Overdue for completed contracts not turned over to the client. Negotiate with the client.		
2. **Service: contracts with government agencies**	Perform planning for closings of contracts in order to avoid massive closings on 30 Sept., and to avoid rapid increase in accounts receivables balance. Prompt response by FOD to the problems reported by clients on uncompleted or deficient work. Prompt billing. Close follow-up of dunning letters.		
	Obtain all contracts for 1972, duly sign.	Major city distrct manager.	Start 1 May 1972. Finish 31 July 1972.
	Obtain corresponding payment approvals.	Major city sales depatment.	
	Issue adequate billings and obtain approvals.	Credit and collection supervisor.	
	Obtain follow-up certification of of service rendered.	Collection men. FOD personnel.	
3. **Service: contracts with private customers**	Determine accounts with balances beyond two months and reasons why these have not been paid.	Same as step 2.	Start 1 May 1972. To continue indefinitely.

Action steps	How to be done	By whom	Date
	Determine why the above contracts have not been suspended, proceeding accordingly, if there are no important reasons.		
	Group all the clients who complain of poor maintenance.		
	Report fortnightly the above to the respective FOD department of the district.		
	Follow-up FOD department in the investigation of client's complaints, through periodic meetings.		
	Visit district offices, in order to obtain a closer cooperation between clients and FOD personnel.		
	Close follow-up of dunning system.		
	Establish in City 'X' the quarterly billing system.		Finish 30 June 1972.
4. **Service: suspended contracts**	Determine reason for suspension and current status of client.	Financial manager.	Start 1 May 1972.
	Consult with lawyers and proceed accordingly.	Credit and collection supervisor.	Finish 1 July 1972.
	Determine if there is any different relationship with the company.	Legal department.	

5.	**Notes receivables**	Eliminate acceptance of notes as a term of the contract. Accept notes in accordance with instructions, avoiding clients with bad credit rating. Discount accepted notes from clients with high credit rating.	Financial manager. Sales manager. Credit and collection supervisor. Chief collector. Cashier.	Start 1 May 1972. To continue indefinitely.
6.	**Intercompanies**	Press for payment of overdues from France. Analyse accounts receivables from Central American branches. Obtain payment assistance through Latin American Region Headquarters. Establish a close follow-up of inter-company receivables.	Financial manager. Assistant to financial manager. Credit and collection supervisor. Traffic department supervisor. Director of finance Latin American Region Headquarters.	Start 1 May 1972. Finish 30 July 1972. To continue indefinitely.
7.	**Other accounts receivables**	Analyse balances, establish overdues and the reasons. Follow-up overdues from personnel, obtain assistance from each department head. Timely submission of monthly expense report. Review the list of productive personnel on trips. Insist on their timely submission of expense report. Prepayment to vendors and others. Monitor whether these amounts are used as credits; otherwise request back-payment.	Financial manager. Department heads. Credit and collection supervisor. Accounts receivables supervisor. Personnel who use form 30—40. Purchasing supervisor.	Start 1 May 1972. To continue indefinitely.

INSTRUCTION FOR USE OF PERFORMANCE APPRAISAL AND REVIEW

Applicable to

OMEGA headquarters and regional staffs.
Managing directors and staff reporting
direct in 'Select' operating companies.

Specific instructions
Name (last name, first)
Position title (self-explanatory)
Date assigned to position (use effective date of transfer or hire)

Office (OMEGA headquarters, region, operating
company, district, etc.)

Location (city and country)
Appraisal date (date on which this appraisal was completed)

1 Major accomplishments

List specific, quantitative, measurable, documented evidence of high performance in relation to the individual's position responsibilities, assigned goals and/or projects, problems solved, etc. Limit to those items which have highest magnitude of impact on key result areas for which the individual is responsible. Include temporary assignments, depending on importance.

2 Areas for improvement

Use the same criteria as outlined under 1. Here we are attempting to measure *specifically* where performance fell short of expectation. The individual needs to know where, as well as how, he can specifically improve his performance. If no performance standard exists in a key result area, it is the manager's responsibility to develop a measurable standard in conjunction with the individual, where the individual is competent to do so.

3 Specific goals to be achieved within the next twelve months

The manager is obliged to develop specific, measurable and timely goals for and with the individual in those areas of major impact to the business.

Progress must be reviewed informally, but often, during the year, to avoid 'surprises' at the time of the annual performance review and discussion with the individual.

4 Signatures

(a) Manager

Person who completes the appraisal form and to whom the individual being appraised.reports. The 'manager' is also the person who will conduct the actual review with the individual who is appraised. This will normally be alone — a man-to-man discussion — positive, frank, *open, two-way exchange*, but warm, cordial and reassuring to the individual. The man being appraised must know that his work, his efforts and his results are appreciated, but he must also know *exactly* and *precisely* where, how and when to improve his performance. Discussions on individual's salary, bonus, etc., are to be avoided. They are not a fit subject to introduce into discussion on performance.

(b) Next high level of management

This is the manager to whom the manager, who compiled the appraisal, reports. Should there be any differences of opinion between the two levels of management, they *must* be resolved before discussion with the individual being appraised by his manager. This will not be accepted as an excuse for delaying either the appraisal form or review with the individual.

(c) Review acknowledged

The individual who is appraised must sign his name on this form. It does not imply agreement with the evaluation. It does prove that the appraisal was actually reviewed with the individual. Where the individual disagrees with the appraisal, he may request and obtain a review with the next higher level of management.

(d) Dates

These should be the actual dates on which:

The manager reviewed the appraisal with the individual.
The next higher level of managment *approved* the appraisal.
The appraisee had his performance review and discussion with his manager.

PERFORMANCE APPRAISAL AND REVIEW

Name ....   Office ....

Position title ....   Location ....

Date assigned to position ....   Appraisal date ....

1.   **Major accomplishments** (in relation to position responsibilities and
                            specific goals)
     ....
     ....
     ....
     ....
     ....

2.   **Areas for improvement**
     ....
     ....
     ....
     ....
     ....

3.   **Specific goals to be achieved within the next 12 months**
     ....
     ....
     ....
     ....
     ....

                            Signatures

                            Manager ....   Date ....
                            Next higher level
                               of management ....   Date ....
                            Review
                               acknowledged ....   Date ....

APPRAISAL RATING GUIDE (to be completed on a separate sheet, but not for discusssion with the individual)

Current performance

1 *Outstanding*

This level is reserved for the exceptional individual, who consistently demonstrates outstanding performance in all significant areas of his position responsibilities. Less than 5 per cent of all individuals achieve this level of sustained competence.

2 *Superior*

Exceeds position requirements on most aspects of his job. Develops creative approaches to the most complex problems. Seizes the initiative in development and implementation of very challenging work goals. Less than 20 per cent of all people are capable of generating this degree of excellence in job performance.

3. *Good*

Performs his job in a completely acceptable manner and fully meets position requirements. Initiative, effort, and results are representative of the work that can be expected from a well-qualified and capable individual.

4 *Minimum acceptable*

Minimum standards of performance are being met. Usually requires close and constant supervision and follow-up. Sustained performance at this level will normally dictate removal from the position.

5 *Unsatisfactory*

Performance does not meet minimum acceptable standards for the position. This level of performance dictates removal from position as soon as possible.

FACTORS AFFECTING PERFORMANCE

Please rate the individual on each of the following factors using:

(+) = Excellent   (S) = Satisfactory   (—) = Needs to improve

Problem-solving ability: To be able to recognize, and clearly define as well as solve, the real problem and not the symptoms.

Decision-making ability: Quality, timeliness and implementation of decisions arrived at, based on clear, rational, logical analyses.

Ability to withstand pressure: To remain calm, rational and analytical despite pressures of heavy workload and time.

Job knowledge: Professional knowledge, tools and experiences to do all aspects of his assigned position responsibility.

Creativity/Imagination: Degree of openmindedness possessed, as reflected in receptivity to new ideas, methods and techniques, as well as finding new ways to get a job done.

Work accomplishment: A measure of the individual productivity relative to what one expects from a professionally competent, experienced individual.

Self-appraisal: Degree to which the individual is critical of his own performance and his efforts to improve same.

Human relations skills: Ability to work effectively and pleasantly with people at all levels: above, on same level and below.

Planning skills: Degree to which an individual plans his work to avoid fire-fighting and being constantly in difficulties.

Organizing skills: Degree to which an individual organizes his work to ensure everything important gets done on time and matters which can be delegated are delegated.

Communication skills: Degree to which the individual communicates all matters of importance to his manager, to those on the same level and to those reporting to him.

Managerial skills: Ability of the individual effectively to administer and control his operations, integrate and build team effort and genuinely motivate his people.

Opportunity-minded: Ability to recognize and implement an opportunity to improve productivity, profitability and results of the activity for which he is responsible.

Result-oriented/Priorities skills: Ability of individual to concentrate personal time, effort and attention to those matters with the greatest impact on business results, as opposed to spending his time on matters of little importance.

Specific comments

5
Developing local resources

One cannot make a silk purse out of a sow's ear. Only good selection will provide the right raw material from which to develop good future managers and supervisors. If the wrong selection is made initially, the most carefully planned training programme, regardless of its length and quality, will not produce an executive of quality.

The critical job is hiring the local managing director. He should be recruited by the international director of human resources. The qualities sought in a multinational executive, as defined in Chapter 6 (pages 141–50), will, however, be difficult to find in developing nations in Africa, Asia and parts of Latin America, for reasons already discussed. Yet, there are increasing pressures from many governments for the management ranks to be filled by locals. Soon multinationals will be *forced* to select locally an unprecedented number of potential senior managers. It is not wise to wait; by the time it becomes mandatory the best potential candidates will have been selected by other companies.

5.1   Selecting and developing local managerial talent

The relatively low educational and economic levels in many developing countries limit the sources of potential talent. The educated élite has frequently no desire to enter industry; its members are wealthy, and prefer a career in government service. University graduates are often hostile to profit-oriented ventures and have had little experience in business planning and problem solving. Their expectations from industry are often unrealistic by Western standards, and they try to overstaff operations for which they are responsible.

Local cultural patterns often produced an intellectual profile deficient in those aptitudes regarded by Western management as essential to top management performance. Testing is no answer: there are cultural/language translation difficulties, and often an absence of management terminology in the society. There is often no understanding of, or an unwillingness to accept, the concepts implicit in economic growth, and the role of capital, profits, surplus, savings and investment in the economy. Those same societies may well have dominant socialistic attitudes, and complex but not very efficient bureaucracies. All this conspires against the emergence of suitable managerial material.

Moreover, curiously, managers in developing countries are conditioned to be highly responsive to the requests made by subordinates. They find it difficult to say 'no': for example, they would never think of the financial consequences of two fifteen-minute coffee breaks a day for a workforce of 2000 employees; to refuse they feel would be regarded as inhumane.

It is not surprising, in these circumstances, that managers in developing countries find it difficult to accept concepts of performance appraisal, review and discussion: many are hypersensitive to criticism, and resist face-to-face discussions about failures, causes of under-achievement and similar problems.

Given a careful job definition, the executive search activity can be most successful in locating local managers who have been employed with and/or trained in the US or European multinational companies. Executive search firms from the developed nations have opened branches or are represented in most major cities of the world. These can be used to supplement the human resource director's own sources. The successful candidate will normally already be employed locally in business or industry. Generally, local executives who have spent their entire careers with a purely local business require a great deal more training than those who have had some multinational training and exposure. The latter will have acquired some understanding of modern management practice.

It may take three to six months to find the right man. The actual selection interview must be tailored to the local culture, using a self-reference criteria correction routine. This can only be obtained through exposure to other executives with reputable companies, preferably in that same environment. For the most part, an attempt should be made to measure the candidate's level of economic understanding and management sophistication. Many of the questions used in the management audit can also be in the selection interview.

Once having selected the 'right' man, an intensive period of training outside his home country is necessary. This period should run from at least six to twelve months, to enable the newly hired senior manager to obtain working knowledge of the company: its policies, marketing and sales strategy and tactics; organization, systems, procedures, and comprehensive techniques of financial management analyses and control. In addition, he should be given intensive training in professional management. Training in managing-by-objectives, management-by-commitment, and managing-for-results is essential. He must learn to delegate work to subordinates, and to measure and discuss performance, individually and collectively, and perhaps above all, he must be taught how to develop his people at all levels.

If a local national is the least bit reluctant to accept either the training, the management philosophy and approach, or the strict discipline required (as emphasized in the selection interview), better to seek another candidate than risk a failure. Most candidates welcome the opportunity to increase their professional management knowledge and experience. Financial rewards should *always* be slightly above the local level to attract the best candidates. If a man is good, he is worth far more than his total remuneration; if he is bad, the losses to the company can be astronomical, and he is worth less than nothing.

5.2   Key to local human resource development is the managing director

If the right man is hired and properly trained to manage the foreign subsidiary, the corporate parent need not worry; but periodic audits are always desirable. His training should be concentrated at the operating company level, within the US or Europe, and should include a general initiation into all facets of the company's business within company environments which most closely parallel the one for which he has been selected to manage. This means roughly comparable in size, complexity, outlook and technical sophistication. This may involve assignments in three or four different companies to broaden the individual's experience. The training must also be geared to the individual's background and tailored to his specific needs. In the OMEGA study, the training of the local managing director was normally developed and personally supervised by the international director of human resources, working in close cooperation with the regional vice-president.

For high-level management personnel who are already employed with a foreign subsidiary, whose functional and/or managerial skills need improvement, training outside the home country is both a necessary and a desirable investment. The training should consist in working closely with his counterpart, whether managing director, financial manager, production manager, or human resource manager. It should include project assignments as well as observation and discussions. These criteria are equally applicable to the newly hired manager and the executive in a foreign subsidiary. The manager responsible for the training of the foreign national should be given instruction in teaching methods and measuring the results of training.

The operating companies in the developed countries must accept the responsibility for giving up part of their time to the corporate family: they must be willing to devote the necessary time to train their counterparts in the developing countries. The international director of human resources can provide the methods, techniques, organization, guidelines, and coordination of the training, but it is the operating company's general manager who must be willing and able to assist in the transfer of technological and managerial expertise.

5.3 Measure results of training

Much has been said about the necessity for training and how to train the local national in the foreign subsidiary. A great deal of time and money must be invested: this investment must be carefully measured and controlled, and the guidelines on training standards observed (see Chapter 4, pages 57–61).

The development of managers in foreign subsidiaries is helped by regular visits to the subsidiary by staff and line experts from other subsidiaries and corporate headquarters. This type of training is most effective, for example, in teaching supervisory and managerial skills to groups. The management-by-objectives approach (as illustrated in Chapter 4, pages 50–5), where concentration on local problems becomes the basis for the transfer of managerial expertise, is a good example of training within the actual local environment.

Generally, where the transfer of technological skills is the primary objective, the training is best given outside the individual's home country. The exception is the training of the newly hired managing director, or the foreign subsidiary's internal candidate for the top position. There is a danger in bringing lower-level managers and supervisors from developing to developed countries for training, particularly from subsidiaries in Africa, Latin America and the Far East. After completion of the training, they become in some cases, 'impossible to live with'. The training received is seldom fully applied: even worse, their increased status almost ruins their interpersonal relationships and productive potential upon return to their home countries. They become dictators and it is difficult to get them to do any work. In such cases it is far better to send the technical expert to the foreign subsidiary.

This problem does not exist in training lower-level management executives from one developed country in another. It applies where the decision has been made to have substantially all the management and supervisory positions filled by local nationals. In one case in Africa, it was found advisable to send experts from developed countries (for long periods, if necessary), to carry out the technical and supervisory training needed and to speed up the advancement of technical and supervisory skills. A great deal of time and patience were required, but the results, for the business, the employees, and in relations with the government, fully justified the cost.

The international director of human resources must be made personally responsible for the international executive trainee and his progress, particularly during any extended period of three months or more spent as a trainee outside his home country. Formal, written training reports should be prepared monthly by the trainee, and submitted within one week of the end of the assignment: of course, assignments of more than four, but less than eight weeks can be covered by one report. Figure 5 : 1 which follows is an example of such a report:

Figure 5 : 1

1. **Period of time covered   From . . . . . .   To . . . . .**

2. **Assignment location and assignment supervisor**

3. **Method of training**

Formal *vs.* informal.
Planned *vs.* casual.
Observing *vs.* participating.
Was there a definite project to work on? If so what did you do and how did it contribute to the operating company?

4 **What was observed and what was learned?**

5 **Critique**

(*a*) Analysis of observations.
(*b*) Constructive, factual, *preferably quantitative* analysis, critique and comment.
(*c*) Comment on the assignment in relation to its degree of applicability in the country to which you will be assigned: considering differences in culture, climatic, political, economic, social, labour and environmental

Figure 5 : 1 (cont.)

factors, including local practices and attitudes. Also consider relative market position of the home *vs.* assigned country: degree of profitability, company organization, product differences, competitive differences, differences in legislation (all facets affecting the business — import, export, labour laws, product needs, etc.).

(*d*) Financial and profit implications of experiences and observations, both with regard to the assigned country and the country of ultimate destination. Specifically, how is each activity measured?

(*e*) Broad overview and comment on assigned country's major problems and opportunities.

Copies of the report should be sent to: international director of human resources, assignment supervisor, managing director (assigned country), managing director (home country), regional vice-president (home country).

The trainee should be provided, by the regional manager, with the complete business plan, forecast, budget and management reports and monthly financial statements of the country to which he will eventually be assigned. This will allow him to make meaningful comparisons with his home country. Those candidates who have been recruited by the international director of human resources should meet with him approximately once a month to review their assignment reports and training progress.

All training should be on a *quid pro quo* basis. The operating company which provides the training must benefit as well as thé trainee and his home country. The high-level management trainee can best contribute by taking on some short-term project: this can introduce a fresh view into the company of assignment and provides a basis for measuring the trainee's progress.

The role of the international director of human resources is vital. He must counsel and guide the executive trainee in his formation, critically review and discuss what was learned, based on the training assignment report, the introduce him into each new assignment. He can be of use in helping the executive to prepare a project to be implemented upon return to the home country. He can also assist in the integration of the new senior executive, conducting special, individually planned seminars to focus rapidly on the major problems and opportunities of the foreign subsidiary, as well as the strengths and individual development needs of each of the members of the senior management team.

If constant improvement is a desired goal in developing local nationals, then the executives on foreign training assignments should be given the opportunity to criticize the training itself and offer suggestions for improvement. Those executives who suggested modifications in length and content of training while undergoing it, ultimately became the most productive executives. That showed an initiative which was also appreciated by the company providing the training.

5.4 Young university graduates

The individual who leaves his home country (particularly a developing country) to obtain a university degree in a highly developed country has a distinct advantage over the local national who obtains his higher education at home. The difficulty in hiring these bright young men is through their unrealistic expectations, in terms of initial starting salaries and rate of advancement. For example, the young man from the emerging nation who obtains his MBA from a good American university may think he should receive an American (USA) starting salary at home. If he is given this while being trained in the United States, he may refuse to accept a significant salary cut when posted home, but the conventional salary levels within the home country must be observed. While it is fair to pay 15–20 per cent above the going rate which a local national would receive for comparable work, higher payments will do the young graduate no good. In any case, the graduate must receive significantly less than his local managing director and the senior staff reporting direct. The realistic young man, who accepts this, will usually turn out to be a valuable employee, with potential for rapid advancement.

An alternative is to hire the best graduates from the best local university, pay them well and give them every opportunity to perform. If they seem likely to be able to acquire the qualities of an effective executive on the basis of their first two or three years' performance, they should be sent abroad for further education, training and development at company expense.

5.5 Manual or unskilled workers and clerical personnel

It is usually not at all difficult to recruit at this level, particularly in developing countries. Many governments now levy a payroll tax, which can run from 1–2.5 per cent of the total payroll. These monies can often be rebated to the employer if he is careful to plan training to improve the skill and ability of his employees. In the OMEGA company, some of the subsidiaries were not taking advantage of these opportunities and were paralysing themselves by high turnover rates, and the payment of payroll taxes with no return: they were also incurring disfavour with the government by not taking the initiative to develop local nationals.

The local managing director must, of course, play the leading part in implementing the right policies. It is not difficult to establish local apprenticeship programmes and courses in clerical and secretarial skills. By working in close conjunction with local vocational and technical institutes, the foreign employer can assure himself of a steady supply of good raw talent, to meet his growing needs for people and expansion as well as building goodwill in the community.

The employer has a major role to play in community and individual development, particularly in the emerging nations. This is expected, and failure to comply may make it difficult to continue doing business. This is precisely why patience, understanding, empathy and flexibility are among the most important qualities of the expatriate executive. When a new operation is started, the expatriates, *prior to* opening their doors and advertising for 'Help wanted', must plan in more detail the training and development of the local nationals. In many countries, the government and employees ultimately become part-owners of the foreign subsidiary. It is highly important to devote whatever resources are necessary to the proper selection and training of the future owner-partners.

5.6 The local human resource manager

Second in importance only to the local managing director is the local manager of human resources. This man shoulders the major burden for the training and development of the personnel, although in a newly formed company it is the responsibility of the managing director.

When the foreign subsidiary reaches an employment level in excess of 250 employees, a local man of top quality, preferably with a university degree and with experience, should be hired by the local managing director in conjunction with the international director of human resources. The local personnel man must establish all local personnel policies, develop training plans and programmes, build morale and teamwork and, in fact, function as the right arm of the managing director. He is at least as important as the financial, marketing or production manager.

Unfortunately, few developing countries have a man trained in most aspects of professional human resource management. In fact, a significant number of developed countries, the local personnel manager is not regarded as a policymaker, or as a member of the senior management team. He is relegated to the routine, perfunctory details of low-level employees, simple records and clerical administration. To combat this situation and to assist in the development of the local personnel manager, a worldwide human resource survey was designed by the international and European human resource directors at OMEGA. The 'Worldwide survey of human resources policies and practices' was initiated by the most senior line executives, in response to requests for more professional management of the human resource function at the operating company level.

A total of 17 companies were selected to participate in the survey. They involved small-, medium- and large-sized companies, with numbers of employees ranging from 150 to 6000. Both developing and developed countries were included. The survey was conducted over a four-month period by the headquarters' staff directors of human resources, through personal visitations of two days each to the foreign subsidiaries. In the local company, the managing director and the local personnel manager were interviewed. A copy of the survey was sent well in advance of the actual visits, in order to enable the local men to prepare the data for discussion. The objectives of the survey (Figure 5 : 2), also sent out in advance, were as follows:

Figure 5 : 2

Extracts from letter sent to managing directors

The objectives of the surveys are as follows:

1   To determine what is actually being done in the individual companies to make best use of our human resources, at both the hourly-paid and clerical-salaried levels, and managerial and professional levels.
2   To identify possible areas for improvement, dependent on the size, complexity of the company, the human resources available, and the constraints, whether financial, political, social, cultural, legislative, or labour-union situation. These might include, for example:
      Recruitment, including development of labour sources.
      Orientation, training and induction.
      Absenteeism and turnover.
      Safety.
      Management and employee communication.
      Management training and development, including manpower planning.

Figure 5 : 2 (cont.)

> Availability of executive back-ups.
> Fringe benefits and costs.
> More efficient utilization of human potential at all levels.
> Compensation programme with regard to local practices.
> Union relation and workers participation.

3 To identify the best practices in other individual companies, for possible applicability.

4 To develop guidelines for managing directors and personnel directors, to improve human resource practices and thus increase productivity, reduce costs and maximize human satisfaction.

5 To develop international and regional policy guidelines for your consideration and approval.

6 To establish a basis for regional meetings of personnel managers to share experiences and take full advantage of ideas and practices learned from this survey.

In order to realize maximum benefit from these surveys, you are respectfully requested to participate and contribute. Within the next few weeks, you will be asked to make your personnel manager available for two-day meetings, to answer questions pertaining to the enclosed checklist. It is rather complete and we feel that advance preparatory work on his part is necessary. It will expedite matters if he can have available, in an organized manner, most of the information indicated in the checklist. Specifically, we would like to see examples of the following:

Written personnel policies.
Organization charts.
Manpower plan and back-up charts.
Samples of employment tests, if any, costs and results.
Typical representative personnel file for hourly paid, clerical and managerial employees.
Company orientation materials.
Concise description of:
   (a) All training programmes for all levels of personnel.
   (b) Orientation materials, such as brochures.
Examples of all forms of management and employee communication, as noted on the checklist.
All data on salary structures and comparison with local wage and salary surveys.
Copies of job descriptions and performance appraisal forms, if any.

Figure 5 : 2 (cont.)

Union contracts, and other examples of employee participation, together with comparisons of other contracts from other companies in your local community.

Concise listing of all employee benefits, as indicated in the checklist.

All employees' statistics as noted in the checklist:

How are the statistics maintained, used and followed up?

Formal safety and security programmes.

All community relations activities and management participation in community affairs and professional organizations.

Records of all management, clerical, and hourly personnel, who have attended outside education and training courses, as well as courses conducted in house.

Follow the guidelines as outlined in the survey.

We fully realize that this is a time-consuming project, but we are convinced that the results will justify the effort. Should you have any questions with regard to this survey, the method used, or the anticipated results, do not hesitate to write or call us. Your cooperation is appreciated and we will call on you to schedule a visit at a mutually convenient time.

Sincerely,
Staff directors of personnel

The following (Figure 5 : 3) is the actual survey questionnaire which accompanied the letter. Ratings were used in the survey as follows: (1) Excellent, (2) Good, (3) Needs improvement.

Figure 5 : 3

WORLDWIDE SURVEY OF HUMAN RESOURCE POLICIES AND PRACTICES

Major categories	Hourly-paid and clerical-salaried/	1	2	3	Managerial and professional/	1	2	3
1. **Does the company have a personnel manager?** To whom does the position report?	If not, who is responsible for the function?				If not, who is responsible for the function?			
2. Up-to-date company organization charts	Include all levels of the organization.				For management personnel only.			
3. Written personnel policies	Yes____ No____				Yes____ No____			
4. Formal manpower planning and forecasting	Used for advance recruitment. Back-up charts. For training needs.				Used for advance recruitment. Back-up charts, ages of senior staff. For training needs.			
5. Employment: recruitment	In advance of anticipated needs. Based on the manpower plan. Sources used. Application form. Personnel requisition and approval.				Regular recruitment of college graduates. Based on the manpower plan? Personnel agencies; executive search. Application form. Personnel requisition and approval.			

Figure 5 : 3 (cont.)

Major categories	Hourly-paid and clerical-salaried /	1	2	3	Managerial and professional /	1	2	3
	Pre-employment testing: costs vs. results. Reference investigation before or after hire. Employment of minority or disadvantaged personnel.				Pre-employment testing: costs vs. results. Reference investigation before or after hire. How positions filled – within or through outside hires, quantify.			
6. Formal orientation and induction procedures	Employment entry programme. On-the-job training. Vestibule training. How long is orientation period? Follow-up. Brochure on company history, benefits, pay etc.				Employment entry programme. On-the-job training. Vestibule training. How long is orientation period? Follow-up. Brochure on company history, benefits, pay, etc.			
7. Training and development	Formal apprentice programmes: how many; what types? Planned advancement to upgrade skills. In advance of openings. Clerical training. Inside or outside company. On company time. Upgrades on seniority or merit. Tuition assistance programme. Formal supervisors' training: Programmes, number and kind. Length of time. In-house or outside.				Early identification of young high potentials. Planned assignments for career advancement. Formal management development: Management-by-objectives (MBO) – how many levels? Task-force assignments. Special assignments. Job enrichment. Outside courses: How many sent? To what programmes? How results measured? Training in other companies.			

Tuition refund plan.
Company library.

How many sessions? Length of sessions?
How results measured?

8. **Communications**

Any recent survey of employee attitudes:
    When?
    How followed up?
Formal employee communications:
    Merit rating and discussion.
    Plant newspaper.
    Bulletin boards.
    Letters to home.
    Small group meetings:
        Frequency.
        Agenda items.
    Written shop rules.
Employee counselling in areas such as retirement, benefits, discipline, dissatisfactions, compensation.
Exit interview programme and follow-up.

Any recent survey of employee attitudes:
    When?
    How followed up?
Formal performance appraisal and review with the individual.
Job descriptions for each position.
Performance standards for each position + MBO.
Career planning and counselling.
Procedure for resolving executive dissatisfactions.
Regularly scheduled management staff meetings:
    Frequency.
    Duration and subject matter.
    How many levels of management?
Exit interview programme and follow-up.

9. **Compensation**

Formal wage and salary administration:
    Local wage and salary surveys.
    Job descriptions.
    Merit rating.
    Annual wage and salary reviews.
    Wage and salary structures.
    Maintenance and update.
    Automatic increases, e.g., cost-of-living, etc.

Formal compensation programme:
    Position descriptions.
    Job evaluation.
    Local salary surveys.
    Salary structure.
    Annual merit reviews.
    Maintain and update system.
    Bonus — who included:
        Mandatory.

Figure 5 : 3 (cont.)

Major categories	Hourly-paid and clerical-salaried/	1	2	3	Managerial and professional/	1	2	3
10 Fringe and social benefits	Life insurance							
	Medical insurance ⎫ Public and private:				Same.			
	Pension plans ⎭				Same.			
	Who is covered?				Same.			
	Amount of benefits.							
	Paid vacations:				Same.			
	Schedule based on company service.							
	Vacation bonus.							
	Number of paid holidays.				Same.			
	Employee loan programme.				Same.			
	Company sponsored events:				Same + planned management social activities:			
	Recreation facility.				Type and frequency.			
	Christmas party.				Wives included.			
	Housing employees.							
	Local benefits surveys.				Same.			
	Fringe benefit costs to company as percentage of total wages and salaries.				Same.			
					Nonmandatory.			
					13th month, etc.			
					Automatic increases.			
					Other, e.g., car, clubs.			
11 Other employee incentives and awards	Cash awards for employee ideas.				Special management awards:			
	Any contests, e.g., quality, housekeeping,				Submitted ideas.			

attendance, etc.: awards, recognition — tangible and intangible.
Announcement of promotions: notice-boards, letters to homes.

Sales contests — incentives.
Any other type of special management recognition.

Management unions, e.g., engineers.
Frequency of labour/management meetings and duration:
    Subjects discussed.
    Reasons for meetings.
    Who attends meetings?

12 Labour and/or union relations

How many unions? Plant, office.
Who negotiates contracts?
Grievance procedure.
Number and duration of strikes, work stoppages and slowdowns in past two years:
    Estimated cost to company.
Shop council or other forms of employee representation.
Local legislation — mandatory, codetermination, etc.:
    Labour represented on board or management committee.
    Restrictions on management rights.
    Compulsory arbitration.
Any other unusual labour conditions — uniforms, free meals, etc.
Time off for union business.
Restrictions on reducing workforce, overtime, etc.
Forced hiring of handicapped.
Payment of worker indemnities for layoff or discharge — amounts and how determined.
    Pending legislation.

Figure 5 : 3 (cont.)

Major categories	Hourly-paid and clerical-salaried/	1	2	3	Managerial and professional/	1	2	3
13 Working conditions and housekeeping	Field. Factory. Office. Locker facilities – showers. Uniforms. Parking facilities. Transportation. Cafeteria.				Size of offices. Private offices. Cleanness of work place. Parking facilities. Cafeteria.			
14 Employee statistics	Turnover and absenteeism: By department ⎫ By supervisor ⎬ number and per cent, By sex ⎭ including total time lost. By age group By length of time employed. Overtime hours worked and paid: field, factory, office, by department and supervisor. Number of employees: Direct and indirect. Percentage increase or decrease in each within past three years. Employee accidents: Frequency. Severity.				Turnover and absenteeism + reasons: Same: Number promotions. Number demotions. Number discharged. Number transfers. Number of management employees: Past three years. To increase or decrease. Same.			

	Working hours lost in past two years. Severance indemnities paid: why, how much, to how many individuals? Activity per employee: 1972, 1973.	Same.
15 Safety and security	Formal safety programme, including field, factory, office: Regular maintenance. Safety rules. Safety committee. Fire prevention programme. Safety inspections. Hazard precautions. Full- or part-time nurse. Identification of accident-prone employees. Safety statistics followed up. Communication of safety programme. Manuals of instruction on how to use equipment. Safety training for supervisors. Proper storage and labelling — solvents, etc.	Not applicable directly; only to extent does top management regularly and periodically review and take interest in total safety programme?
16 Community relations	Any organizations for employees only, sponsored by union or employees themselves: Purpose. Frequency of meetings.	Company and individual executive involvement in community affairs: Local fund-raising. Membership in professional organizations: Rotary.

Figure 5 : 3 (cont.)

Major categories	Hourly-paid and clerical-salaried/	1	2	3	Managerial and professional/	1	2	3
	Strength of membership.				Management groups.			
	Action programmes.				Chamber of commerce.			
	Effect on management.				Local manufacturers' associations.			
					Code committees.			
					Product safety committees.			

17 Other major activities
(within responsibility of personnel function not included)

The response was enthusiastic, and the comment was frequently offered that the advance material provided an excellent guide in the formation of a complete personnel programme. The major topics included are illustrated (in Figure 5 : 4) as follows:

Figure 5 : 4

MAJOR TOPICS FOR ANALYSIS OF PERSONNEL POLICY AND IMPLEMENTATION

1   Personnel manager

Group level.
Company level.

2   Organization charts

Management.
All levels.

3   Personnel policies

Written.
Informal.

4   Manpower planning and forecasting

For advance recruitment.
Back-up chart.
For development.

5   Employment recruitment

University graduates recruitment
  regularly.
Based on manpower plan.
Sources.
Application form.
Personnel requisition and approval.
Pre-employment testing.
Reference investigation.
How positions filled:
    From within?
    From outside?

6   Formal orientation and induction procedures

Employment entry programme.
On-the-job training.
Length of orientation.
Follow-up.
Company brochure.

7   Training and development

Identification of young high potentials.
Planned assignments for career
  advancement.
Formal management development:
    Management-by-objectives: what
      levels?
    Task force assignments.
    Special assignments.
    Job enrichment.
Outside courses.
Intercompany transfers.
Central library.
Tuition refund.

8   Communications

Employee survey.
Formal performance appraisal and review.
Job descriptions.
Performance standards.
Career planning and counselling.
Resolving executive disatisfactions
    (procedure?).

Figure 5 : 4 (cont.)

Regular management staff meetings:
  Frequency.
  Duration/subject-matter.
  How many management levels?
Exit interview programme and follow-up.

9 Compensation

Formal compensation programme.
Job description.
Job evaluation.
Local/national salary surveys.
Salary structure.
Annual merit reviews.
Maintain/update systems.
Bonus eligibility:
  Mandatory.
  Nonmandatory.
  13th month, etc.
Automatic increases.
Cars, clubs, etc.

10 Fringe and social benefits

Life ⎫
Medical ⎬ insurance.
Pension plans.
Paid vacations.
Number of paid holidays.
Employee loans.
Company sponsored events.
Local benefits survey.
Fringe benefit costs to company.

11 Other incentives and awards

Special awards:
  Sales contests.
  Sales incentives.
  Submitted ideas.

12 Labour and/or union relations

Frequency, duration and costs of strikes.
Management unions.
Frequency of labour management
  meetings and duration.

13 Working conditions

Size of offices.
Private offices.
Cleanness of workplace.
Parking facilities.
Cafeteria.

14 Employee statistics

Turnover and absenteeism.
Number of management employees:
  Past three years.
  Increase or decrease.
Employee accidents.
Severance indemnities paid.

15 Community relations

Company/individual executive
  involvement in community affairs.

Shortly after the personal visit and discussions, each local managing director and his personnel manager received a report on the observations of the staff human resource directors.

In order to take advantage of the momentum gained through the positive response of the subsidiary companies, personnel policy and practice was designated one of the two major themes for the annual one-week senior management meeting. This meeting included 22 managing directors and all senior staff supportive personnel from headquarters. Briefing material was sent out in advance of the meeting, to prepare the managing directors to apply the principle of contestation for the small group discussions and subsequent reports at the general meetings. The briefing material included the following:

Typical survey report — developed country.
Statistical rating summary of the 17 companies using the 16 categories defined in the survey.
Comparative rating of companies, solely according to the strength of the personnel programme.
Summary, by category, of the 17 companies.
Recommended international personnel policies.
Suggested guidelines for implementation of international personnel policies.
Example of a professionally done human resource programme — developing country.

Samples of these exhibits are included in Appendix A (pages 316—56).

A professional presentation was made at the management meeting, stressing the magnitude of the financial and human considerations involved in an improved approach to human resource management. The individual discussion groups responded well and discussed the practicality of the intended policies and the suggested guidelines for implementation. Each group was assigned two major subjects. A managing director was chosen by his peers to be the reporter and to present his group's conclusions and recommendations at the general assembly meetings. Overall, there was excellent acceptance and recognition of the fact that improvement was both necessary and possible. The conclusions were summarized by the international director of human resources and presented orally at the end of the meeting. Then a follow-up written summary of the conclusions was sent to the managing directors.

At the time of writing this book, 24 companies had requested specific assistance to strengthen their local personnel functions. The conclusions (Figure 5 : 5) were as follows:

Figure 5 : 5

SUMMARY OF AGREEMENTS RELATIVE TO ACCEPTANCE OF RECOMMENDED INTERNATIONAL PERSONNEL POLICIES AND GUIDELINES FOR IMPLEMENTATION

December 1974

1   Personnel Policies

The policies [see Exhibit 5, Appendix A, pages 331—2] were generally

Figure 5 : 5 (cont.)

accepted as written. There were a few differences of opinion as to the implementation of these policy 'guidelines'. It is recognized that implementation is a long-term process, possibly up to three years in some companies, but nevertheless a beginning must be made, particularly in those companies whose individual reports indicated a need for improvement.

2   Agreements on areas requiring attention and implementation (resulting from group discussions and general meetings)

Improve manpower planning and forecasting, particularly in executive manpower and management back-ups.
> Organization charts to be made available for all levels of management and updated as often as necessary, but at least once annually.

Recruit good people, even in times of recession.
Provide for executive back-ups by working in close cooperation with staff personnel director.
Job descriptions for all levels of management down to the first-line supervisory level.
Salary structures — updated annually and a good local programme for administering a total compensation system.
Pay will be based on job responsibility and accomplishment, and not seniority.
Total compensation and fringe benefits will be competitive on a local basis only — no attempt to be made to equate one country with another.
Performance standards to be developed for all management positions. These will be used to identify high-potential as well as marginal performers.
Marginal performers are to be released after six months' trial period if they fail to meet performance standards.
Each manager will be entitled to an annual performance appraisal and discussion of his contribution to the business.
Each company will have complete employee records systems. According to local needs, separate confidential files should be maintained for key employees at the discretion of the local managing director.
> There will be separate job application forms for hourly and clerical employees, supervisors and managers.

While many companies do gather employee statistics, they are not used

Figure 5 : 5 (cont.)

effectively as a tool for management control over its investment in human resources.

All companies should have local personnel policies, complementary to international personnel policies [as defined in Exhibit 5, pages 331—2], but adapted to local needs. As a general rule, the larger the company, the greater the need carefully to define more areas for local personnel policies.

Strengthen employee orientation and induction procedures and provide for a local court of appeals, wherein aggrieved employees may have their job-related problems reviewed by the next two higher levels of management. This excludes matters where formal grievance procedures are already established and matters of a contractual nature.

3   Managing directors have requested staff assistance in the following areas

Help to develop professional personnel managers at the local operating company level.

At least one annual visit to the smaller companies by the staff personnel director, or his designated representative, to provide counsel and guidance in personnel management.

Develop a special handbook for newly formed and small companies, to serve as a guide for handling personnel matters.

Provide uniform format and explanation for gathering and proper use of employee statistics. In some companies, the accumulation may be the responsibility of the financial manager, but it is recommended that the follow-up for management control be the responsibility of the local personnel manager.

Assist local companies in improving executive manpower planning by:
    Participating in annual organization and manpower reviews.
    Participating in the solution to the problem of executive back-up on a company-wide basis.

Design a uniform performance appraisal plan and teach local managers how to conduct performance appraisal discussions with those reporting to them.

Conduct and follow up management-by-objective (MBO) seminars on request from managing directors. Recognize that it takes three to five years successfully to implement MBO in a large company. Do not attempt MBO with first-line supervision.

Coordinate all training activities among the various operating companies.

Figure 5 : 5 (cont.)

Managers to be trained in operating companies, and not headquarters. Trainees to be evaluated and asked to evaluate training received.

Train teachers in methods of instruction, to ensure transference of technology and management skills to the trainee.

All training costs and expenses to be consolidated, measured and controlled.

Assist local companies in the formulation of supervisory and management development programmes. Large companies to invite smaller companies to participate in their internal supervisory, managerial and functional training programmes.

Provide guidelines for communicating and explaining reductions-in-force to employees and managers.

Provide guidelines for managing companies with employees' and workers' councils.

Conduct regional or area conferences for local personnel managers.

4   We accept your challenge and we will deliver a quality product on time (including service)

To do this, we need from you, the managing directors, the following (plus support and guidance):

Tell us if there are any unresolved differences of opinion or disagreements with the handout materials.

Prepare any modifications you feel are necessary, together with your reasons for so doing.

Let us know, as far in advance as possible, when you want our help and assistance.

Make your key people (including your personnel manager), available from time to time, with sufficient advance notice from us, to attend meetings on personnel practices, to teach others from smaller companies and other regions.

Resolve now to improve management of your human assets, to get a better return on human capital while improving employee satisfaction.

Make a beginning in those areas where improvements were suggested.

5.7   Summary

Creative ways had to be found and sold to senior line management fully to develop local human resources. If a good selection has been made, both of the local managing director and his manager of human resources, half the battle is won. The task is not an easy one, but the careful preplanning and the expense, time and effort are more than justified.

Application of concepts, such as the 'Worldwide survey of human resource policies and practices' (pages 123–30), have a snowballing effect. One success leads to another; nothing succeeds like success. As top-level local executives are hired, trained and developed, they can assist other developing and developed countries to progress. The multinational company cannot afford to do less. If it is to be successful in its goals of expanded markets, higher profits, improved individual satisfaction, and a distinct measurable positive contribution to the various societies in which it operates, development of local human resources is a top priority.

The next chapter focuses on the qualities of an expatriate executive which are necessary for the successful transference of managerial and technological expertise to the local nationals.

PART THREE
THE MAN ON THE SPOT

6

The expatriate executive

In the transfer of managerial and technological expertise, the major element and most frequent obstacle to success is the expatriate manager himself. He needs particular attributes and skills, developed to an unusual degree. Essentially, the same human qualities which make an executive accepted and successful in his home country will guarantee his success in a foreign country, but the need for these becomes more pronounced in a foreign environment, and they must be coupled with essential managerial skills if catastrophe is to be avoided, for failure is more obvious and dangerous than it would be at home. In order of importance, the qualities are:

Adaptability/Flexibility

To assume a high-level managerial position in a foreign environment requires physical, mental and psychological adaptability. It may be necessary for the expatriate to change eating habits, social protocol, possibly even life style. He cannot remain aloof from his new environment and the local people: he must assimilate their culture, traditions, habits and customs, and not spend all his spare time in a ghetto of his own countrymen. He must develop an understanding and an appreciation of their cultural heritage: their hopes, aspirations, motivations and ambitions. Flexibility is also vital. Managerial styles fully acceptable in his country may be virtually unknown in the new environment.

High tolerance for frustration, and patience

If people do not respond instantly as expected, the foreign executive, particularly the American, tends to become very frustrated. The indigenous government, service industries and employees have their own way of doing things: the employees are usually eager to improve their skills, but they frequently do not realize the commitment required of them. Precision, concern for productivity, punctuality, dedication to work, rigid self-discipline, are new concepts to many people — particularly those in developing countries. If this is recognized at the outset by the expatriate executive, he will be far better prepared to cope with the situation.

Establishing a new plant operation in Peru or India will never generate the same speedy results as the establishment of a new factory in West Germany or France. And there are many gradations in between. Attitudes and behaviour patterns derived from centuries of preconditioning cannot be changed in six to twelve months. It is not that people are less intelligent or unwilling to cooperate, but that they must be taught *gradually* to recognize the need for change, and then meticulously and painstakingly take those steps necessary to effect change. Once they recognize the necessity for change and its possible benefits, they will change.

Empathy/Understanding

To place oneself in the shoes of another person is a formidable task; but by trying to understand their educational, political, social and religious backgrounds, it is possible to acquire an insight into why a person acts as they do. Expatriates can benefit from a foreign culture as well as contribute to that society. Their technology and managerial skills may result in a higher level of productivity and an improved standard of living for the host country, but the expatriates must first be personally acceptable to those they will serve: if an individual is rejected, so are his ideas and his expertise. Empathy demands a thorough advance study of the host country. It is equally important in joint ventures, mergers, acquisitions, buying or selling, starting a new company, or negotiating a licensing agreement.

High intellectual capacity

It is essential to be able rapidly to assimilate knowledge and experience, and to be able to relate that to developing a commonality of interest and goals. A high level of intelligence, perception and imagination are vital. Technological or managerial experience alone are insufficient. Indigenous people will look to the expatriate for leadership in more than just the solution of technical and business problems. In many countries, the relationship between employer and employee goes well beyond a fair day's pay for a fair day's work. Even the very clever will find it an exhausting task to operate effectively in so alien an environment, and this is one of the main reasons why so many multinational companies are pursuing the policy of staffing foreign operations with local nationals at the most senior levels of management in the subsidiary.

Some unfortunate experiences have shown how true this is. For example, it has been common practice for many multinational companies to place their own financial executives in foreign subsidiaries. Millions of dollars have been lost through this well-intentioned move. The most competent expatriate financial manager will find difficulties, because while the fiscal laws say one thing, actual practice is something quite different. It may well be, for example, that relationships with a government-owned central bank or the minister of finance will be far more important than the financial expertise of any expatriate, however distinguished. Of course, there must be strong internal financial control of subsidiary companies, but, given the guidelines and control, a local national financial manager is far more effective than an expatriate financial manager. The same is true for managing directors, human resource managers and marketing managers.

A company's success is often largely dependent on its relations with local government; and the selection of a local executive, with high intellectual capacity, can be more valuable than bringing in an expatriate, with superior technical skills and management sophistication.

Ability and willingness to learn the language

Fluency takes time, but even before his arrival, the expatriate should learn the basics of the local language. The mere fact that the expatriate tries to speak the language, however poorly, is seen in most countries as a positive sign of his willingness to integrate. No communication will be possible with most people unless the rudiments of the language are learned. There is no excuse for an expatriate executive in a local operating company not being reasonably proficient in the language of the host country within two years of his arrival.

The expatriate executive must become deeply involved in the business from the very beginning. A number of expatriates fail through blind acceptance of the reports of a management team. Particularly at first, it is necessary for the expatriate to check what he is told: without the language, the expatriate manager can and will be misled. The results can be disastrous for the company.

Problem-solving ability

The expatriate is left to his own resources to solve local problems. Being often far removed from headquarters, he must improvise. Problem-solving ability is defined as the ability quickly to recognize and identify the real cause of the problem, and not just the symptoms. This, of course, is where the technological expertise of the expatriate is invaluable. Using a systematic approach avoids having to live with difficult situations. The expatriots cannot assume that all people in the world think and act as he does: they have neither been trained nor equipped to provide his type of systematic, rational approach to solving problems. Where there is a problem of sufficient magnitude, the expatriate manager must not remain aloof until it reaches the crisis stage. The job is demanding because it requires personal involvement until local nationals can be properly trained in real problem identification and follow-up and implementation.

Opportunity-mindedness

This is defined as the ability to recognize an opportunity when it arises. Local nationals have to be trained to view problems as opportunities, that requires imagination. In one Far Eastern country, for example, job completions were considerably behind schedule. Salesmen insisted they could not sell because of the company's inability to deliver. Close investigation revealed that competitors were experiencing far greater difficulty in meeting commitments. Hence, a positive sales tool was developed: a number of clients were visited, to explain that this subsidiary's delivery was eight to sixteen weeks better than competitors'. A problem was turned into an opportunity.

Again, in one Middle East country, customers complained about high service costs. An imaginative manager viewed this as an opportunity, and was able to get the end users of the product to contribute to its proper maintenance. He got the service contracts at the right price because the owner of the equipment now had his customers share the cost of servicing that equipment.

Opportunities must be recognized, clearly defined, acted upon and sold to all concerned. The expatriate must have the necessary ability, but he can be helped by opportunities to bring a new approach to old problems.

Results orientation

Sometimes an expatriate is so influenced by his environment that he forgets all the good management techniques he brought with him. Instead of changing the environment, he becomes part of it. Too often, he forgets he is there to inculcate a results orientation among employees of a subsidiary company. He may get discouraged and fall into the trap of thinking 'it cannot be done here'. He may accept any excuse for failure to achieve results, even when it is clear that those results are realistic and obtainable in that particular environment. He may get caught up in the social life, and forget that his mission is to do more than obtain goodwill. To avoid this syndrome requires long, hard hours of work, sometimes seemingly with little result. But perseverance and determination to succeed will result in improvement.

The introduction of a budgetary control system, for example, is a new experience in many countries, particularly where cost and expense controls have been virtually unknown, and only the select few in a company have ever received information on the financial performance. The local financial manager has a major responsibility to teach financial analysis and control to all levels of management. This takes time. It requires monthly reports, discussions, thorough analysis of all items of significant cost to the business. Some simple, straightforward techniques, such as in-depth analysis of accounts receivable, sales versus inventory levels, increasing borrowing, late billing, high interest costs and poor collections, may never have been considered. Hence, the totality of the picture has not been apparent, and management controls are nonexistent. Progress demands change: growth demands change, and costs can get completely out of control if all managers at all levels are not taught a results orientation in their work.

Decision-making ability

This is defined as recognizing when a decision has to be made. It includes the ability to make the right decision based on inadequate information. It includes the timing of the decision, obtaining, as far as possible, acceptance of the decision by all concerned, and the cooperation of all whose joint efforts are necessary to implement the decision. There is a tendency among managers in developing countries to defer or postpone urgent, but awkward, decisions in the hope that the situation will improve. Too often, a delay merely ruins the profit performance for the company.

In some countries, people have been hired on the basis of poor forecasting, so that two months later there has not been enough work to keep the new employees busy. Current social and political pressures, however, will prevent their being laid off: it is costly to make a bad decision, based on over-optimistic sales prognostications. Good, timely decisions, properly and promptly implemented, are vital. All managers must support the decision once made, regardless of whether they agree with it or not. Otherwise, it will never be known whether the decision is a good one or a bad one. If all try to make it work, it will become quickly apparent if the decision was a bad one. It is better to have a bad decision, well implemented and supported by all, than a good decision not supported and poorly implemented.

Communication/Teaching/Listening skills

Mere possession of knowledge, skills and experience is not enough. How many of us have had brilliant professors at our university, who could not teach, could not communicate, could not transfer their expertise even to students from the same cultural environment? The difficulties involved in the transfer of technological and managerial skills to people with a totally different cultural heritage are the same, only magnified a hundredfold.

A shirtsleeves executive is required: one who can analyse a situation, show how a process is to be done, by breaking the job down into simple, logical, orderly steps; write it down, observe the application, make the necessary corrections, patiently and with understanding; then, repeatedly, follow up, giving all kinds of encouragement for any measurable progress. Immediate feedback of results is absolutely necessary to ensure retention of learning. It is also important to recognize accomplishment with more opportunity for achievement. This is a most essential motivation, as defined in 2.2 (pages 32–3). A helpful technique is to set the individual (at all levels of the company) to repeat exactly what he has understood he is expected to do, and how to do it. Then, he should write it down, commit himself to dates, measure his own progress. This is time-consuming but highly rewarding.

Most people want to please their employer. It is up to the employer to give all the tools and training necessary to do this, within the framework of the individual's level of understanding and ability to do the work. This is determined by an understanding of the environment which made him what he is. It necessitates treating people as human beings – not as instruments of production.

Integrity

The expatriate must be honest with himself, his company workers and his management. It was mentioned in 1.1 (page 5) that, in many parts of the world, the so-called 'conflict-of-interest' is nonexistent. Bribery is a common practice. The multinationals must not only introduce ideas of honesty, such as not using company assets for personal gain, they must also take care that they do not succumb to what are regarded as common business practices in a foreign environment. There are many opportunities to cheat, receive bribes, and engage in devious practices, which eventually can destroy the local subsidiary.

Establishing a high level of mutual trust and confidence in a foreign country requires the highest business principles and moral standards. If a man does not know something, it is best to admit it, and not to try to bluff his way through. This only results in a lack of credibility: once this happens, the expatriate may as well pack up and go home.

A frequent problem is the making of promises to local nationals, which are never intended to be kept. This may momentarily placate the individual, but he will completely lose confidence in the expatriate. For example, the promise of a pay increase, and that it will be done by such and such a date, or 'don't worry, I'll take care of that'. While a sincere intention is good, *all* promises, even implied, must be kept. It is a reflection of a man's integrity, and this is especially important in a developing country.

Priorities skills

This is the manager's ability to concentrate his time and efforts on those activities which produce the greatest return to the business. To state it another way, most managers spend 80 per cent of their time on matters which have less than 20 per cent impact on profits. It means the cultivation of priorities skills, the ability to delegate matters of lesser importance to subordinates, and to avoid spending time on items of trivial importance. This quality has been called the 'cash-register' mind: it is the kind of mind that ensures efficiently run businesses.

In developing countries, issues of a seemingly trivial nature often occupy more of a manager's time than he would desire; but failure to respect these local issues and traditions means a disordered sense of priorities, because the end result may be a costly slowdown. For example, one senior manager chose not to attend the employees' annual Christmas party because of other commitments: the employees accordingly chose not to attend work for a period of time. This cost more than the benefits derived from a cost-improvement programme for the next six months. In some countries, failure to say 'good morning' to each employee may result in a slowdown: priorities must be oriented to achieve the best results in human satisfaction as well as profitability

Professionalism

It is essential also to be a professional manager in order to earn the employee's respect and loyalty. True in any environment, this is most important in a foreign country. The skills of planning, organizing, integrating and measuring, as described in Chapter 5 (see pages 112–37), must be possessed by the expatriate executive: he must also be able to teach these skills to others within their cultural framework. These are some causes of managerial failure abroad, as witnessed by the authors:

Arrogance, inability and/or unwillingness to listen.
Dishonesty, bad judgement, succumbing to the existing standards of the new environment.
Bad decisions.
Weakness of character and personality.
Could not or would not delegate.
Did not trust anybody.
Failed to verify information received, did not get sufficiently involved in the business.
Managerial obsolescence.
Bad organization.
Became too friendly with the workers.
Inability to teach managerial concepts, lack of understanding of local people.

Successful managers tend to possess most, if not all, the qualities in exact opposition to these failings. The priority of each attribute varies, but the human skills involved need to be learned quickly. Small things, laudable, in themselves, can cause a lot of trouble if handled badly.

In one European country, the newly appointed expatriate managing director went early to the factory one morning. His trip was not well received; it was regarded with deep suspicion, because in that particular country the top men never started before 10 a.m. To make matters worse, he started to speak to the workers: that was an almost unforgivable sin. He then attempted to get his managers (those reporting direct) to make their own decisions, to accept the responsibilities and results of their actions: this created suspicion and mistrust. Managers naturally expected the top man to make all the decisions, big and small, and do their thinking for them. The managing director realized his mistakes in time and proceeded to modify his behaviour. He began an extended programme of conditioning, to change established attitudes and expectations of managerial behaviour. The company eventually became highly successful.

If the executive properly understands his own attitudes, assumptions and beliefs about other individuals and groups, he is more readily able to detect the usefulness and limitations of these feelings. If he can go a step further, he begins to accept that viewpoints, perceptions and beliefs may differ radically from his own. He can then proceed to create an atmosphere of security and approval, where subordinates feel free to express themselves without fear of censure and ridicule. Sensitivity is the counterpart to and prerequisite for understanding. Dr Cecil G. Howard of Georgia Southern College has carefully analysed the most essential skills for successful overseas performance. He has classified these into technical, human and conceptual, and related the skills to the environment, the organization and the individual. He would add, to the points above, the following interorganizational conceptual skills:

Capacity to institute the desired style of *management within* an organization.

Knowledge and experience in implementing *change in the organization.*

Ability to understand and adapt to a desired *style of management.*

Capacity to adapt to and engineer change in ownership, management, technology or *production.*

Tolerance and prudence in implementing change concerned with expatriate know-how transferred *to the organization overseas.*

Understanding of the problem of transferring *technology to an international environment.*

Demonstrated intelligence and ability to think through problems; judgement, innovativeness, imagination, analytical and planning *capabilities. Ability to teach others.*

Receptivity to technological change.

In addition, he has listed the most important human and moral attributes:

Competence to cope with and adapt to different attitudes, values and perceptions.

Ability to identify and cope with environmental hostility, adversity and complexity.

High facility in interpersonal relationships with peers, subordinates, superiors, and other expatriate, third-country nationals from countries other than his own.

Fitness in withstanding illness and fatigue.

Presence of vocational and other outside interests.

Awareness of the impact of internal, social, political and economic decisions on the individual's and organization's goals and objectives.

Sense of responsibility for developing individuals and groups.

Demonstrated self-control of one's own goals, attitudes and perceptions.

It may appear to the reader that the selection process for overseas executives emphasizes a 'superman'. While this is not entirely true, it does mean that only the exceptional executive must be given an overseas assignment. A mediocre person will fail.

6.1 The human resource in acquisitions and mergers

It was mentioned in the Preface that less than 50 per cent of multinational ventures achieve the desired results. Stock analysts may pass this off as vulnerability to political and economic instability and discount the real value of a multinational company's stock because of it. All too often, however, the failure has a human cause and this cannot be emphasized too often. Assuming a legitimate business reason for the multinational venture, the human differences become even more pronounced when attempts are made to merge:

Family-owned with corporate business.
National with multi-national.
Private with governmental.
Large companies with smaller companies.

The management audit described in Figure 6 : 1 (page 151) is a prerequisite to merger discussions. Many companies overlook the human element, even though they say: 'We bought it for its management talent'. They cannot describe how this talent was assessed. They often do not know in depth the backgrounds, in education and experience, of the top 15 executives in the prospective company. They cannot identify, nor do they attempt to assess the calculated risk of bringing in a family-owned company, which may well have in it authoritarian management style, paternalism, nepotism, disorganization, managerial obsolescence, lack of controls and lack of capital investment. Most companies after all are willing to sell only when they are in trouble.

Managers from smaller companies are unaccustomed to cost and expense controls at top levels; to precise measurements and 'bureaucratic' paperwork systems. In some situations, the owner-manager would rather see his business fail for his new owners than see someone else run it more successfully.

If, despite all precautions, the decision is made to buy, merge or make a joint venture, the acquiring company should not use a task force from the home office to 'investigate' the company. People might interpret this as a threatening gesture, and leave. Most owner-managers will leave anyway within two to three years after their company has been purchased, because they cannot adjust to so much change.

If one man from the parent corporation is given the responsibility for the successful integration of both companies, he must find the strengths of both companies and evolve, and sell, a plan for merging these strengths. He must be fully acceptable to the president of the acquired company, and must serve as his assistant and not his boss. If he assumes line authority, he may become too critical of how the company was run and act too impulsively, making many management and organization changes in too short a period of time. This could destroy the company, even though it may become necessary to replace all the senior executives of the acquired company over a period of time.

If the decision is to appoint one man from each company, to prepare and implement a plan for the complete integration, each should be a senior executive, and both should be totally acceptable to the presidents of the acquired and acquiring company. In this case, as in all others, the new multinational parent company must learn immediately to respect the traditions and protocols of the country and adapt to the new environment *before* introducing change. This can take six to twelve months for a superior executive.

To assess properly the degree of risk, and to evaluate the actual differences in management, Figure 6 : 1 demonstrates an audit, both of the *acquiring company* and *the potential candidate for acquisition*. These

---

Figure 6 : 1

ASSESSING THE HUMAN RESOURCE FOR COMPARATIVE STUDY
MANAGEMENT AUDIT

Objective criteria (as determined by physical presence or absence)

Written statements of long-term objectives and short-term goals.
Formal organization structure covering all levels of management.
Personnel policies.
Position descriptions.
Performance standards.
Performance appraisal.
Formal compensation system.
Training and development at all levels.

Figure 6 : 1 (cont.)

Employee statistics.
Employer record system.
Manpower forecast and plan.
Business plan.
Budgets.
Cost and expense controls.
Productivity records.
Formal communications system.
Local union contracts.
Incumbent qualifications in relation to job responsibilities.
    Age.
    Years of experience:
        Within company.
        Outside company.
        On present job.
    Internal and external training received.
    Salary progress.
    Formal education completed: number of years, degrees, day school
        or at night.

Subjective criteria (from personal interviews of top 15 executives)

Management philosophy.
Business charter.
Degree of delegation of authority and individual accountability.
Management style of company.
Frequency of management meetings ⎫
Content of management meetings ⎬ at all levels.
Each executive's understanding of:
    His own job responsibilities.
    Relationships to other jobs.
        At same level.
        Levels above.
        Levels below.
Contribution of his job to profitability.
Priorities of work.
How he develops his people.
How his priorities relate to overall problems and opportunities of the
    company.

Figure 6 : 1 (cont.)

His concept of line and staff relationships:
>With regard to his own position.
>With regard to other positions — above and below.
>With regard to degree of integration which exists in his company.

Written goals and plans for achievement, including action steps, timing, measurement of results.
>Interrelationship of individual goals.

The executive's understanding of the foregoing criteria.

His own assessment of how well he and his company are achieving these criteria.

criteria are presented to give the prospective buyer of a foreign company some idea of the magnitude of the problem in attempting to integrate two companies. Add to it the complexities of a foreign environment, with all that this implies, and it is small wonder that so many individual and collective failures occur.

The attempt is not to discourage foreign acquisitions, but rather to bring into perspective the need to assess carefully the high degree of risk involved: by proceding slowly and cautiously, to minimize the chance of failure. One general manager, who is highly successful, noted that the key to success is to develop a plan for the merger for *after it happens, before it happens*. That is to say: clearly define the new organization, the venture objectives, and what will happen to the top people in both organizations. The plan must be detailed, and written and agreed to by both parties.

The outcome of a merger can be successfully predicted: the major cause of failure is the inability of management to integrate the two companies. It can be as bad as, or worse than, the transplant of a live organ from one human being to another: it is always a shock at best, and often rejected.

The treatment of former managers, shareholders and employees will vary, depending on the situation in any given company at any given time. That is why it must be spelled out. Many multinationals acquirers want to put their own team in right away. This can be fatal to the acquired company. As a general guideline, if, by the acquiring company's standards, more than half the key executives are candidates for immediate replacement, it is best to abandon the acquisition entirely.

While there is no set pattern for success, there are many sure ways of failure. Just the fact that there are major differences in size and distribution of power; different reporting relationships; lack of trained managers of 'change'; wrong assessment of the managerial competence available in both companies; and the total incompatibility of management styles — all are more than sufficient to cause failure; just the difficulties in communication alone are significant obstacles to success. The consequences of failure do untold damage to individuals and to both companies. Specifically:

The 'goodwill' of the host country is lost.
The image of the foreign expatriate is tarnished.
Selection and development costs increase.
The host country will not forget an 'injury'.
Profits decrease substantially.
The development of the host country and its people are retarded.

6.2   Why do companies use expatriates?

Foreign-service employees, and particularly US expatriates, are not cheap. They can cost two to three times as much as a local national on their total remuneration package. The list of customary payments is intimidating: base salary (often higher than a local manager's), foreign-service premium, cost-of-living allowance, housing allowance, tax equalization, education allowance, relocation expenses, benefit contributions, currency fluctuation, etc. Yet there must be some valid reasons for companies to continue to use foreign-service employees, and to neglect this potentially rich source of cost reductions.

A multinational corporation often feels the need to be represented in the host country by a man with sound company experience and a knowledge of the business and industry. They want someone who knows the policies and procedures of the parent company and, even more important, knows whom to contact in order to get what he needs quickly and effectively. Communication is easier and this, together with the other advantages, is of prime importance in the early stages of setting up a new overseas subsidiary. It is a crucial time and the firm does not want to run the risk of failure.

In the early stages of a country's development, there may be a shortage of good local, national managers, for reasons already analysed. Multinationals usually make every attempt to protect their investment in a subsidiary, and they may feel that its efficiency and profitability are endangered by the lack of management talent, either because current employees lack *any* potential for senior management positions or because there would be too great a time-lag while the local nationals were being trained. Some complex problems may need rapid solutions and cannot afford to wait on the normal processes of recruitment, selection and training.

Although it is the responsibility of every expatriate in a subsidiary company to develop his own back-up man, there are occasions when his specific task is to train local nationals for higher positions. This is more likely to be training of a technical nature, or in a particular functional expertise, and the foreign-service executive may even have the responsibility of selecting the people to fill the key positions. His assignment will be of a temporary and well-defined duration. This approach will find favour with highly nationalistic governments, who suffer foreign managers unwillingly, and it will be a demonstration of the company's good faith.

The expatriate may be accountable for the development of top-flight, internationally minded executives from subsidiaries, who will be ready to take up key jobs in regional and international headquarters. He himself will be a high-calibre executive, with a general management background and probably specific functional expertise. His will be an advisory role: running seminars, providing an evaluative and counselling service to the subsidiary management. His assignment will be a roving one, lending the same assistance to all the subsidiaries, since the future headquarters staff will be drawn from these managers. The appointment of such an executive can be an encouragement to local nationals, as they see their promotional opportunities opening up.

Some international companies may blatantly wish to retain control of the subsidiary (either financial or managerial) and put their own man in for this reason alone. US multinationals have, on occasion, lost patience with their slow-moving, low-profit European subsidiaries, and have sent in a single expatriate, or a team of dynamic management experts, to sort things out. This does not always have the desired effect: the local management sometimes dig their heels in, dismissing all new-fangled methods, leaving the unfortunate foreigner feeling at a loss. A series of expatriates may be sent to wield the hatchet: theirs are not usually long-term assignments.

In a young or newly acquired subsidiary, the headquarters may want a home-country or third-country national who is familiar with the company, to occupy a key position, in order to ensure that the subsidiary is complying with overall company objectives, goals and policies. A local company may be competent, making a satisfactory level of profits, and yet be lacking that panache which will assure it a growing share of the market. It may lack imagination and new products. This is even more likely to happen where the R & D function is centred in the corporation's home country or when marketing is closely controlled. The subsidiary placidly waits for new products, production techniques, publicity practices, and may need some encouragement. An outsider may provide that impetus to accept, and seek, new ideas.

Some multinationals consider a tour in the international division an indispensable part of the executive's development and career plan; and an overseas appointment may be the stepping-stone to a senior position in the corporate structure – a kind of grooming for stardom.

These are some of the reasons why multinationals still use foreign-service employees. In any one case there may a combination of reasons: 'The company made an even bigger loss this year, all the managers have resigned, the treasurer's been using our funds for his own benefit – go and do something about it'. In any event, the position of an expatriate is a delicate one. If he is in a subordinate position, he may be suspected of being a spy for top management. He will feel isolated from the seat of power and have fears about reintegrating later into the parent company. The firm must be even more careful about selecting someone for overseas service than it would be for domestic operations. To talk of sending an expatriate overseas does not imply one type of assignment only: it can be temporary or indefinite, confined to one country or to several, can entail frequent visits or be on a project team basis. The multinational can use any combination of these arrangements, and they will be examined in 6.3. In any event, a basic policy on selecting, developing and rewarding their foreign-service employees will be required: otherwise they may well end up negotiating each single transfer, causing inequities and a heavy administrative workload.

6.3   What are the elements of this policy approach?

The key to a successful policy is the planning of the company's own manpower needs, of its executives' own career development, and of the appropriate remuneration structure. Too often this sort of thing is left to chance: for example, no provision is made for a back-up man for a subsidiary's president; when the latter leaves unexpectedly, the company is either forced to promote an inadequate subordinate, recruit a local national from outside (which usually takes time), or bring in an expatriate.

The multinational must prepare a manpower plan, which will identify the current and future needs for international staff, determining the number required and available, the qualifications required (is it technical expertise, marketing, finance, or general management skills?). This information needs a time-frame which will act as a constraint on management's plans: it is useless to send the proposed general manager to the Harvard Advanced Management Programme if he is needed next week in Venezuela. On the other hand, the company should not over-react to urgent calls for help: there is always a tendency for subsidiaries to exaggerate the urgency of their needs; and when assistance has been provided, either to ignore or delay implementing the solution. Any request for managerial assistance should be carefully evaluated, in the light of necessity and the company's current commitments. Sudden decisions to transfer an individual overseas are usually profitable neither for the person nor the company, and the company can sometimes be justly accused of manipulation.

Once the company has made some progress in identifying its man-power needs, it can start to identify and develop executives with high potential for work in international management. The person best suited *to do this* is the international human resources director, himself often an itinerant expatriate. Fulfilling this plan is by no means as easy as it sounds. It demands a good knowledge of all the top operating executives and foreign-service employees to be able to spot those with potential for promotion. A manpower inventory is a useful tool in analysing employees' experience and qualifications: if, it does not exist in the company, it can be a major task to initiate one, however simplified. There is resistance to change to be overcome. Is an inventory useful? Who should have access to it? Is it too difficult to implement? Once over these hurdles, issuing the inventory and analysing the resulting data is time-consuming. In the meantime, hiring, firing, promotion and transfer decisions are still being made. So, although in a ideal world, before making decisions, one would wish the system to be well set up, with the fullest and most appropriate information available, one does not usually have the time to wait. A director of human resources, in a situation where virtually all data is lacking, is forced to make certain hypotheses and move forward on several fronts at once. By meeting and evaluating the company's executives, he will gain an idea of the weak spots in the top people – and, by inference, their subordinates (on the premise that people usually hire subordinates in their own image) – and where he should therefore concentrate his initial efforts in developing management education programmes. Knowing subsidiary managing directors' salaries, with the help of a few national management salary surveys, he will have some idea of how competitive his company is: what are the differential salary relationships between the different levels of management, and what sort of package he should give a foreign-service employee. This is the crudest possible portrayal, and anyone would feel uneasy operating such a poor system for any length of time; but it illustrates a *modus operandi* until the right information is forthcoming.

The human resources executive can himself carry out a mini-survey of executives' attitudes to international service. Does it attract them? If not, why not? Does the fault lie in the company's philosophy? For instance, when international operations of corporations were in their infancy, top management tended to consider international operations as less complex and demanding than domestic. They did not, therefore, send their best men – quite the opposite. This gave the American expatriate abroad a bad name, both with local nationals and with his colleagues back at head office. Is the financial inducement considered insufficient? Is this justified?

Choosing the right expatriate

All this background information helps in choosing the right people for international assignments should the need arise. Any business which takes its international assignments seriously, should send its most highly qualified and most adaptable executives, not those who have failed at home. The formidable list of qualities needed has already been examined (see pages 141–50). There may already be comprehensive job descriptions in the international operations, which lay out the accountabilities of all key managerial positions. If these do not exist, however, the human resources executive should define the proposed responsibilities of the job with the man's immediate superior (and/or the person who wants the expatriate to take the job on: this may not be the immediate superior) and the executive himself. There must be complete agreement on the parameters of the position, the overall objectives and short-term goals the expatriate is expected to achieve. It is unfair to send someone on an overseas assignment without a clear idea of what he is supposed to contribute. This is particularly so if his immediate overseas superior is in conflict with the person who sent him. He will be working, in that case, in a hostile environment (since his new colleagues are likely to back his boss), and will later be censured by both bosses for failing to make an appreciable contribution. No one is then going to make allowances for the fact that he was prevented from meeting his objectives. It should be remembered that even if the expatriate has only an advisory status, he and the company should work out a realistic set of goals. Whether taking on a line or staff job, objectives should be realistic, and fair, and this will be the company's responsibility. However experienced the executive is, he may not know what he is really up against, especially if he has not had an international assignment before. However much the company wants its subsidiary to become profitable in one year, if it has been making a loss three years running, the expatriate will be under unreasonable pressure to take short-term measures, which may ultimately harm the long-term future of the subsidiary.

For this reason, the human resources executive, the new line manager and the expatriate should define the strategy the latter should adopt in his new assignment. With the accountabilities well described, it is useful at that stage to develop in some depth a tentative workplan for the expatriate's assignment, and discuss his timing and approach to certain problems. This avoids misunderstandings which may arise later, if the expatriate tends to tackles difficulties differently from his superior. It should be clear what authority the expatriate has to get the job done. For example, is he to follow the hierarchy closely, or has he the right to report to a member of corporate staff? The latter is more common in a project-type assignment, for the expatriate may be solving a major technical problem, with implications for the rest of the corporation; or it may be a pilot project, which if successful, can be applied to other parts of the company. The organization chart does not always show up the nuances of reporting relationships, and if these are not well defined the expatriate may run into trouble if, in good faith, he exceeds his authority.

The objectives set for the expatriate's assignment will vary according to the proposed length of stay. The responsibility for dealing with a subsidiary will probably demand an indefinite transfer: it is perfectly feasible to design a new plant in under two years. In any event, these constraints, such as they are, should be determined before the executive moves overseas.

If there are any weaknesses in the executive's background and qualifications, this is a good opportunity to send him on a short preassignment training course: often there is not enough time to carry this out, but at least the executive can be forewarned of this area of potential weakness and may be able to protect himself accordingly. This is all the more important because his performance on assignment will be evaluated according to certain predetermined criteria and (relatively) objective measurements. These criteria may be those used for domestic assignments, or special factors may be added to take account of the diverse situations the expatriate may encounter internationally.

Preparation before moving abroad

The planning steps outlined above apply to executives going on extended business trips as much as to expatriates on indefinite transfers, but a broader plan should be made to prepare those employees and their families who are embarking on a stay of two or more years.

Although it would seem self-evident that some sort of training should be provided for executives being transferred overseas, a recent survey showed that 23 per cent of companies provided no programme at all, and another 37 per cent provided the training on an occasional basis only. In the education programmes, which 40 per cent provide on a regular basis, the three most common subjects were cultural background, company objectives and language training (an average of 120 hours). Living conditions, personal security, the behaviour of the spouse, evaluating housing and schools, were also usually covered. Most companies used their normal office training staff to conduct the courses, but 36 per cent had their own special overseas training staffs, while another 32 per cent used outside consultants of one sort or another (this is practically always the case for language instruction). Only 30 per cent automatically included the wife or husband of the executive in the training programme, and 27 per cent made that optional; involving the children was extremely rare.

Positive assistance for the expatriate and family once in the host country is much less common. Only 12 per cent of the companies conducted a formal process of familiarization with a local national: some 42 per cent assigned someone to look after the expatriates on an informal basis. This is a less than satisfactory practice: unless the local national is particularly conscientious, the tendency is to provide a minimal service; perhaps the documentation for work permits and residence visas, or telephoning accommodation agencies. Paradoxically, if the executive is unable to speak the local language, he has a better chance of being helped. A person needs to be in charge of all arrangements, otherwise responsibility tends to be shuffled from one person to another. The expatriate may raise questions only when he is in difficulties, by which time it may be too late: over, for example, signing rental agreements, importing/buying a car, furniture arrival in the host country. He may already have fallen foul of the local bureaucracy and the company may be unable to retrieve the situation.

Once the company has established the need for pretransfer training programme, it has to choose one of several 'models' of cross-cultural training. There are basically three models:

1 *The intellectual model* is a non-participative type of programme, consisting of lectures giving general information about other nationalities, and often tests to determine the degree to which the executives have assimilated the knowledge. It relies on drawing an ideal picture of the typical local national: when the latter does not come up to expectations, the expatriate becomes frustrated, since he has no alternative image or mode of action to fall back on.

2 *The area simulation model* attempts to create situations that the executive is likely to meet, and there is considerable use of role playing. Unfortunately, simulated situations can never be exactly the

same as the real thing, and the executive may eventually produce stereotyped reactions.

3 *The cultural awareness model* is a more recent training technique which attempts to develop in participants (executive and family) an awareness of the influence a culture has on an individual and how they will differ from any other given nationality. The prospective expatriates think about and discuss their own backgrounds and experiences, and how these affect their behaviour today. Helped by trainers, they use generalizations about foreign cultures, which enable them to focus on significant attitudes and behaviour in other nationals. It is particularly important for the husband and wife to live through the training together. There may appear to be some disadvantages: the cost is high (though markedly less that the cost of the executive being ill-equipped in the new culture for a long time): the training lasts for a full month to six weeks before transfer. A major advantage is that when the executive is transferred to the new culture the attitude and behaviour change he has learned will be immediately reinforced.

This sort of training for the family can minimize the cultural shock that usually hits transfers, particularly that involved in intercontinental moves. In addition to general information, a checklist (see Appendix B, Exhibit 14 pages 385–95) should be given to the family to give them some idea of what they should expect and what possessions they should take with them. This avoids the unpleasant surprises that often await families transferred abroad. Even in highly industrialized countries, customs and terminology can differ. For instance, in the US, even an unfurnished apartment still contains a cooker, a fridge, electrical fittings, etc; in France, this is not the case. Another instance is the cost/size of housing: although a US expatriate may be warned of the high cost of housing in say, London or Brussels, he may just not have registered that for twice the price he will get only half the square footage: therefore there will be no point in shipping over all the family possessions, for there will be nowhere to put them. The sample checklist also indicates typical acitivities to be carried out by the company and the prospective expatriate.

Repatriation to the home country

Even before the executive leaves on his foreign assignment, there must be some preparation for his return. Except in very unusual circumstances, the transfer is temporary and the expatriate is aware that he will be responsible for hiring and training his replacement, usually a local national.

Knowing that in any event his tour of duty is limited, he will have more incentive to ensure that he chooses a good back-up man in plenty of time, in order to leave the job 'clean'. Incentives to return can be built into the financial rewards package: these are treated in more detail later. The company should also make some guarantees to the individual: that if he performs successfully (which should be readily discernible from the mutually agreed criteria), he will be placed, on his return, in a position of at least comparable rank to his overseas assignment; that he will receive, at a minimum, the equivalent of the salary increases he would have received had he remained in his old job in domestic operations. This is not the molly-coddling approach it would appear at first sight: it lessens the natural fear of any executive that he will be forgotten while abroad and thrown on the scrap-heap when he returns. Although a company may expect any self-starting, ambitious executive to jump at the chance of an overseas assignment, it is likely to be the most ambitious who will weigh up most carefully the pros and cons of *any* position that a company may offer them. These precautions, of course, are less likely to apply to executives who are hired directly to work as expatriates. Although they may be in a better bargaining position, from the point of view of remuneration they are less protected should they ever wish to return to their home country.

Something should be said about the problems experienced by expatriates and their families when they are finally repatriated. It is commonly accepted that expatriates suffer from cultural shock when transferred from one country to another. It is not generally recognized, however, that when returning to their home country they experience what one writer calls 'reverse culture shock'. This can stem from many reasons: a drop in total income (however much the company tries to separate base salary from allowances, the executive still tends to consider his total net income as basic); a loss in prestige and status (the big fish in a little pool syndrome); where the expatriate is of mediocre calibre he tends to fear obsolescence and that he will be put into a low-paid job; the individual may prefer the overseas life and its frills (presumed or actual) and threaten to leave the company if he is transferred to domestic operations; a sense of insecurity may develop if the executive has been away some time and is out of date with headquarters' procedures and professional developments in his function; he may also come under pressures from colleagues above and below him, envious of his international background, which they think may fit him for a more senior job sooner than themselves. If the company does not have a policy of rotating people through international management as part of their development for top jobs, there may be some difficulty in placing him in a suitable position. The expatriate's family may have worries too: how to find a suitable school in the home country; how much harm will the uprooting have done to the child? An executive's wife may have become accustomed to high-level social life, entertainment and club memberships, extensive domestic staff: a drop in status and standard of living upon their return may seem somewhat depressing. The more the expatriate and his family enjoyed their posting (and any company hopes they will have integrated well into the subsidiary company), the more likely they are to resent a further uprooting.

How can the company alleviate some of these difficulties? Some of the preplanning has already been mentioned. The company should also remember how isolated the expatriate can become overseas. He should be kept informed of what is happening in domestic operations, and in the country generally, so that he and his family know what to expect when they return. The company may also want the executive to retain his sense of corporate (or domestic) identity. A rivalry between international and domestic operations sometimes exists – particularly as overseas operations often grow faster, because of larger and less saturated markets, and build a self-image which compares favourably with domestic. This is a perfectly healthy and acceptable trend, until the company wants to bring the internationally-minded expatriate home. Then they find he is no longer in touch with domestic thinking. A more satisfactory approach is to send regular information to the executive, while he is overseas, on company policies, objectives and plans, new products and services, new acquisitions and plants, organization structure, and modifications in domestic benefit plans and services. He may even be asked to participate in a project concerning the domestic division: in effect, he keeps a foot in both camps, and remains relatively objective about the merits and demerits of each side's point of view.

If they have not been home for some time, the biggest surprise, on their return, will be to find that things have changed, when they had subconsciously assumed they were coming home to a familiar environment. The office location, colleagues, superiors, subordinates, may have moved. The whole family will need reorientation on the social/economic/political scene: if they left the US in 1965 and returned in 1970, the social climate of the country would have changed considerably. They should meet informally, new colleagues, superiors, familiarize themselves with the company's departments and offices, and be brought up to date on company policies, etc. This can be achieved, amongst other methods, through interviews, discussions, tours, seminars, social gatherings. These will all help to reduce the pressure on the executive and his family when returning home: the strains produced by a dissatisfied wife and children can be a considerable hindrance to the executive's performance.

6.4   A case study

An interesting example of conscious planning of expatriate careers, and of the strains of a multinational life, is seen in the European Research Centre (ERC), set up by SKF at Jutphaas, in Holland, in 1972. Its task is to undertake major research projects and make the results rapidly available to all SKF's European plants, thus eliminating the duplication which had frequently taken place before. The research at ERC can be controlled to ensure that it has a highly practical application. Although SKF is a multinational company, with very mobile executives, it was still something of an experiment to launch a centre where twelve experts from six different countries manage the research teams.

SKF's policy is to develop their managers and broaden the scope of their expertise by a systematic job rotation in domestic and international operations. This, of course, can cause problems in the expatriate's home life, however enthusistic he may be about his work. There are many good and bad points about ERC, the significance of which varies considerably from one expatriate to another, depending on his nationality and his own motivations.

SKF stresses that its centralized computer system enables them to pick the best and most appropriate people from any of their subsidiaries to fill the top jobs, in line with their management development needs and strengths. Most expatriates benefit from high net pay, stemming from a 35 per cent tax relief they receive for a period of five years. They all view their jobs as challenging; the people and the facilities making a good working environment. There is a sense of reward deriving from the recognition by SKF's plants of the high quality of their work. Ideally, some of the executives (including the centre's leader) see their jobs at ERC as a big step towards top jobs in SKF management, although not all of them are so optimistic, particularly if they plan to stay in research. ERC's multinational environment means that the project and department leaders who have worked there will be very marketable as international managers. A lot of other advantages pointed out by the ERC expatriates were of a more personal nature: they get to know people with different values and cultures, learn more tolerance, make a real effort to communicate more clearly, have the opportunity to learn new languages, gain greater self-confidence and social ease, broaden their character, can travel more, eat a variety of foods, and so on.

There are naturally a few negative aspects to working at the ERC. There is the fear of being forgotten, while other people reach the top in Sweden; the research hierarchy is limited, because other SKF research facilities are less high-powered than the ERC. They worry about finding a job whose *net* pay is higher than the one they receive at ERC. The French, Germans and Swedes, in particular, find the Dutch landscape dull and the country as a whole very crowded. Many of the expatriates' wives do not speak Dutch, nor, in some cases, English. They are therefore very isolated and tend to flock together, reinforcing their inability to cope. This is, of course, a common problem for all expatriates: American ghettoes in smart suburbs around the world are frequent. Parents with children over 12 tend to want them educated in their home country system, and this too can become a problem. These strains can prove too much for an individual to carry on working at ERC; in fact, in the first two years since its inception, eight Swedes and one Englishman have left. All this must add to the risk of ensuring a consistently high standard of work.

The experiences of these expatriates are not intended to be comprehensive, but are merely an insight into the sort of reactions a multinational headquarters can expect from the executives it sends on overseas assignments. Even if they are highly motivated and ambitious, they always have lurking doubts about their future careers; and current concerns about their personal lives.

6.5   The alternatives to an expatriate programme

There are two major options open to a company not wanting to follow the full policy approach to expatriate management outlined above. Many companies arrange prolonged visits by experts from the headquarters offices and other subsidiaries. These cover the whole range of expertise: functional, technical and managerial. The visitors will be expected to perform two tasks: problem-solving and audit. They will probably, on many occasions, be called in to solve a particularly knotty problem, especially where it is causing the subsidiary to lose a considerable amount of money. They may help to train the local personnel to solve similar problems on their own and install systems for use in the longer term. The audit function of the visiting experts will involve a careful appraisal of the standard of management talent in the local company, and of its financial and technical operations. In both cases, the visitors should provide the local management with a list of recommendations and a plan for implementation, which will have been worked out with the management team. The main problem with this approach, of course, is that unless provision is made for close monitoring of the implementation, and it is carried out, the foreign problem-solvers will return a little later to find that nothing has been done. It ultimately becomes a time-consuming and expensive process.

Another option is for the parent company to pick an individual or team, to lead a project assignment in the subsidiary company. This would only have a temporary status: possibly three weeks to six months or more, but in any event less than two years. The duration of the assignment, that is, project completion, would be determined well in advance, and the team member(s) would have a temporary-transfer, overall remuneration package. There are some problems for which project work is particularly appropriate, either for a full expatriate team, or an expatriate leading or advising a local management team. Such problems include building a new factory, introducing a new product, or a new budgetary control system, or a major cost improvement project, or a new management information system.

Although these temporary expedients are useful there is an initial phase when any subsidiary company will need one or several expatriate managers, on indefinite assignment. Where a multinational has recently acquired a subsidiary, or if the local company is growing very quickly, the parent company should be prepared to use expatriates. This will be so when the subsidiary has more than 250 full-time employees and/or sales volume over $4 million annually. Until the parent company is fully satisfied (probably for a period of 2–4 years) with financial results, sales volume, percentage market share, productivity, net profit, growth potential, and the management of human resources, the expatriate should remain. He will ensure that all the control systems, both management and financial, are fully understood and implemented at all levels. The most likely position for an expatriate is that of managing director. The financial director is often an expatriate, but it is debatable whether this is ideal, since he may not be in full command of all the complex local legislation. Other positions include the engineering or production managers, or a senior executive advisor, with the authority to ensure that parent company objectives, policies, directives, programmes and goals are followed and implemented.

Although this discussion about the expatriate manager is by no means comprehensive, it is intended to give a company embarking seriously on overseas operations – whether for the first time or not – a general survey of the field, with some ideas on conceiving and implementing its own plans.

7

The local manager

Both developed and developing countries are becoming more sensitive to the influence of foreign investment. Hostility to foreign economic power may manifest itself in various ways: forbidding investment by foreigners, strictly controlling it, or nationalizing foreign companies. The same attitudes may lead to a control of the way foreign companies use manpower, particularly executive and technical talent.

7.1 Nationalism and the multinational companies' attitude to local nationals

As the multinational companies grow in size and power, local governments have become increasingly uneasy about these monsters in their midst. In 1971, the value-added of all MNCs was $500 billion — or 20 per cent of world GNP, *excluding* centrally planned economies; and 650 MNCs accounted for $773 billion in sales. This has given them unprecedented influence over economic events in foreign countries.

The signs of nationalism

In recent years, trends towards the liberalization of trade and the growing interdependence of nations have paradoxically adversely affected the position of some multinationals. Efforts to harness nationalism to economic development have resulted in regional nationalism, exemplified by EEC, EFTA and LAFTA. Such associations focus their members' attention on the benefits of economic, social and political cooperation, but outsiders are, of course, carefully excluded. Such groupings enable the members to:

Define and jointly maintain their economies.

Provide larger, more economic markets.
Generate sufficient capital to develop industry.

The economic groupings have been more successful than the political —
thus, the EEC has become little more than a customs union: there is still
no surrender of political sovereignty. Nevertheless, some legislation that
flows from these groupings, such as that on free movement of labour in
the EEC, can significantly affect all multinational corporations, even if
they are not prejudiced by being 'outsiders'. For these groups do, almost
inevitably, tend to operate against the interests of outside countries and
groups, particularly in times of economic uncertainty. Some recent
examples:

The Andean group closed some of its sectors to direct foreign investment
    and gave foreign investors three years to divest themselves of 80 per
    cent of ownership.
Strict regulation of applications by non-EEC members for work permits in
    France (the US rules are even more severe).
Non-issue of work permits in France for six months in 1974.
Non-renewal of several thousand work permits by Germany in the summer
    of 1974 (the burden fell on Yugoslav and Turkish immigrant workers).
The recent requirement by Australia that UK citizens should obtain
    residence visas.
The referendum, held in Switzerland in October 1974, on a proposal to
    reduce by 50 per cent in three years the number of foreign workers
    (again hitting mainly at the lower-paid immigrants: 35 per cent of the
    Swiss labour force was foreign).
Restrictions placed on the percentage of a company's payroll that can be
    allotted to expatriate staff in Venezuela (thus limiting the number of
    highly paid expatriate managers in any one company).
New Zealand's extremely strict exchange controls and restricted immig-
    ration.

In general, restrictions on the use of expatriates are designed to ensure
full employment among nationals. Thus, there is an onus on a foreign
company to prove it has made reasonable efforts to find a local manager
before it employs an expatriate or third-country national. In Africa and
Asia, similar attitudes prevail, but more markedly. In Africa, the recent
colonial past has left a fear of political as well as economic domination,
and specific legislation to promote the employment of local nationals in
top management positions is very common. There may also be discrim-
inatory personal income tax or an expatriate employment quota.

To a multinational corporation concerned with the most efficient use of resources, financial and human, such regulations may seem unnecessarily restrictive, but if a company expects benefits from its activities abroad, so does the host government. Many governments are disappointed with the large corporations. They feel that multinationals have not only excluded local nationals from top management, but have made no efforts to prepare them ultimately to run the company. They are sceptical about the autonomy of a subsidiary, even if a qualified local national does take over. A recent study revealed some of the devious means employed by multinationals to keep their expatriates in control of a company, despite the anxiety of the local government to prevent it:

Bribing local officials, to enlist their support in ignoring the existence of qualified local natoinals for managerial positions.

Interfering in local elections, to ensure that their views would be heeded during a party's term of office. (This does not necessarily mean the degree of involvement by ITT in Chile, but substantial financial support.)

Deliberately hiring below-standard local nationals, to minimize the threat to their own managers.

Such practices naturally reinforce the deep sense of injustice felt by foreign countries. Another irritant is often the obvious, perceived gap between a corporation's policy declarations and its practice. If asked, a corporate senior executive will usually affirm that the company is dedicated to equal opportunities at the top, regardless of race, creed, national origin, or sex. But international employers often fail to integrate their local managers fully into the company's career structure. This is confirmed by two studies, to determine the degree to which multinationals carry out their avowed policies: by K. Simmonds, 'Multinational? Well, not quite' (*Columbia Journal of World Business*, Autumn 1966); and H. V. Perlmutter and D. A. Heenan, 'How multinational should your top managers be' (*Harvard Business Review*, November—December 1974). However significant the subsidiaries may be in terms of sales or profits, they are inadequately represented, both at the corporate level and in the subsidiary top-management team. Nevertheless, steady pressure from host countries, either legislated or implicit, has eroded the multinationals' ethnocentric position, and local nationals are, with good reason, increasingly rising to top executive positions.

The move to local managers

Although many more local nationals are now moving into the top jobs, both in subsidiaries and at corporate headquarters, this is not because of

disinterested concern on the part of multinationals. There is an acute
shortage of talented expatriate managers. The qualities needed for a good
expatriate are many; and as companies take the running of their
international operations increasingly seriously, so they become more aware
of the shortcomings of some of the executives they would formerly have
sent overseas. Indigenous managers are a source of hitherto untapped
managerial potential. Training and developing them has become a top
priority. Paradoxically, the very technical and specialist expertise which
has until now prepared US managers for overseas duty, is making it
difficult to recruit, pay and retrain the top generalists needed to run local
operating companies.

The shortage of qualified local nationals is not, of course, only due to
previous neglect by multinationals. It also reflects the low prestige
accorded to business in many parts of the world. The more highly
educated sections of the population tend to prefer the liberal professions.
The United Kingdom has the second largest number of multinational
companies in the world after the US. After years of under-investment in
management training and development, when the need for top-calibre
executives is correspondingly greater, there are signs that the supply of
business graduates to these large firms is likely to remain at a low ebb.

A survey made in 1972 by the British Institute of Management,
'Graduates in Industry', has some alarming implications for effective
human resource management. Nearly 33 per cent of undergraduates who
leave manufacturing industry to go to business school do not return, and
amongst those who do, there is a high turnover. There is also a noticeable
tendency to move into small firms: 35 per cent of business graduates
choose to work in companies with less than 500 employees, apparently
because these offer more money and more job satisfaction. Multinationals,
therefore, will have to try very hard to attract the generalists they need.
This is borne out in the findings of a survey, by M. Fores and D. Clark of
the Government Economic Service, on educational achievement in
manufacturing management: 'Why Sweden manages today' (*Management
Today*, February 1975). This concluded that, at both senior- and
middle-management levels, Swedish manufacturing managers were more
highly educated and competent than their British counterparts. It would
appear that Swedish education is more likely to have a practical
application to business situations, resulting in better problem-solving skills.
This trend is also noticeable in a similar comparison between the UK and
certain Western European countries. It would appear that engineering
(particularly production engineering) and management careers are not
attractive to those entering undergraduate courses, which in turn
compounds the problem of companies looking for future technically-based

managers. These two surveys have been mentioned, to show that even in a highly industrialized economy with large investments overseas, like Britain, it cannot be assumed that there will be a ready supply of expatriate managers. Conversely, the low income and standard of living of most UK executives may provide an incentive to move abroad, and surveys do show that British managers are more mobile than other Europeans

If he is of the right managerial quality, the local national has many advantages, of course, over an expatriate, from the point of view of the multinational. He understands the local environment, and will know many businessmen and government officials. Not only can he add continuity to the subsidiary operations in the eyes of the local community, he can also have an important role in public relations. In developing countries, it is critical to maintain good close relations with the government, which is likely to be centralized and may be one of the largest customers for the foreign company. In some cases, government officials will refuse to do business with anyone in the subsidiary, other than a local national of high social standing, and of managing director status: this is true in Latin America and Asia. A local national will have a much better idea of how to deal with the bureaucracy and how to minimize the inevitable red tape. His status will help to ensure that the company can obtain hard currency, send cash remittances to the home country, or import heavy equipment and machinery, which can be difficult in countries such as India, Egypt, Mexico or Brazil.

These are some of the purely business reasons for a company to put qualified local nationals into key managerial positions. Other considerations also arise. If a country (either its government or public opinion) does not welcome foreign companies and their expatriates, the sight of local managers running the operations may allay some fears. Alternatively, they may feel, with some justification, that industry and commerce form an integral part of their plans for development and are better managed by one of their own nationality. Moreover, a company must develop a sense of responsibility towards the communities in which it operates: training local nationals, so that they can accept positions of greater responsibility, or increase their technical skills, either for use within the international company or in locally owned industry, is a service that benefits everbody. Such a policy will be welcomed by the government, the local business community and unions, and will lead to better relations with them all.

Expatriates are extremely expensive — perhaps two to three times more costly than a local manager in the same position. The expatriate often starts with a higher base salary, to which must be added cost-of-living and housing allowances, a foreign service premium, tax equalization, education allowance, home leave, and maybe club memberships and other similar

DIFFERENT TYPES OF ORGANIZATION ARE APPROPRIATE TO DIFFERENT STAGES OF THE COMPANY'S DEVELOPMENT

	TYPES OF ORGANIZATION			
CHARACTERISTICS OF ORGANIZATIONAL DEVELOPMENT	Polycentric	Ethnocentric	Regiocentric	Geocentric
1	Exporting operations. Foreign manufacturing growth. Local managers run local companies.			
2		Foreign diversification. Early manufacturing growth (first 2–6 years after start-up or acquisition). Subsidiaries controlled by expatriates.		
3			Stabilization of growth overseas. Regional headquarters rationalization: mixture of nationalities.	
4				Local managements need subsidiary companies and corporate headquarters with third-country nationals. Mature or declining international oligopoly.

Figure 7 · 1

extras. The cost apart, too many expatriates can also become an embarrassment *vis-à-vis* local nationals: their presence leads to envy and resentment, which are counter productive. Moreover, the failure rate of expatriates is high: 30–50 per cent of US expatriates do not complete their assignments in developed countries; and the proportion rises to 70 per cent in developing countries.

Companies which take all these factors into account not only use local nationals in isolated managerial jobs, but gradually modify their organization structure and corporate philosophy. Figure 7 : 1 shows the fairly predictable pattern of the role of the local manager, which changes as the multinational grows. In the export phase, local nationals are better equipped to handle matters in their own country, but they find it difficult to compete when international firms become involved in acquisitions, joint ventures, or start up plants. Expatriates play a large part in the organization of any ethnocentric company. If the firm does not expand further, local executives will be asked to run the subsidiary operations. If rapid growth continues, however, US multinationals eventually group their companies into regional headquarters, which are usually headed by US expatriates, but offer opportunities to subsidiary executives to hold some of the top jobs at the regional headquarters. The next stage is staffing the international and corporate headquarters with executives from their subsidiary companies. This is the geocentric organization, which is still something of a rarity. The company will want to build on all the managerial expertise available to survive in a saturated or declining market, and a sufficient supply of qualified local nationals may not be available. There is no reason why most corporate headquarters should not contain a mixture of home-country nationals, ex-local nationals and third-country nationals. In fact, a better initial use of international human resources could probably prevent or slow up the gradual decline of an industry or company.

It is unlikely, however, that multinationals will develop to a geocentric stage, unless some concerted effort is made to ensure that multi-nationalization takes place and it is right for the human resources function to provide the necessary impetus. Figure 7 : 2 gives some idea of the areas it is most important to tackle first and who should be responsible. It goes without saying that the chief executive officer's full commitment to the programme is essential. Changes in organization structure, such as mobile headquarters, may be necessary to facilitate a move to geocentric multinationalism. In Figure 7 : 2, timing has not always been included, since it depends to a large extent on the current stage of the company's development: where the timing is stated, it is usually the minimum time needed when staring from an ethnocentric environment. In addition, the

Figure 7 : 2

PLANNING FOR MULTINATIONALIZATION

Key action areas	Priority issues	Responsibility	Deadline
1 Manpower planning	International manpower inventory (home-country and subsidiary executives).	International director of human resources (IDHR).	1 year.
	Identification of potential:	Regional vice-presidents (VPs).	
	For top-operating company jobs.	IDHR.	1 year.
	For international and corporate headquarters jobs.	Local managing directors. Regional VPs.	
	Performance appraisal:	IDHR.	3 years.
	Functional skills.	Immediate superior.	
	Skills as an expatriate.		
	Top level assignments for high potential foreign nationals:	IDHR.	2–3 years.
	In other operating companies.	Regional VPs.	
	Regional headquarters.	Chief executive officer (CEO).	
	Corporate headquarters.		
	Emphasis on personnel planning:	IDHR.	2 years, then continuing process.
	Subsidiary.	Managing director.	
	Regional headquarters.	Regional VPs.	
2 Recruitment and selection	Recruitment:	IDHR.	1–2 years.
	Foreign nationals in US.		
	Foreign business-school graduates.	Foreign subsidiary managing director.	
	Foreign executives for key jobs in subsidiaries.		
	Foreign nationals from other multinational companies.		

3	Organization and manpower	Process in developing local nationals. For each subsidiary, 10 best and 10 worst performers. Plans to correct performance deficiencies. Assignments and goals to broaden individual managers. Individual career planning and assignments.	Most senior corporate staff. IDHR. General managers. Regional VPs subsidiary companies.	Once annually.
4	Training	Management training programme: All headquarters executives. All subsidiary managers: 2 levels below managing director. All foreign-service employees. Planned job rotation for corporate executives: Overseas. Functional. General management. Language training. In-house vs. outside opportunities.	IDHR. CEO. Regional VPs. Managing director. IDHR. Regional VPs. IDHR. IDHR.	2 years.
5	Compensation	Worldwide compensation policies: Job descriptions and evaluation. Review of all salary structures. Review of all allowances and incentive compensation. Identification of inequities between home-country expatriates and third-country nationals.	IDHR. Regional VPs. CEO.	3—4 years.

Figure 7 : 2 (cont.)

Key action areas	Priority issues	Responsibility	Deadline
6 Participation	Foreign participation (ownership): In subsidiary company equity. In parent company. Foreign-national managers as members of board of directors: In subsidiary. In parent company. Advisory group of company executives on multinationalization progress.	Parent company board of directors. CEO. Parent company board of directors.. CEO. CEO.	
7 Measuring effectiveness of multinationalization programme	Availability of key executives when and where needed as: Executive back-ups (all levels). Growth and expansion. New business ventures. Planned replacements.	Most senior corporate staff. IDHR. General managers. Regional VPs subsidiary companies.	Once annually.

company undertaking a multinationalization plan should decide how far it wants to go: for example, if it is planned to open up top foreign assignments to local nationals, should there be a minimum number per year? Will this be reverse discrimination in favour of under-qualified local nationals, or will it encourage managements to develop their subsidiary managers more quickly? It should be stressed that each company will have to work through its own plan, appropriate to its needs. Although some individuals have specific responsibilities, every opportunity should be taken to involve executives at corporate and operating-company level. The mere existence of such a plan will have a significant impact on the motivation and attitudes of foreign nationals, and will convince them that they are no longer second-class citizens.

Designing a sound organization structure is not just an exercise in administration: it can produce tangible benefits for a company. The organization not only becomes more profitable, but can achieve balanced growth. Current responsibilities are separated from development work, which in turn ensures that the business does not become obsolete and remains flexible and adaptive to change.

7.2 The organization design will influence the local manager's effectiveness

An organization structure which will help people to work more effectively, while achieving the benefits outlined, must contain certain key elements. It needs first of all to be *logical*, to make sense to the people who have to work it. A UK subsidiary of an American engineering company underwent one of its frequent, self-inflicted reorganizations and emerged with the purchasing manager reporting to the public relations and technical director (already a horrid combination!). This seemed incoherent even to the long-suffering employees. The apparent reason for this change was that the technical director: (a) was a long-service employee, who knew a lot about the company's raw materials; and (b) fancied himself as a sharp negotiator (unluckily he was suffering from self-delusion). Fortunately, the company continued to work satisfactorily, because everyone knew there would soon be another reorganization, and this anomaly would be cleared up.

A structure should be *understandable*. If it is clear and relatively uncomplicated, it can be easily communicated and understood, which increases the likelihood of its acceptance and use. It will also be *explicit*, avoiding possible ambiguity in terms and relationships: a geographical responsibility, for example, should spell out the exact territory under the executive's direction. The practice of 'promoting' long-service assistant foremen to the job of planning engineer in another medium-sized UK company gave everyone the impression that *some* planning was taking place, though planning what and how was never defined: this did little for the morale of the people involved.

Certain principles are of particular relevance to the local manager operating in a multinational environment, because multinationals' structures, with their diverse and confused origins, lend themselves to *ad hoc* and unsettling solutions. The following rules are vital:

Local national to report to one manager.

Spans of responsibility to be selected according to type of work, interrelationship of positions being managed, and complexity of roles.

Fewest possible levels, consistent with well-designed responsibility spans.

Positions to be designed in terms of responsibility for specific, measurable results.

Use of self-measurement, with feedback of results going first to individual doing work.

Elimination of assistants-to, coordinators, and other positions with unclear responsibilities.

Open communications channels.

The well-designed organization structure should strike a happy balance between flexibility and stability, to enable the business to grow steadily and to adapt easily to the changing environment.

No doubt all this seems self-evident, and a common basis for any sound organization. There are, however, recurring problems in the relationships between national managers and their corporate headquarters which stem in large part from the insufficient attention paid to these issues by multinationals.

Headquarters executives are considered by subsidiaries to be ignorant about conditions overseas. They lack understanding of the importance of social, cultural, economic and political conditions. This may be relatively unimportant if they leave the subsidiary alone to take most major decisions. If, however, with this background they exercise close control on decision-making, they can and do make basic operating errors. Often they cannot understand the differences between the US and European countries, and between these countries themselves, and fail to identify fundamental consumer and market characteristics. Local managers will accept controls willingly only when they know that headquarters' decisions are founded on a thorough knowledge of foreign conditions.

American multinationals disregard the human element. Keen young American managers tend to emphasize the importance of management programmes and techniques, particularly marketing. Executives from headquarters spend too little time with subsidiary managers, getting to know them and their problems. The subsidiary manager tends to feel isolated, without a supportive relationship with headquarters' executives. This leads to misunderstandings and loss of goodwill in the host country.

There are often delays in decisions from headquarters. This is one of the most frequent complaints made, not only by the subsidiary managers, but by potential customers, suppliers, and outside agencies. Companies miss many opportunities, or even make losses, because headquarters delay urgent decisions. In spite of the improvements in air travel, mail and telephone, procrastination in decision-making increases rather than decreases. Corporate management may suffer from some psychological blockage: because fast communications exist, 'we' can take our time making the decision; and 'they' can implement our instructions immediately on receipt. Speedy communications can even be a disadvantage when used as a means of control. Antony Jay relates the story of a British admiral after the Suez operation grunting: 'Nelson would never have won a single victory if there'd been a telex'.

Reporting systems are too cumbersome. Most subsidiary managers agree that far too many reports are requested by headquarters: worse, there appears to be little acknowledgement or even use made of the information, to the extent that visitors from head office sometimes appear totally unaware of its existence. Interestingly, while subsidiaries view the information demands as onerous and as evidence of close control, corporate executives see their requests as minimal, and as a means of *avoiding* control. Reporting requirements should be related to the size of the subsidiary: too often they are made the same for the small and large company.

Local nationals suffer from a low level of credibility. While corporate executives often ignore recommendations made by local managers, at the same time they tend to ask for more and more information. This is particularly noticeable in highly centralized companies and leads to national managers trying to cultivate 'a friend in court' — at least one individual who will accept their ideas. Conversely, local managers may not have the global outlook, and information, necessary fully to understand the headquarters' decisions.

The impact or occurrence of these problems will depend to a great extent on where the major decisions are taken, and how these decisions are controlled. We will discuss how the difficulties inherent in international relationships may be somewhat mitigated by choosing the appropriate organization structure.

Where are the decisions taken?

There is a distinction to be made between the different types of organization adopted and the relationship between the local manager and headquarters: close or open. In spite of seemingly wide divergences of opinions and practices, there are pressures, external and internal, on multinational companies to move towards a norm of behaviour, both in terms of company philosophy (Figure 7 : 3) and of organization (Figure 7 : 4).

Figure 7 : 3

A MOVE TOWARDS GEOCENTRISM

External pressures

Technological and managerial know-how increasingly available in different countries.

International customers.

Local customers' demand for best product at fair price.

Host country's desire to improve balance of payments.

Growing world markets.

Global competition among international firms for scarce human and material resources.

Major advances in international transport and telecommunications.

Regional supranational economic and political communities.

Internal pressures

Desire to use human *vs.* material resources optimally.

Lowering of morale in affiliates of ethnocentric company.

Evidence of waste and duplication in polycentrism.

Increasing awareness of, and respect for, good men of other than home nationality.

Figure 7 : 3 (cont.)

Risk diversification in having a worldwide production and distribution
  system.
Need for recruitment of good men on a worldwide basis.
Need for worldwide information system.
Worldwide appeal of products.
Senior management's long-term commitment to geocentrism, as related to
  survival and growth.

Figure 7 : 4

CHARACTERISTICS OF A BALANCED RELATIONSHIP BETWEEN HEAD OFFICE AND THE LOCAL MANAGER

Organization

Subsidiary organization in some way similar to parent company.
Parent company appoints local board, but local manager may nominate
  candidates.

Communication

Quarterly or monthly reports in some detail.
More general reports in other functions.
Head Office forms and language for financial reports.
Frequent visits to and from head office.
Visits of all functions/many ranks.
Occasional worldwide meetings, regular for chief executive officers.

Decisions by regional centre or head office

Major- and medium-scale capital expenditure.
Raising funds.
Entering new product range/market.
Final approval of future plans, budgets, dividends.
Appointment of senior executives, with consultation by local manager.

Grouping the organizational units. Domestic operations have usually been arranged within one of three frameworks:

1 *Functional*. Operating activities are coordinated by separate functional heads. This is used most often by companies producing or selling one major product or with highly integrated production processes, for example, cars, steel.
2 *Regional*. Operating activities are split along regional lines, with manufacturing, sales or servicing activities for a particular geographic area coordinated by a regional head. This is most common when production or services can be duplicated in different regions, e.g. service industries.
3 *Product*. Operating activities are split along product lines under product divisions. Product organization is most frequent among diversified companies whose products need essentially different production technologies and are sold to different customers.

A company commonly functions as a national entity before it extends its activities to foreign countries, either by export-sales, or licensing agreements. Later, it may move to assembly and production, through branch operations or subsidiaries. So it has to consider whether these new elements necessitate a change in its basic organization structure. There is no set answer, but some dominant patterns did emerge from one study:

Functionally organized. Foreign operations integrated into functional units. This was rare, except in companies who were limited primarily to export sales.
Functionally organized. Foreign operations assembled into one separate, overall international unit, or reporting separately to the parent company top management for example, AKU (1964) and Volkswagen (1964). Domestic operations were organized on functional lines.
Product organization. Foreign operations integrated into product divisions or product groups, for example, ICI (1964).
Product organization. Foreign operations reporting directly to top management, or as assembled as a separate international unit, for example, Dunlop (1963) and Schweppes (1964, pre-merger).
Regional organization. Total operations (foreign and domestic) grouped into components under regional heads, for example, Massey-Ferguson (1965), Singer (1965), Standard Oil (New Jersey) (1964).

The US companies seem to use an international division more frequently than European companies as an addition to their domestic operations.

In some cases, companies integrate their foreign operations into an existing structure: functional, regional or product. Where this is not the case, the rationale depends on the breadth, type and length of experience in foreign operations. A factor which is pertinent, particularly to top-management organization, is the extent of international activities, measured as a percentage of total sales or profits. If foreign operations are limited to export sales, it seems most appropriate to integrate them into a functional or product-sales organization. If the company has invested in overseas units, they may continue to be independent. When manufacturing operations start up abroad, the novelty of such an organization will dictate a separate international unit, run by executives with special expertise – so the regional structure takes over, at least for a time. When the mystique of international affairs wears off, then international activities may be integrated into the functional or product structure. This approach (with variants) is becoming more popular as foreign operations and their growth strategies mature.

A case study

Corning International had been experimenting with a matrix structure of dual reporting relationships and reponsibilities – which ran counter to the usual principle of one-man, one-boss. Corning is a leading manu-facturer of speciality glassware and related products. 1973 sales were $946 million, of which $289 million came from international operations. Since 1963, non-US sales grew from 10–30 per cent of the total. They foresaw 50 per cent international in 1975–76.

Since 1965, Corning has had area managers in charge of operations, responsible for profits, for the geographic regions: Western Hemisphere (outside US), Asia/Pacific, Europe. In 1972, Corning introduced four business managers into their structure, whose responsibility was to review the long-term and strategic possibilities for Corning worldwide, regardless of the geographic boundaries of the area managers' operations. To assist them in their tasks, Corning created seven 'world boards' (corresponding generally to Corning's US product divisions), which coordinated specific product strategy. The business managers, instead of the area managers, liaised with the US divisions and with executives of foreign affiliates, who sat on the world boards. One business manager was concerned with licensing, worldwide; the others divided up the business-linked world boards between them.

A world board met two or three times a year, in the US or another region; it included the appropriate business manager, representatives of the US television division, and executives from the foreign affiliates concerned. The last had dual responsibility; to their president and thus area manager, and a shared responsibility as a world-board member for strategic, worldwide planning and coordination, on matters such as pricing and location of manufacturing facilities. Local management was supported by the provision of a global strategy and a harmonization of all group activities. Area managers could attend world boards, but usually did not, although they received minutes and maintained contact with the business managers.

What was the rationale behind this innovation? It was an attempt to prevent the international group from cutting itself off into a separate company, and to use the strengths of the US company by building a corporate staff on both a US and an international basis. The senior staff executives thus had dual responsibilities in areas such as manpower/personnel resources, controller, legal and treasury officers. Business managers became necessary because area managers were too involved with current operations to liaise effectively with domestic division managers: they had neither the time nor the people for planned growth. Their major opportunities were in mature business, leaving little time for long-range or diversified-growth planning.

What was the initial reaction? There were some strong reservations among the area managers who were used to line relationships. Instead of liaising with the domestic divisions on a problem, they now had to liaise with all four business managers. If an area manager wanted to arrange the price of a worldwide product, or a brand name, or market a product in someone else's area, he had to consult the appropriate business manager, whereas before he had taken a unilateral decision. The business managers, in theory, did not have the time to dominate or interfere with area managers' operations. An initial step which met with wholehearted approval was to run an organizational development programme when structural changes were being implemented. It aimed to unfreeze personal relationships and to help managers to agree their goals together. It was considered quite successful. Nevertheless, as area managers operate from their regions and do not sit on world boards, a gap did exist between them and the business managers. Some confusion between their respective roles existed because it was not always clear whether a proposed action was strategic or operational.

The aim ultimately was for business managers to make available, at the beginning of each three-year planning cycle, a set of business priorities, for each area. The area managers then developed specific plans, in harmony with world plans. The organization was ultimately changed, but the point is that experimentation in different forms of organization does become necessary to arrive at a better solution.

Developing the regional centre

As the regional structure appears to be the common step amongst mature international companies, it probably deserves a little further examination. Although the first step towards regionalization, is to set up what is often called an international division, a further development is the area, or regional, centre (Figure 7 : 5). The general purpose of this move is to control and coordinate the activities of subsidiary companies and to offer staff services to support and advise on subsidiary operating programmes. There is some evidence to show that firms are increasingly using such a structure.

Although it is a mixed blessing, according to many subsidiaries, one advantage of this pattern is that the head office is in closer contact with local companies, particularly in marketing. A strong and experienced team can plan strategically the development of the area, and help practically in carrying out acquisitions or establishing new companies. Whenever a company is in difficulty, executives from the region can take over line management. With this back-up a local company can take greater risks in planning for growth: in fact, the weaker or less independent a subsidiary, the more it will appreciate a regional centre.

One activity best carried out in such a regional centre is management development. If promotion policies include opportunities for local managers outside their home countries, regional centres will be an advantage: assignment to the regional centre will be extremely valuable. A regional centre can provide useful services by undertaking long-range planning for a whole area, where the subsidiary companies may not have the resources or knowledge to undertake major studies.

Setting up regional centres, however, has dangers. Many local companies resent it, seeing it as an extra link in the chain of communications. The regional headquarters reduces the autonomy of the local managers, some of whom see it as a demotion, cutting their contact with headquarters, some try to bypass the regional executives, telephoning or writing to the international president, claiming some form of special relationship. Naturally, this causes friction. Any company contemplating setting up area headquarters should ensure that the executives involved have sufficient skill in human relations to convince the local managers of the value of the change. If regional executives do in fact deliberately block communications with other levels or divisions, resignations among key local staff will result. Multinationals with area centres have found that a major danger (only avoided by frequent reviews) is that regional staffs increase while the head office still retains the same number of employees as before.

TYPICAL REGIONAL ORGANIZATION (a multi-product company)

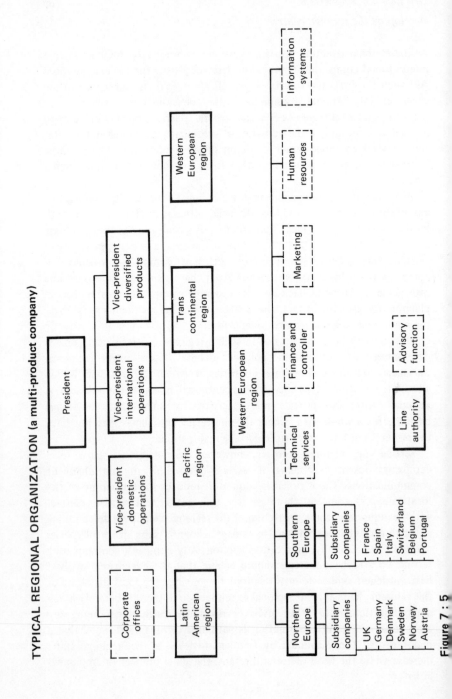

Figure 7 : 5

Regional centres may, in the long run, cause more difficulties than they solve. Even if a team of experts is needed to support weak companies, this does not necessarily warrant a full central staff. Undoubtedly, as local companies mature, and corporate executives gain a more complete knowledge of international operations, there will be a move towards product-structured organizations, and this is likely to be reinforced by the marked tendency towards diversification.

Using the central staff

Where do the corporate staff departments fit into an international organization structure? Relations between the international unit and its domestic counterpart (from which corporate staff are usually drawn) can sometimes be strained: friendly rivalry is the kindest interpretation that can be put on some of their activities.

In principle, a staff department comprises a group of specialists who make their expertise available to other departments or divisions, and who have an *advisory* role. This role will change according to the department: financial and legal advice, for example, tends to possess a mandatory quality. Local managers have often been confused about who is their real boss when the central staff establishes contact, by letter or by visit directly, without clearing it with line managers. This is the reverse of the undermining of regional staff by national managers. This ambiguous situation should be clarified if there is not to be a tremendous loss of energy and time: the usual solution is for staff departments to be created within the international division (less necessary if there exists a strong regional centre staff) or else the international division is reorganized into a functional or product structure.

The need for unified financial policies has often led to the controller's office assuming a line function. Legal departments usually try to assume the same degree of control, but are in fact less qualified to do so, because foreign law differs significantly from US law, and issues usually have to be referred to foreign counsel. That problem can partly be avoided by using international law firms, with headquarters in the US with foreign affiliates — although legal departments still want to be informed of every step, causing complications and delays. Their intervention will be better appreciated if they offer creative solutions rather than bureaucratic formulae. Patent and trademark matters are usually handled on a centralized basis, and there is little margin of manoeuvre for the subsidiary manager. Although product/production services can be coordinated to some extent by corporate HQ, marketing, human resources and public relations staff can only be influential if they are seen to be unusually competent.

Where does all this weight of organization structure leave the subsidiary manager? If well designed, it should help him do his job, without undue interference from overbearing or well-meaning regional or corporate staff: a good balance between centralization of policies and decentralization of decisions (Figure 7 : 6).

TEN RULES FOR DECENTRALIZATION

1   Decisions take place as near to the action as possible.
2   Is most effective when the individual with the most relevant knowledge and a quick understanding of the problem can make most decisions.
3   Works only if authority is really delegated; not if the manager has to report every detail, or the details must be checked prior to the decision.
4   Higher line and staff executives must have confidence that the local manager will make good decisions most of the time.
5   Demands realization that the sum of many individually sound decisions will be better overall for the firm than decisions made and controlled by head office.
6   Corporate staff must understand that their role is to provide experienced assistance and advice which will better enable subsidiary managers to make sound decisions.
7   Need exists to have general business objectives, policies, plans, organization structure and relationships known, understood, followed and measured: but top management must realize that subsidiaries have different ways of carrying out policies.
8   Senior executives must realize that if they have genuinely delegated, they cannot retain the authority themselves.
9   Will be effective only if the responsibility that accompanies the decision-making authority is really accepted and supported at all levels.
10 Demands a personnel policy based on performance evaluation, defined standards, promotions based on merit, and dismissal for inadequate performance.

Figure 7 : 6

Handling decentralization

Although the local manager in international operations can never have complete autonomy, restrained as he is by the fact that he is part of a larger unit, he has certain built-in advantages over his domestic counterpart. These factors mean his operation will be more decentralized in practice, if not in theory:

Distance. Not a substantial factor, but the travelling time involved to make an on-the-spot decision would mean – may be costly – delays. (No distance, however, will save the national manager located in subtropical climes from a swarm of top executives of a British multinational descending on him between the months of November and March!)

Information on local customs. The need for knowledge of local customs, laws, buying habits, work habits and local conditions has meant that firms leave fairly broad discretion to the subsidiary manager.

Nationalism. International companies usually wish the local company to be a beneficial part of a host country's economy, and this leads them to ensure the local manager has enough latitude to be seen as an effective leader to his compatriots.

Subsidiaries. Foreign operations may largely consist of wholly or partially owned subsidiaries, and the legal structure gets in the way of more complete centralization. Many a local president has used this complication to seize more power for himself than was desired by the corporate chiefs.

Although the national manager may be expected to contribute to the overall formulation of company policy and strategy planning, these remain essentially centralized. The chief executive – with the help of his executive office, which should include the international division president – will determine overall objectives, the allocation of financial resources, establishment of budgetary controls, and key staffing (executives who will lead major domestic and foreign components). In fact, even the president will have to present most of these proposals to his main boards for approval.

M. Z. Brooke and H. L. Remmers, in *The strategy of multinational enterprises* (Harlow, Longman, 1970) use the terms 'close' and 'open' relationships between subsidiary and head office to describe centralization and decentralization. The terms express the type of relationship which actually exists, in contrast with the degree of control stated in company policies and pronouncements. The relationship between subsidiaries is not static: there are several forces which can make a relationship more open or closed (Figure 7 : 7). The common element appears to be the *sense of*

PRESSURES TOWARDS A NORM

Towards decentralization		Towards centralization
Local/political pressure. High living standards. Personnel management.	**Host country**	Low living standards. Low education level. Expatriate management.
Good results/planning. Higher sophistication. High managerial turnover. Containment of problems.	**Subsidiary**	Poor results/unsatisfactory planning. Failure to grasp profit opportunities. Local management alienation.
Geographical organization. Marketing orientation. Ability to delegate.	**Corporate office**	Product group organization. Technical orientation. Emphasis on global strategy. Use of operating manuals. Development of modern techniques. International rationalization.

Figure 7 : 7

missed opportunity occasioned by either extreme of relationship. Too close a relationship will lead to a loss of personnel (including any high-calibre local manager) and a low standard of performance in the company. On the other hand, if a subsidiary is too autonomous, and does not accept the technological developments or EDP equipment produced by the home country, opportunities for new and profitable application will be missed. Brooke and Remmers have developed the tendency of the *normal line* where influences cancel each other out, but recognize that the practice is more centralizing than the theory.

Although some external factors are not controllable, some elements result from the power structures of the companies concerned and can be modified. More significant than physical distance is organizational distance, where powerful units intervene between the managing director of a subsidiary and the company's top management. This was the case with the Omega company, where a strong president of international operations had equally strong regional centres reporting to him: it produced a closer relationship than was perhaps intended, and by strengthening the solidarity of international staff led to a covert international *vs.* domestic confrontation. Even if top managers wish to leave the local manager considerable initiative, the interpolation of a regional centre's additional management levels, collecting information and issuing procedures, *in practice* leaves him little autonomy.

Another factor is the confidence of head office in the local manager. If he can show by his performance that he is capable of running an independent unit, he may be allowed more latitude. Too often local managers are kept in leading-strings for so long that they are likely to make mistakes when let loose, which of course proves to headquarters that they cannot be trusted on their own, and so new controls are promptly instituted. The increased possibilities for rationalization across frontiers, intercompany trading, sourcing, coordinating purchasing policies, mean a closer relationship for the local manager.

Companies whose origins are 'colonial' or manufacturing tend to close relationships. Commercial and investment companies have a more open relationship, as long as short-term financial returns are adequate. Whatever their background they are all in a fluid situation, moving towards some central tendency of behaviour. Some of the pressures are shown in Figure 7 : 7. A local manager who is a strong personality can achieve a greater degree of autonomy for his company: it is doubtful if his approach will really be accepted, since he is a threat to the system. Even if his performance is outstanding, pressures will build up against him, and though this may not result in his removal, it will have a decisive effect on the firm's choice of successor. The size of company will have some impact on the relationship: small firms tend to a more open relationship. This is geared to expense: a small firm can afford to maintain close contact less than a large company.

Any relationship between the parent company and the local manager contains overtones of discipline and support. Moving a regional centre close to the subsidiaries may be viewed as supportive by headquarters and disciplinary by the subsidiary: this will be covered in more depth later in this chapter when discussing communications (see pages 195–8). Paradoxically, an open relationship can run into difficulties if the local company does not get the support, that is the benefits, of belonging to an international company.

How are the decisions controlled?

How do companies enforce their decisions? What means do they use to persuade the manager to perform well? And what are the implications for the local manager of the organization structure and the control mechanisms used in his company? There are two significant methods of controlling other people's decisions: one is called, euphemistically, motivation, and the other is by setting up monitoring systems, either formal or informal. One relies on the individual executive managing his own performance, while the other method is based on an externally-imposed set of controls (although often fondly referred to as 'communications', it it can tend to be a one-way street, as many local managers have complained).

Combining the 'carrot' and the 'stick'. However decentralized an organization may be, one of its prime objectives must be to ensure that its individual managers conform to organizational goals and work in the desired direction. Effective decentralization depends on managers sharing similar commitments to hard work, and self-determination. An employee spending half his time running his own business (without headquarter's consent) may show proof of great diligence, but will not earn the gratitude of the multinational chiefs, for it detracts from his increased performance in their business. So they must devise a system that rewards the manager's efforts on their behalf.

Rewarding managers financially for higher performance has to some extent fallen into disfavour, due partly to a misunderstanding of Herzberg's theories on 'hygiene' and motivating factors (see Chapter 2, pages 29–34). His basic point is that if a man is well paid (or at the least satisfactorily), heaping riches on top of this will not result in better and better results; but neglecting this need will lead to a fall in productivity. It can be considered as akin to diminishing marginal returns. However, recognizing a manager's need for achievement, self-esteem and recognition in the design of his work and the opportunities for self-enrichment will pay off for the company. An astute mixture of 'carrot' and 'stick' is the profit centre: a unit of the organization where the man running it will be judged on its profitability and rewarded (or penalized) accordingly. The implication is that a man will work much harder if he feels as if he is running his own business (entrepreneurs being well known for their devotion to the work ethic). Another means of appealing to the individual used by highly respected firms is the 'training-ground' concept. They are so prestigious that just working for them will enhance the manager's knowledge and management ability. These companies are thus able to persuade the individual to forego his immediate financial needs for more intrinsic personal rewards. This method is probably more likely to appeal to younger executives, ambitious for any opportunity which will assist their career progress.

The foreign executive will be less amenable to the threat of sanctions than the American executive, since his salary and promotion chances may be less closely linked to his performance – as will the possibility of dismissal or demotion. He is unlikely to put in extra effort for an even more highly taxed income. He will, however, expend greater energy and enthusiasm on increased responsibility, since the complexity of multinational corporations offers him a new challenge.

American executives will benefit from favourable tax laws and the home-country stock options benefits, which are less accessible to national managers. Both the American and local senior managers will be spurred on to improved results, since their careers and perhaps investments may be committed to the firm: this puts them under an inbuilt pressure to perform.

Nevertheless, financial rewards should still be seriously reviewed: after all, some of the company's executives may find that a high salary, with accompanying fringe benefits, acts as a stimulus. The story goes that Harold Ross, the editor at the *New Yorker*, had tried unsuccessfully to lure the old *Herald Tribune*'s top writer to work for him. Finally a new managing editor enticed the man away by offering him three times his *Tribune* salary. 'My God', said Ross, 'You're a genius – I never thought of offering him money'.

Designing the control systems. Within the framework of the organization structure and the guided motivations of the multinational's dispersed local managers, there exist several mechanisms which assist the direction and coordination of the company's activities. Although they are not substantially different from those used in domestic operations, their effective use can be more complex, for the following reasons:

1 Distance between headquarters and the foreign subsidiary conditions the type of control. Is the cost of close control over a small subsidiary worthwhile? Probably not, but the mere fact of major differences in the countries' backgrounds creates a demand for explicit, detailed information.
2 The differences in tax systems and risks involved in foreign investments cause multinational corporations to centralize financial decisions, where there is an overall view of the business, on items such as remittances, composition of the subsidiary's liabilities, and transfer pricing. Tax and risk-minimizing schemes will distort the subsidiary's

results too much for them to be a good measure of performance. The complex solutions tend again towards centralization of decision-taking.

The functioning of the control systems should be briefly described.

1   *Planning activities*. The final operating plan offers a choice between alternative courses of action and uses of resources. This is an initial control, but it also commits the local manager and his team to carrying it out; their performance will be judged to a large extent on how well they carry out their commitments. Reports are established – for follow-up and control – to measure how closely the plan is adhered to. These mean that timely corrective action can be taken if all does not go well. The main component of this system is the annual budget: operating budget (sales, expenses, cash-flow) and capital budget.

2   *Capital budgets*. Usually there is a distinction between a review required for a major (non-recurring) investment and the more routine investments required for the normal development of the subsidiary. Although most subsidiary investments are self-financed, headquarters want to maintain ultimate control over the local company, and usually limit the amount of expenditure that can be carried out without referring to the local manager's superiors.

3   *Control activities*. These measure how well plans are implemented and what corrective actions should be taken. The feedback of information (mainly financial) is through reports, prepared by subsidiary managers, who also outline what corrective measures have been taken on variations. Headquarters can thus evaluate the situation and provide any necessary support. Usually *complete* results are reported at least quarterly. These activities are intended to exercise headquarters' desired control by exception.

4   *Measurement of performance*. This helps determine future allocation of resources to the subsidiary, and facilitates the coordination of interdependent activities. Performance is ultimately measured by profitability, although *long-term* profits should be included. The yardstick tends to be either a fixed or flexible budget, or a specified profit rate, such as the rate of return. Foreign subsidiaries are usually regarded as profit centres. The dominating measures are a combination of profit and growth.

Although many of these activities seem burdensome to local managers, who resent them as a reflection on their ability, they are consistent with the need to meet the organization's objectives. Interpersonal relationships, and communication, however, can have even greater impact on a subsidiary's performance and commitment to overall corporate goals.

Communicating with the local manager. Communication can be either informal or formal, voluntary or involuntary. However important the planned information processes, their informal aspects are also very significant. If properly used they reinforce the collective spirit and minimize the isolation felt by managers running foreign subsidiaries: they reduce his sense of being only a buffer between top-management demands and his employees' reactions. If headquarters staff do not actively discourage it, recognized regional groupings may develop, where managers discuss common problems and formulate common strategies. In companies where head office forbids this, such groups still emerge (informally, even clandestinely) and their consensus is more likely in this case to be against the corporation's interest. Informal links with central services may exist, either because someone there is viewed as a source of promotion, or as assistance on product or functional problems; links amongst expatriates of the same nationality are common. These help to make the formal structure more personal and enhance group cohesion, which can often work in favour of the company, sometimes in spite of a poor organization structure.

The formal communications network should leave little to chance, because employees will derive most of their information about the company from these contacts; as Murphy's law runs, 'anything that can be misunderstood, will be'. The process includes: issuing written instructions, operating manuals, statements of corporate policy, reporting and control systems; circulation and discussion of plans; meetings, interfirm comparisons, visiting firemen and company conferences.

Certain organization structures facilitate communications, others do not: the greater the organizational distance, the more difficult communications. Speed and reliability are affected by the number of levels in a hierarchy and thus regional centres may slow down the flow of information. If, however, a regional headquarters is able to make most major decisions and sort out pressing problems, it need not be a limiting factor. The more extended the multinational's chain of command, the more likely its policies are to be reformulated, reinterpreted, misinterpreted and wilfully misunderstood on the way. This may apply to policy manipulation, or data collection. An executive in a subsidiary may prefer to neglect to ask his superior's advice, and to act in what he feels to be the best interests of the company, on the basis that they would only tell him to follow policy: he can always claim ignorance of policy if trouble strikes later.

A UK subsidiary used the confusion caused by constant reorganization at local and at international level to make its labour figures appear better than they really were: unexplained difference in American and English definitions of direct and indirect labour, the changing of department job titles made the UK labour ratios look competitive with other European subsidiaries. What had been intended as a simple control system, yielding basic, comparative information for the multinational's subsidiaries, confused headquarters for a considerable time.

What are the reactions to communications systems of the national manager and his headquarters? The major means of communication is report compilation for headquarters. This, however, is often a one-way street. Subsidiaries prepare information (usually with a deadline), but receive' no feedback, either on a regular basis or from headquarters' visitors. Reports tend to be standard for all subsidiaries, thus running the risk of being irrelevant and time-consuming for many local companies. In smaller subsidiaries, located in far-flung parts of the globe, the need to produce such reports in the company's common language can be a formidable task, out of all proportion to the benefit to the company. Of course, while companies view these reports as a tacit slur on their ability to operate autonomously, headquarters will claim that the reports make real control unnecessary, forcing the subsidiaries to evaluate regularly key aspects of their business.

Multinational have usually made a large investment in their subsidiaries and inevitably keep a close watch on them. Resentment would probably be less if headquarters made sure that they were speedy in imparting *their* information to subsidiaries and that the right information went to the right people. The single copy of a voluminous report that stays in the local managing director's pending tray until he has time to read it is fine, unless it is the marketing director who really ought to have the information in it. It is more useful to circulate (upwards and downwards) brief minutes of meetings (such as research; marketing; production committees), so that there is a general awareness of ideas which would otherwise be buried or ignored in a report. Internal newsletters, with matters of interest, opinions and information, can be sent to operating company executives. Of course these have to steer clear both of the self-congratulatory, inflated style usually produced for public consumption, and of the trite, patronizing style too often used in employee bulletins.

Meetings of executives of subsidiaries, with regional and headquarters staff, can be another effective way of communicating. Directives become more palatable, and local managers can be more certain that *their* ideas and opinions are being properly transmitted and received. Group meetings can be particularly useful in promoting a greater sense of unity amongst different subsidiaries, and in developing a broader, more international approach to management problems. They are a forum for highlighting and airing grievances that otherwise might become festering sores, particularly if the grievances relate to what other subsidiaries are or are not doing.

Policy documents and procedure manuals often form part of the communication process. Again, this is a very one-way affair, to the extent that executives do not consider them as true communication. Where no written documents exist, there can be a strong set of traditions and conventions. These can be even more inhibiting than written rules, because they are often related to the powerful position of a few individuals. Such executives seem to think that everyone is aware of their responsibilities and obligations and there is no need for further formalities. New and younger executives, however, are likely to be increasingly bewildered and confused when they fall foul of an unwritten code: 'We want aggressive managers, full of initiative', it is said; but the young manager is then left in no doubt that seniority in the organization is what counts. Policies can take the form of a company philosophy, or they lay down the areas and levels of decision-making which belong to the local manager and the parent company. Procedure tends to overlap, particularly in the financial area, which in turn is the function most likely to possess formal and written rules, to which all subsidiaries must strictly adhere. Subsidiaries sometimes feel the attention to detail is overdone and take their satirical revenge accordingly (Figure 7 : 8).

Figure 7 : 8

HOW ONE SUBSIDIARY TOOK THEIR HEADQUARTERS CONTROL MECHANISMS TO HEART

Expense account completion

In view of the new attitude of the internal revenue service, reimbursement for entertainment expenses will not be made by the company unless the following requirements are met:

Where meals are involved, *please submit menu*, with items ordered and prices checked. If menu is in a foreign language, you must attach an English language copy, signed by an interpreter and certified to by a notary public.

Figure 7 : 8 (cont.)

Under miscellaneous entertainment items, a receipt signed by the person receiving tip will be required. For taxi expense, furnish name of cab company, cab number and name of the driver. Also state the point of departure and the point of arrival and the mileage between the two.

When home entertainment is involved, the total number of drinks, if any, and total number of ounces of liquor, if any used, must be shown (separated by brands). Cost of liquor must be computed on a 'per ounce' basis, and only the amount actually used should be carried on the expense account. When food items are involved, a fair estimate of the leftovers must be deducted from the cost.

When 'laundry' and 'cleaning' are charged under miscellaneous entertainment items, the amount must be prorated to include only the portion of dirt accumulated during the entertainment.

Under 'gifts', a signed receipt for gifts must be obtained from the cash recipient. In the case of flowers sent to a patient in hospital who dies before receipt can be obtained, a simple, notarized statement from the nurse in charge, giving the date, time, type and number of flowers received will suffice. In the case of mixed bouquets, the type and number of each flower must be shown. Greenery need not be listed, as this is usually furnished free.

An original and two copies of all expense accounts for reimbursement must be submitted. The original must contain all information. The first carbon copy should show all amounts but no names, the second copy should show all names but no amounts. Your office copy, if you desire to keep one, should show neither amounts nor names.

We have been discussing communications between the headquarters and the national manager, to the exclusion of any other communication needs. Although a corporate headquarters may consider its needs to be paramount, it constitutes only one of a dozen interactions which a local manager must sustain (Figure 7 : 9). They should therefore try to simplify and speed up the *two-way* flow of information as much as possible.

Determining the right approach

After the possibilities offered of different organization structures and communications channels, what do most companies want from these systems? What is the end result required? And how does one determine which is the best approach for one's own company?

There are two major considerations in structuring any international operations: the company headquarters (or regional centre) and the local

COMPLEXITY OF LOCAL MANAGER'S COMMUNICATIONS NETWORK

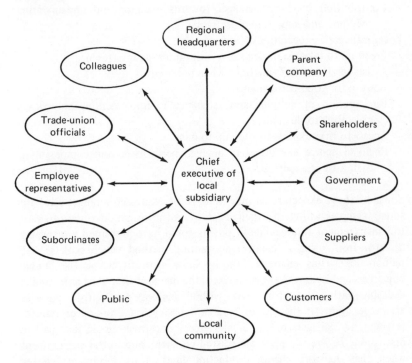

Figure 7 : 9

manager. The latter is too often disregarded, and yet ultimately he is the person on whom the company's profitability depends. His attitude to the company will influence his performance. This is not to say that a professional manager will not produce good results, but he may not, if disaffected, produce that extra effort which will spur the company's growth to new heights or, indeed, channel in into new and profitable ventures. Although one could assume that the two participants would want the same things from an ideal organization, this is by no means the case:

Corporate headquarters expect the structure to facilitate:

Acceptable and growing level of profitability.

Information which can act as a danger signal and which will alert them before a company gets out of control.

Local manager motivated to company growth (or any other specific company policy).

Contribution by local manager towards planning and implementing medium- and long-term objectives.

Local manager's expectations:

Freedom to take major decisions without *undue* interference.

Assistance from staff functions when required.

Reward for good performance.

Participation in defining and assistance in implementing company's objectives for his unit.

Access to firm experts to keep up to date.

Regional centre executives to be high performers, and competent in their area of expertise.

Some of these expectations may seem to be expressed ambiguously, but some examples will clarify their meaning. An information system to alert top management to a decline in profits could have prevented a managing director from using a 'creative accounting method which sank a $2.5 million loss, thus enabling him to show a profit. Once the annual objectives and budgets have been fixed, the manager should be able to take decisions within those parameters without his boss constantly being wise after the event. If there is to be a new policy, on sourcing or transfer pricing, the managers of the local offices concerned should take part in discussions *before* the plans are foisted on them, and not at the moment when they have to change production lines or to revamp accounting practices. The communication lines should be sufficiently free for the local manager to be able to contact acknowledged firm experts on specific topics, such as engineering, without his superior feeling resentful that his authority may have been usurped.

These are the sort of things that the participants in an organization might legitimately expect. But how does one adopt the right approach? There is no single right way which can be applied to every organization, but there is usually an appropriate form for the individual corporation. So what the president and his staff need is an assessment of criteria which must be satisfied before the structure is sound for them. Any major reorganization may take some years to complete; units and their responsibilities cannot be altered overnight. This does not mean, however, that the approach will be disorganized or piecemeal: the corporate staff will continue to survey the operation, and make sure it stays on course. Figure 7 : 10 illustrates the planning elements which a company should use when designing their international organization.

Figure 7 : 10

ELEMENTS IN PLANNING AN ORGANIZATION STRUCTURE

Common principles of organization

Define objectives, policies, responsibilities and authorities.
Group activities to ease supervision, and coordination to achieve results.
Assign responsibilities that can be effectively handled by one person.
Define line, and staff, relationships and ensure these are clearly understood.
Delegate as much authority as possible, while still retaining effective
    control, allowing decisions to be taken near to place of action.
Judge and reward individual for results of his actions when he has a clearly
    defined job with appropriate authority.

Major criteria for success

Identify company's business.*
Evaluate each business.
Assess environmental factors.
Define key decisions for successful operations.*
Determine planning requirements.
*See Figure 7 : 10a

Company plans and goals

Clarify objectives.
Ensure objectives are logical and practical.
Ensure involvement of executives in setting objectives.

Constraints

Consider inherent problems and feasibility of changing present organization
    structures.
Assess strengths and weaknesses of current human resources and potential
    for change.
Evaluate management philosophy and its impact on executive behaviour.
Analyse existing management procedures and effect on organization
    structure.

Figure 7 : 10 (cont.)

Other influential factors

Strong, effective leadership.
Compensation.
Executives' value systems.
Company's climate.

Figure 7 : 10a

CRITERIA FOR SUCCESS/USEFUL ANALYSES

1   Identify company's business

Evaluate functional differences.
Compare skills required.
Analyse physical flow.
Analyse composition of return on investment.
Analyse customers.
Compare profit and loss (division, area, product).
Analyse foreseen opportunities.

2   Evaluate each business

Identify requirements for marketing and distribution current and future.
Analyse manufacturing processes and technology.
Assess economics of each business:

      Typical profit levels and return on investment.
      Profit sensitivity.
      Usual margins.
      Cost elements.
      Capital requirements.

3   Define key decisions for successful operations

Rank decisions by impact.
Analyse sensitivity.
Analyse capital spending patterns.

Figure 7 : 10a (cont.)

Analyse new products.
Analyse cost centres.
Carry out interindustry comparisons.

Principles of organization

The principles of organization expressed here are well known guidelines, applicable to almost any situation, using mainly good sense and business experience. To a large extent, they reinforce the 'rules' of decentralization in Figure 7 : 6, and rely on each individual's responsibilities being kept simple and clear. They are thus a useful yardstick against which to measure the feasibility of the alternatives likely to be suggested.

These principles confirm that an international corporation is forced to decentralize to some extent, in order to avoid a stifling bureaucracy, whereby a few executives at headquarters hold most of the control and make most of the decisions. A middle course is desirable: between a span of control that encourages major geographical areas with 20–30 operating companies, reporting direct; and a relationship where the top man will have little better to do than to interfere with daily activities.

Criteria for success

One of the critical factors in determining whether the organization will be successful is defining which business it is in. Most major companies have been involved in the corporate identity crisis, and many presidents have indulged in it, as a result of reading of IBM's switch from business machines to information provision. Although this may be useful in encouraging lateral or creative thinking, it does not replace sound analysis and judgement of the company's source of strength. Muddled thinking in Dunlop's case (according to its chairman, Sir Reay Geddes, rubber and its accessories absorb shock, cushion, grip, bounce: extension of these things bind Dunlop's activities together) contributed little to their profitable future. The separate nature of the company's divisions and their functions and their corresponding interdependence, with a due regard for the complexity of their relationships, must be carefully analyzed. What are the differences between functions or divisions? Do they show similar or dissimilar new specifications or job profiles? Where are the most profitable areas of the business now? And where would the company commit its resources in the future? Are production methods geared to customer needs? Who and where are the customers?

Once the company has decided what its major businesses are, it becomes necessary to evaluate each one: how, if at all, do manufacturing processes and technology differ? What are each business's marketing and distribution needs? What are the key factors in each business's economics: typical profit levels, return on investment, margins? Costing structure? Investment needs? Which products are most susceptible to price changes? Particularly important in the multinational environment is the likely effect on each business of different countries' economic trends, government relations and their implantation of competitive companies.

Having laid the groundwork, there are certain key decisions which will have a telling effect on the successful operations of the company. Is success more likely to come from the right decision in capital investment, R & D or new production techniques? Or will results really come from the right pricing policy? And high service standards? Or is the utilization of personnel the critical factor (as it is in consulting, for example)? None of this means that taking a wrong decision in non-critical areas will not matter; but identifying the areas where good decisions will have most impact can make the difference between success and survival.

One of the main criteria for success is effective planning. The company itself will have to determine its planning requirements. Central planning staff may be needed, but in a holding company, with autonomous units, most forecasting can be done easily by operating executives. Questions will have to be asked. Is the company business so volatile that short-term planning is most effective (with a contingency plan to fill in the longer-term gaps)? Can the organization's development be foreseen over the next 10–30 years? Is coordination needed or a unit precisely allocating the company's resources?

The answers will decide whether a company should be organized around geographic regions, or functions, customers/markets, or products. The significance of certain activities and functions (whether or not they are currently carried on) will be highlighted. Top management's functions will become clearer, both to themselves and to their subordinates. This will help them to clarify the company's objectives and future planned activities. A set of policies and objectives, ritually repeated, may have existed, even in writing, but such objectives are often not quantified and express pious hopes rather than the reality of the business environment. This is more likely if the objectives have never been committed to paper, but are tacitly assumed by those in the know: goals are likely to be incompatible one with another and probably unworkable. Success in setting the goals will probably be greater if the subsidiary manager participates, to some extent, with his immediate boss, rather than relying merely on central planning. Such an approach gives the necessary decentralization of any multinational company a better chance of working.

Once corporate management has formulated its ideal organization structure, it comes up against practical constraints, primarily the existing organization. Whatever intellectual satisfaction may be derived from designing the perfect abstract structure, it will fail if its proper implementation is contingent on removing the current corporate financial vice-president and revamping *his* organization, when he is the most powerful officer after the president. Does the existing structure work well or not? Does everyone know what are his responsibilities and how far he can go in exercising them? Are there persistent delays with identifiable trouble spots? How are conflicts resolved? Are decisions made quickly, or do they drag unnecessarily? Is the organization inert, unwilling to change, reacting rather than initiating? Is the present structure more or less decentralized than the proposed one? Is there to be one chief executive or a president's office? A move to stronger staff functions; or is all the power to remain in the line operations? The geographic structure to remain; or a move towards a product organization? All these objective assessments have to be woven in with the informal organization which always exists, either working in line with corporate goals or pulling in the opposite direction. In the latter case, it may be a major threat to the success of any new structure.

The structure of a company is made up of people, and a new structure may put strains on existing human resources. If a competitor has low-calibre people, then the pressure is less, but there may be special functional or professional needs, particularly if the company wants to expand its overseas operations very rapidly. If the level of key personnel is weak, this may be attributable to lack of promotional opportunities, or inability to recruit outsiders who will stay; all the best people have left. A lot of positions may have been created specially for certain people, who have built their own empires, thus creating a block to effective change.

The management philosophy of a company can have a significant impact on the company's effective operations. It may not be explicit or formal, but it can still exert a strong influence: there may even be two philosophies in contradiction with each other, one negative and one positive, the official and the unofficial version. None of this is critical unless the existing philosophy is inappropriate to the new proposed structure. In this event, the corporate management must recognize that a change in attitudes will take a considerable length of time, and must resign themselves to progressing more slowly in real terms than might be expected from the structural changes.

For all the talk of changing the organization structure, it may be as easy and efficient to alter the management processes. If control systems (budget, plans, reports) are cumbersome and irrelevant to subsidiary managers; if decisions are taken slowly and too far up the organization; if the communications network is poor; if the reward/performance ratio is considered unfair: modifications can be made without the upheavals which accompany most major reorganizations.

Although these constraints exist in any organization, they can often become positive factors when altering management structures and processes. They are, of course, not the only influences on executive behaviour and successful performance. Amongst others, the value systems of managers and executives can modify the quality and quantity of their work and that of their subordinates. In this context, any company should analyse the implications of a change in these values. Until recently, the work ethic has motivated managers: work in itself, and company loyalty, were signs of virtue; and leisure time was filled by comparable activities (even moonlighting). The younger generation not only value leisure time more highly, they expect greater job satisfaction and greater financial rewards from their employer. If they do not get this, they soon move elsewhere. Employers can benefit from these changes, but only if they are prepared to be more flexible in planning careers and financial rewards; in giving decision-making authority, and job scope. Although this phenomenon is now manifesting itself mainly in the lower ranks of employees, it will inevitably have an effect on management development and career planning, the organization structure, and what top management can legitimately expect it to achieve.

No single right approach has been detailed here, but rather a series of questions which any company can pose itself, to help to improve its current processes and structures.

8

Compensating the foreign-service executive

A key problem facing multinational executives is that of financial rewards for their foreign-service employees. It is evident from Figure 8:1 (see pages 211–19) that formulating these policies is by no means a clear-cut or easy task. Thes examples have been chosen to show the variety of philosophies and approaches, but they by no means represent the whole of current practices. The renumeration policies for nationals of the company's home country (working abroad) and for third-country nationals (the expatriates from country X working in country Y for a company based in country Z) are often very different and reflect to a large extent the ethnocentricity of a great many multinationals. In our table, only two companies, B and D, cope with this problem: one by suppressing most expatriate allowances to all foreign-service employees; and the other by the use of a matrix on cost-of-living and housing allowances, which can be used equally well for expatriates and third-county nationals. There are problems arising from the significant differences in the remuneration practices of each subsidiary: these may be competitive within the local environment, but cause great difficulty to the multinational transferring several expatriates to Europe to do the same job. Any communications network, formal or informal, will pick up apparent discrepancies in financial rewards, and the company had better have a satisfactory explanation.

One reason why companies have sometimes failed to establish comprehensive expatriate remuneration policies is that with a few expatriates (usually home-country nationals) there was no problem; then it just seemed to grow. Another reason, of course, is the complexity of multinational operations. If a multiproduct, multidivision firm operates in several countries, with several units in each country, the problems of maintaining equity or competitiveness on a local scale for expatriates are enormous. They are magnified when the expatriates and local nationals from different functions, backgrounds and countries start making invidious comparisons on remuneration.

The complexities of existing practices may inhibit the achievement of the multinational's overall objective on financial rewards: they are often conflicting. The company will probably wish to achieve some form of internal equity, by function, division and country. It will probably be impossible to achieve all three at once and the company will be forced to choose one as a priority. Linked with internal equity is the concept of external competitiveness, which will differ according to the industry sector of each division or subsidiary company. A further aim will be to minimize the cost to the company of total remuneration and of individual benefits. Unfortunately, this cost-reducing element often dominates companies' thinking: hence the negotiations that ensue between a prospective expatriate and his new boss or the personnel executive. These in turn give rise to all sorts of indefensible precedents, which may end up by being more expensive, since the company may later on be forced to set policies which reach the standard of the highest negotiated compensation deal. American companies and, increasingly, European ones, also stress the relationship between good performance and high rewards to their incentive plans. It must also be admitted that even a well-defined set of policies and procedures, rigorously implemented, can still fail to achieve the original goals, because they will be the result of a compromise between the top people in the organization. Some (such as current high-level expatriates) have a vested interest in maintaining or increasing their total package; while others, who may never before have left their own shores, try to limit the expatriate's sense of uniqueness (and his consequent financial demands).

When a company intends launching an integrated expatriate remuneration policy, certain issues should be carefully reviewed in the light of current and future company developments. The international division(s) of the company may be in a period of rapid expansion, which will put a premium on flexibility, not only because the number of expatriates will increase, but because the number of third-country nationals will probably also multiply. If the overseas subsidiaries are stable, slow growing, perhaps because of stagnating or declining markets, the flow of foreign-service employees will remain steady, unless top management intends to revamp the operations or diversify abroad in the near future. The company should consider the implications of a sudden push for growth, in terms of personnel planning and financial incentives to executives for relocation. Their present executives may not be prepared to transfer, or indeed may not be right for international assignments, so the company may have to go outside and offer an attractive total remuneration package. This, of course, will apply equally to a company whose executive ranks are stretched through constant growth.

Once the company has identified its anticipated personnel needs, it is better able to relate its remuneration package to the type of people it plans to send abroad. Will it be the technician, sent to solve a specific problem? He will gain little in terms of career advancement after a spell abroad, unless the company has handpicked him for promotion. That is unlikely and he will need a great deal of financial encouragement to sell his home, take his children out of school and move, for example, to Zambia, to work on a construction project. The career international manager, on the other hand, views every change of location as a sign of progress on the way to a top corporate job: the incentive is built into the job, and as long as the executive feels that manpower planning is being well handled, he will feel sufficiently secure and not demanding increased allowances every time there is a slight rise in the cost-of-living. He is in a similar position to the junior executive, with only a couple of years' service and few family responsibilities. The middle-aged managing director of a subsidiary, a local national who has never worked abroad, will be far more reluctant to move. He will have to sell his house, disrupt his social life, revise the schooling and university plans of his children: he is going to need considerable financial inducement to move. The company needs to design the remuneration package in line with the needs of the personnel they are most likely to send abroad.

The corporate staff may want to reassess their staffing policies abroad. Do they currently have ten expatriates or hundreds: do they intend to continue this pattern? Does the company prefer to have expatriates in a few key positions and have the rest of the subsidiaries and headquarters staffed by local nationals? Are there a lot of foreign-service employees in each subsidiary? Are these tendencies going to change? How many overseas posts does the company anticipate will be filled by foreign-service employees during the next five years?

The final consideration, when thinking through an expatriate programme, is the company's attitude to the average length of assignment. Does it believe in the 'firefighter' approach, where an individual is definitely on a temporary assignment: he is there to solve a specific problem and no more? Or do they send out executives to fill key slots for a few years and then bring the expatriate home? Are expatriates internationalists, going from one foreign assignment to another; or sent to one foreign post, staying there until they retire (the colonial practice)?

All these issues will affect the way in which a company builds up its total package, but the *key element* in all these approaches is undoubtedly *flexibility*. The policies and practices must be adaptable enough to change without tinkering with specific aspects, thereby putting the whole system out of balance. For instance, before 1971, unless a company had subsidiaries in politically or economically unstable countries, very little thought was given to changes in exchange-rate parities; and certainly not to the prospect of the US dollar. It took a considerable time to work out a satisfactory response to these phenomena.

8.1   Components of an international remuneration programme

It may be useful to look at the basic elements of a remuneration policy for foreign-service employees, in the light of the different approaches used in Figures 8 : 1a and 8 : 1b and the trends shown in surveys conducted in the US and elsewhere. The major elements to be considered are: base salary, position allowance, foreign-service premium, cost-of-living allowance, housing allowance and tax equalization.

Base salary

There are three common ways of setting an expatriate's salary; some companies use all three methods, but this depends on the national origin of the foreign-service employees.

1   His salary can be tied to his home-country salary range; if the company is US-based, this is the most common for US expatriates.
2   The foreign-service employee's salary can be linked to the assigned country's salary range: this is a more frequent condition of a third-country national's employment than of the multinational's own expatriate, although he may be tied to the home-country scales for benefit contributions and salary administration purposes.
3   A third-country national's salary can to be linked to US salary levels (if this is a US multinational). Countries wanting to develop an international cadre of managers, and trying to become more geo-centric, are moving towards this approach.

Some companies wish to avoid the problems involved in remuneration for losses on exchange-rate fluctuations. But, in a survey of company practices carried out by the authors in 1973, 88 per cent (362 companies) still used the home-country ranges to set expatriate salaries: though, to be fair, the majority of those were US companies; there has always been the tendency to view US salary levels as higher then other countries; they have thus taken the easy way out. Nowadays, however, salary levels, in Europe particularly, have crept up: American executives still come out ahead on total remuneration, because of the higher incidence of incentive and capital accumulation plans (85 per cent of 600 leading US companies have

Figure 8 : 1a

Category of compensation	COMPANY A (Banking)	COMPANY B (Light engineering, European based)	COMPANY C (Electronics)
Base salary.	International executive tied to home country. Third-country nationals equated to US scales for salary administration purposes.	FSE receives salary of assignment country. Exception to this rule are countries with much lower salaries, Poland, UK.	Grade and salary for similar job in US. Subsequent merit increases recommended locally. Performance criteria same as those in US. Applies to assignments over two years.
Foreign-service premium.	Relocation adjustment allowance (RAA) is lump-sum payment for international relocation, equal to three months' annual salary (maximum $36 000). RAA paid on each relocation to compensate psychological disruption.	No premium paid to compensate disruption in relocation.	Compensates initial disruptions and provides incentive to work overseas. All FSEs receive percentage of base salary: from 15 per cent (Europe) to 30 per cent (Far East).
Cost-of-living allowance.	US State Department index. No negative adjustment for countries where COL lower. Allowance increased where index increases.	No COL for industrialized countries. Some COL for developing countries (indices: UN, Wiesbaden) higher for lower-level expatriates.	Use outside consultants and US State Department. Provision made for negative COL adjustment.

Figure 8 : 1a (cont.)

Category of compensation	COMPANY A (Banking)	COMPANY B (Light engineering, European based)	COMPANY C (Electronics)
Housing allowance.	Expatriate pays maximum contribution to housing and utility of $4500 annually (15 per cent of $30 000)	FSE responsible for housing costs up to 15 per cent of base salary. Company pays 80 per cent of any excess up to 25 per cent of gross salary.	FSE reimbursed 75 per cent of rent/utilities cost exceeding US norm (also operates negatively). Housing norm: 12 per cent of base salary up to $20 000 per annum, plus 6 per cent for salary portion above $20 000 per annum.
Hardship allowance.	Area differential (AD) covers hardship and special factors (cultural, political, etc.). AD ranges from 0 per cent (most of Europe) to 40 per cent (Argentina) of base salary. AD declines.	No hardship allowance.	Hardship comprised in foreign-service premium.
Position allowance.	No position allowance.	No position allowance.	Not applicable, since all FSEs paid on US salary base.
Tax equalization.	Company reimburses tax and benefit contributions on 60 per cent salary and allowances in assigned country which	FSE pays full taxes of assigned country without compensation.	Company withholds hypothetical federal tax on base salary employee initially earns on assignment. Company pays actual tax liability in host

	exceeds hypothetical US federal and state taxes.		country and US on salary plus allowance.
Home leave.	FSE and family are granted annually equivalent of economy round trip to home country, with freedom to choose where he spends vacation.	FSE and family paid trip home every other year, except in inconvenient locations (Djakarta, Manila).	FSE and all family members eligible for one trip per calendar year of assignment (excepting years of arrival and departure); not deferrable. Minimum of three weeks (US vacation policy applies). Economy-class air travel and reasonable incurred living expenses during travel from assignment to point of origin. Lump sum US $100 each FSE and wife, plus $50 per dependent.
Education allowance.	Maximum US $2000 per annum per child if educated in home country. Incurred tuition costs paid in assigned country. Employee chooses country of education.	US $1500 per annum allowed per child, whether in assigned or home-country school. Child's trip home paid in alternate year to that of home leave.	FSE's children to attend local state school, unless inadequately accredited. Local private school: all reasonable tuition costs, books, uniforms, etc., plus cost of transport. US or other private or state school: all reasonable costs, to a maximum of $2000 per annum per child. If in same continent, maximum of three trips home per year (economy air).
Relocation allowance.	Company pays FSE 75 per cent of cost of furniture removals in lieu of shipment. No additional allowances.	$1500 allowance paid at time of transfer. Removals, cars, furniture paid.	Specific documented losses resulting from relocation are reimbursed to a maximum of $2000.

Figure 8 : 1a (cont.)

Category of compensation	COMPANY A (Banking)	COMPANY B (Light engineering, European based)	COMPANY C (Electronics)
Exchange-rate fluctuation compensation.	Company reimburses losses sustained on executives disposable income, calculated at 60 per cent.	FSE bears cost of any parity changes, since his salary unrelated to home-country scales.	No reimbursement for losses sustained as a result of currency fluctuations.
Benefits coverage.	Selected FSEs participate in multinational's home-country benefit plans. TCNs remain in home-country plans, if possible, or assigned country. Additional coverage if these plans inadequate.	Company maintains and pays expatriates coverage in home-country benefits, wherever possible. FSE pays compulsory benefit contributions in assigned country.	FSE continues when possible in US plans. Base salary (plus bonus) used as 'notional salary'. Benefits: retirement, group life, accident, long-term disability, medical, travel, accident, major medical, social security.
Cars, clubs, etc.	No cars or club memberships. FSE receives low-interest loan for car where costs are prohibitive (for example, Singapore).	Local policy on cars and club memberships followed. No low-interest loans.	Cars and club membership only granted where *position* warrants it. FSE not automatically eligible.
Split compensation payment.	FSE paid, wherever possible, 60 per cent of salary, and allowances in assigned countries.	Salary and allowances paid entirely in assigned country.	FSE paid in assignment location the amount of salary that local national would be paid for that job. Minimum salary always paid in US, to enable benefit and tax deductions to be made.

Figure 8 : 1b

Category of compensation	COMPANY D		
	Temporary transfer	Indefinite transfer	
Base salary.	Temporary transfer usually lasts less than one year. FSE receives same base salary as prior to transfer. Salary reviews and adjustments during first year according to base-country policies and procedures.	If assignment becomes permanent after one year, FSE salary will be calculated according to assigned-country salary range for his new position. FSE will receive at least minimum of assigned-country range. If assigned-country minimum salary exceeds base country by more than 20 per cent, FSE will receive minimum rate, with adaptation allowance reduced by this surplus amount; but he will always receive minimum appropriate adaptation allowance (AA). If base-country salary exceeds assigned-country salary, FSE retains base country salary, while surplus amount deducted from AA (FSE still receives minimum AA).	
Foreign-service premium.	FSE receives *up to* 15 per cent of current salary. Premium remains fixed during temporary transfer.	When assignment becomes permanent, adaptation allowance replaces FSP, COLA and housing allowance, based on US State Dept., Wiesbaden, Swiss Bank Corp. UN, and Financial Times indices, and outside consultants' estimates of qualitative factors.	
Cost-of-living allowance.	COL ranges from minimum 10 to 43 per cent. COLA determined according to base-country category and assigned-country category (five categories of living costs).	FSE receives AA (percentage of base-country salary), which reflects quantitative differences between base and assigned country and qualitative differences (distance, cultural, climate, etc.).	

Figure 8 : 1b (cont.)

Category of compensation	COMPANY D	
	Temporary transfer	Indefinite transfer
Housing allowance.	Company pays 90 per cent of differences between actual housing cost and 15 per cent of base salary.	Minimum for intracontinental transfers is 10 per cent and for intercontinental is 20 per cent. Matrix table of percentage AA is applicable to US and TCN expatriates. Additional housing allowance is applied to Hong Kong, New York, Paris, Singapore and Tokyo, because of volatile situation (temporary formula applies). AA remains constant for three years, then reduces 20 per cent annually (though never more than annual salary increase).
Hardship allowance.	No hardship allowance (tacitly included in FSP).	No hardship allowance (included in AA).
Position allowance.	Not applicable, as FSE still paid on base-country policies.	Position allowance is that portion of assigned-country salary exceeding 120 per cent of base-country salary. Position allowance is adjusted as is base salary. Position allowance discontinued if FSE returns to base country.
Tax equalization.	Temporary transfer premium, COL, housing and education allowances are after-tax amounts.	Company calculates hypothetical income-tax and compulsory-plan contributions due in base country on assigned country base salary, position allowance and latest bonus.

	Company reimburses taxes and compulsory benefits contribution paid in assigned country which exceed FSE's normal base-country tax on salary and bonus. Company ensures deductions and compulsory benefit contributions are made. FSE responsible for his income-tax declaration.	Company calculates hypothetical tax and compulsory contributions due in assigned country, on assigned-country base salary, position allowance, last bonus, adaptation education allowance and home leave. Difference between two sums is tax allowance.
Home leave	No home leave up to the end of interim period, until the end of first year, *if* assignment is extended for further six months.	After interim period of temporary transfer, employee and eligible dependents will be paid air-economy round trip fares to base country. FSE and dependents entitled to one trip per year subsequently.
Education allowance.	Company pay actual cost of adequate primary and secondary education in assigned country. If local schools inadequate FSE may enrol children in base-country schools and company pays up to the maximum they would have paid for best FSE schools. Once-a-year round trip for child (plus home leave provision).	Company pays actual cost of adequate primary and secondary education in assigned country. If local schools inadequate, FSE may enrol children in base-country schools and company pays up to the maximum they would have paid for best FSE school in assigned country. Once-a-year round trip for child (plus home leave).
Relocation allowance.	Lump sum equivalent to one month's pay when transferring out and at repatriation. Travel expenses for FSE and family, one month's living and lodging expenses, reasonable removal	Lump sum equivalent to one month's pay when transferring out and at repatriation. Reasonable costs of removal, travel expenses for FSE and family, one month's living and lodging expenses, property, brokerage

Figure 8 : 1b (cont.)

COMPANY D

Category of compensation	Temporary transfer	Indefinite transfer
	costs for short distances, for long distances may give lump sum, no reimbursement of legal or brokerage fees.	and legal fees for property disposal in base country, rental accommodation fees, etc.
Exchange rate fluctuation.	Company guarantees constant exchange rate between base- and assigned-country currency for period of assignment on salary and premium transferred by or paid to FSE in assigned country.	If assigned-country currency be problematic in terms of convertibility or parity changes, FSE reviews currency guarantee in US dollars or base-country currency. Constant exchange rate (fixed at beginning of transfer) guaranteed between base- and assigned-country currencies on portion of salary employee receives in assigned country.
Benefits coverage.	Company will maintain employee in base-country private plans. Company will maintain FSE in base-country social security plans or will provide compensatory private benefits.	Company guarantees benefits at same level to FSE and family as they received pretransfer. FSE can select to remain in private plans in base country. FSE participate in compulsory and private-benefit plans in assigned country.
Cars, clubs, etc.	Cars and club memberships granted in accordance with local practice and FSE not automatically eligible.	Cars and club memberships granted in accordance with local practice and FSE not automatically eligible.

Split compensation payment.

Where possible FSE paid 100 per cent in base country for first-year salary and allowances. If assigned country requires, FSE will receive a minimum salary there.

Normally paid 100 per cent in assigned country by assigned company.

Abbreviations

1. Adaptation allowance = AA
2. Area differential = AD
3. Cost-of-living(allowance) = COL(A)
4. Foreign-service employee = FSE

5. Foreign-service premium = FSP
6. Relocation adjustment allowance = RAA
7. Third-country national = TCN

the latter; while in the UK only 30 per cent have plans, made inoperative
by wage freezes and high taxes).)

In Figure 8 : 1, Company A's expatriates, US and third-country
nationals, are tied to their home country for salary increases, benefits
coverage, vacation policy and home-leave point of origin. For comparative
purposes third-country nationals are assigned to US salary ranges, but revert
to home-country salaries when repatriated. Company C has made specific
provision only for US expatriates, while presumably each third-country
national becomes a special case. Company B adopts a hardline approach on
the whole issue of expatriate remuneration: the expatriate's salary is the
assigned country's and he is cut off completely from his home country
(except in rare cases). The last one, Company D, makes the distinction
between the temporary transfer (up to one year, with a possible extension
of six months) and the indefinite transfer (two years plus). In the former
case, the foreign-service employee remains tied to his 'base' country
(where he had resided for five years or more before the transfer), and
when his transfer becomes permanent he switches to the assigned-country
salary and administrative procedures. This distinction, and the appropriate
policies, recognize that when an individual is initially transferred, the
company may not always know exactly how long the assignment will last:
this approach will avoid a lengthy and possibly useless administration
process; and allow an overlapping period when the final decision can be
made, by which time the individual will have become accustomed to the
new assignment conditions.

Position allowance

This is a special allowance companies often pay when the salary range of
the expatriates' home country is lower than that of the assigned country.
The allowance usually aims to bring his base salary to the minimum of the
assigned country's salary range. This practice enables the portion of salary
which exceeds what the individual would receive in his home country to
be identified, and he is thus psychologically ready to accept its removal
when he is repatriated.

In Figure 8 : 1, only Company D grants a position allowance, and then
only in the case of an indefinite transfer, when the allowance is linked to
the adaptation allowance the foreign-service employee will receive. The
company identifies the portion of assigned-country salary which exceeds
120 per cent of the base-country salary range (that is, the maximum of the
range) and the foreign-service employee will receive at least the minimum
of the range in his new country. This amount is deducted from his
adaptation allowance, with the proviso that he will always receive at least

the minimum adaptation allowance appropriate to the transfer. The aim of this allowance is to allow the individual the same living standard as the local national in a similar position.

Foreign-service premium

Although the premium (together with a hardship allowance) has been used by most companies since the early days of overseas assignment, there may soon be some modification in this approach. Although many articles and reports have appeared, acclaiming the imminent demise of the foreign-service premium, statistics from financial-reward surveys do not bear this out. In a 1974 survey by the Conference Board, *more* companies paid foreign-service premium in all or most locations – 69 per cent *vs.* 67 per cent – while the proportion not paying any premium went from 16 per cent in 1972 to 15 per cent in 1974. The discussion is thus less about abolishing the premium than on aspects of phasing it out: it rests largely, therefore, on the reasons companies have for paying a premium.

In companies with a well-structured remuneration system, a premium may be used to prevent the job evaluation system from being distorted and to maintain equitable and competitive rewards. Most companies see the premium as an incentive to change location and as a compensation for the psychological and physical disruption caused by breaking up a home life-style and adjusting to a new country and its customs. If the premium is renewed at every new location, the employee is encouraged to remain flexible in his attitude to further transfers.

The payment of the foreign-service premium varies considerably. It is usually calculated as a percentage of base salary, and a large number of companies pay a flat 15 per cent of base salary. The lowest is zero and the highest is 35–40 per cent: the high ones probably contain an element of hardship compensation. Although over 50 per cent of responses to a 1974 *Business International* survey did not impose limits on a premium, others used either specific dollar limits (up to $12 000) or sliding-scale formulae, ranging in complexity. Many companies set their premium according to geographic areas: this is where the range of premiums is likely to vary widely. Sometimes they are calculated by company location (usually by country, but occasionally including provincial cities, when the distance from the capital would give a sense of isolation). Others work it out by groups of countries, usually by proximity (for example, Latin American, Europe), awarding more for intercontinental moves than intracontinental ones.

The gradual change in company thinking has probably been precipitated by dollar upheaval in 1970–71, causing personnel executives to look more carefully at all aspects of executive international remuneration. It also owes a lot to the expansion of overseas operations by many multinationals; the increasing use of local managers; and the implicit questioning of the rationale behind using expatriates. Other factors have also intervened in corporate thinking. An assignment in many parts of the world is by no means as much of a hardship as it used to be. There is sufficiently accurate data for determining the economic cost-of-living in an overseas location; and the foreign-service employee therefore has less need of a high premium into which living costs have been woven. The sense of isolation that often accompanied an international assignment has been much reduced by improved communications, home leaves and business trips. An overseas tour is being regarded increasingly, by companies and executives, as part of the individual's career development; therefore financial inducement in the form of a premium is less necessary. One disadvantage of the premium has been the tendency for expatriates mentally to incorporate it into their base salary, and to resent its removal when they are repatriated. To leave them with the premium when they returned home would prevent executive mobility, because they would be more highly paid than their colleagues in comparable jobs. A yearly addition to the premium (at the same time as an increase in base salary) could be modified after a certain period: the foreign-service employee will have become acclimatized; and the need to provide an incentive to move will have passed.

There are several approaches to this problem, which should be carefully reviewed by the company's financial experts. An initial reaction may be to eliminate the foreign-service premium completely, but not unless both the company and the executive see a foreign assignment as an integral, and advantageous, part of the individual's career development. If this condition does not exist, the company may have difficulty inducing its executive to relocate overseas. The premium can be fixed at the time of transfer and the amount will remain constant during the assignment. A further cost-reduction can be made by limiting the premium maximum, either in specific money terms or by a sliding scale. Some companies have adjusted their premiums downwards, according to location, or sometimes on a worldwide basis, reasoning that better communications and improved overseas environments will compensate for the loss of the premium. An increasingly popular idea, which will reduce costs and encourage mobility, is to phase the premium out over a period of years. The expatriate will thus adjust to the local environment, or if he is transferred again, will receive the full premium for his new location. In any event, the company will review periodically the expatriate's status and his need for a premium. A few companies have explored the idea of replacing the premium by a relocation allowance. This is considered an incentive to the executive at the moment of transfer, when most disruption takes place in his life and that of his family. A lump-sum payment is made at the moment of transfer to the new location and also when the individual returns to his home country. This is not the same as the usual relocation allowance paid by companies to cover moving costs, replacements, etc. (also covered in Figure 8 : 1). The relocation allowance facilitates mobility and its administration is simple: it does not apply to the expatriate who prefers to remain abroad because of his high continuing premium. The relocation allowance is the same amount for any move, and is usually a substantial sum (perhaps 25 per cent of base salary). On this basis, the allowance will be cheaper than a continuing premium for a long-term assignment; but it will be more costly for a short-term tour.

A hardship allowance is sometimes included with the foreign-service premium, although companies whose subsidiaries or sites are in difficult locations tend to separate the two elements. The most common reasons for awarding a hardship allowance are difficult climatic conditions, political instability, alien culture, health risks, risk of danger to physical safety, language problems, and, of course, an area considered to be a war zone.

In Figure 8 : 1, both Company A and Company D pay a lump-sum relocation allowance, judging that the executive needs it most at this stage of his assignment, and that he should adjust thereafter. They differ from Company A, which pays an allowance of three months' salary, to a maximum of $36 000, while Company D pays only one month's salary. In addition, Company D pays a foreign-service premium of up to 15 per cent to the temporary transferee, which remains fixed during the assignment. Company B pays nothing, maintaining a firm policy that overseas postings are part of their personnel planning process and no incentive to relocate is needed. Company C continues the traditional system of increasing premium with salary, ranging from 15–30 per cent; they include any hardship allowance in this premium, as indeed does Company D. Only Company A makes a specific allowance for hardship (understandably 40 per cent for Argentina, with 25 per cent for such places as Guyana, and India), while the allowance declines after four years by 5 per cent per annum.

Evidence shows that companies are far from eliminating the foreign-service premium, and that many still believe a premium should be paid for the upheavals involved in overseas transfers.

Cost-of-living allowance

The traditional way of discharging costs was to add allowances to the base salary. The 'balance-sheet' approach to the equalization of living costs is, broadly, used today by a large number of companies. The aim is to ensure that the expatriate is no better or worse off, in real dollar terms, than he would have been if he had stayed in his home country. Negative calculations can also be included in this: base salary, plus foreign-service premium; plus harship differential (if appropriate) cost-of-living, positive or negative; employee's share of the deduction for housing; deduction for the income tax equivalent to the expatriate's liability in the home country. All this equals *net* monthly income.

This means a distinction can be made between incentive payments (such as foreign-service premiums) and those which are compensation for the different cost-of-living prevailing in the assigned country. If the balance-sheet approach works out well, it ensures an objective and equitable calculation of expatriates' costs. Whatever the initial goodwill, many companies are not prepared to put in the necessary administration to deduct car or housing negative costs. Expatriates do not always welcome the companies' deduction of estimated tax bills, because their personal situation may permit them to get a more favourable deal than that allowed by a calculation of hypothetical taxes.

One of the major allowances involved in the balance-sheet or cost-equalization approach is cost-of-living. The reasoning is that an expatriate will live at the same standard *as he does at home*, buying the same products, etc., and that this will keep him and his family happy. It ignores the fact that the foreign-service employee and his family should aim to change their living patterns after a certain period in the country, by adapting to the local environment: there would then be a good case for reducing the cost-of-living allowance.

The expenditure patterns of a normal US family are developed by the Bureau of Labour Statistics, and the State Department compiles a cost-of-living index, based on embassy reports. This index, plus those of Organization Research Counselling and National Foreign Trade Council, who base their figures mainly on the State Department, is that most frequently used, in spite of many criticisms: executive expenditure patterns are very different from the normal family expenditure pattern; the salary ranges are modest, with a low ceiling of $20 000 annual salary for calculations; executives have a different life style from government personnel, for whom the State Department's index is really intended. Difficulties certainly do exist in transferring the State Department's spendable income pattern to a company's remuneration package. Free housing or a housing allowance used to be included in the cost-of-living figures: even now that those figures are separate, they often bear no relation to the complex and volatile housing markets around the world. In addition, data is often out of date when it is finally issued. The spendable income level used for calculating cost-of-living can be the main factor causing allowances to vary between one company and another, even though they are in the same city and at the same salary levels. Although most companies use 50–60 per cent as their basis, many use complex sliding scales which distinguish between low and high salaries. The *Business International* survey showed that at a salary level of $10 000, the difference between the lowest and highest paying companies was 34 per cent and at $30 000 it was 75 per cent. So some of the supposed impartiality and equity of the system has worn off.

The examples in Figure 8 : 1 show a variety of responses to the problem of paying cost-of-living. Only Company D has effectively met the challenge of paying third-country nationals allowances which are appropriate to their base country. Company A uses the State Department index without modifications, including spendable income levels; makes no adjustment where the cost-of-living allowance would be negative; and automatically increases allowances when the index moves up. Company B takes a much harder line, giving no allowance for industrialized countries and *on occasion only* uses the UN and Wiesbaden indices for developing countries, giving the lower-paid executive a higher percentage allowance.

COST-OF-LIVING ALLOWANCE AS PERCENTAGE OF HOME-COUNTRY SALARY

Move to	Move from				
	Category 1	Category 2	Category 3	Category 4	Category 5
Category 1	15	10	10	10	10
Category 2	22	15	10	10	10
Category 3	29	22	15	10	10
Category 4	36	29	22	15	10
Category 5	43	36	29	22	15

Cost-of-living ranking of COMPANY D location

Category 1   Berlin, Brussels, Geneva, Paris, Tokyo
Category 2   Amsterdam, Copenhagen, Oslo, Stockholm
Category 3   Beirut, Caracas, Hong Kong, Lisbon, Milan, New York, Sydney,
            Singapore, Vienna
Category 4   London, Madrid, Mexico City, Rio
Category 5   Buenos Aires, Johannesburg

Figure 8 : 2

Company C uses two sources and does build in a negative factor should other parts of the balance-sheet show a positive balance. Company D makes the distinction between temporary transfer and indefinite assignment. Temporary cost-of-living allowances are high, ranging from 10—43 per cent, applied as a percentage of base salary, according to the type of move. There are five categories of living costs: thus a move from category five to category one brings the highest allowance (See Figure 8 : 2). The indefinite assignment is remunerated by an overall adaptation allowance, covering premium, cost-of-living and housing. The

FOREIGN SERVICE POLICY: ADAPTATION ALLOWANCE AS PERCENTAGE OF HOME COUNTRY BASE SALARY (valid from 1 July 1973 to 31 December 1973; parities as of 1 July 1973)

Move from	Move to										
	A	B	C	D	E	F	G	H	I	J	K
A Amsterdam	—	30	27	17	32	15	19	19	17	20	26*
B Berlin	18	—	25	15	25	18	19	19	19	15	22*
C Brussels	15	25	—	17	21	17	17	17	15	17	15*
D Copenhagen	22	32	34	—	34	20	19	22	22	15	29*
E Geneva	20	25	23	17	—	20	17	17	12	17	22*
F London	37	44	43	31	46	—	28	24	29	34	43*
G Lisbon	39	47	44	36	44	27	—	12	22	31	36*
H Madrid	43	47	48	41	45	24	24	—	32	38	43*
I Milan	36	43	39	34	36	22	19	20	—	31	34*
J Oslo	28	35	37	20	37	23	22	24	24	—	31*
K Paris	14	22	17	17	20	17	17	17	15	19	—
L Stockholm	25	32	34	18	34	20	19	22	22	15	31*
M Vienna	32	37	41	34	38	22	21	22	25	29	36*
N Beirut	43	50	48	40	48	29	29	26	31	38	40*
O Buenos Aires	63	70	68	59	68	49	45	39	48	56	56*
P Caracas	45	52	50	42	50	31	29	24	33	40	42*
Q Hong Kong	35	42	44	35	44	20	30	25	30	35	44*
R Johannesburg	57	64	68	55	68	47	47	43	50	52	56*
S Mexico City	56	63	61	52	61	40	38	32	43	49	49*
T New York	31	38	40	31	40	21	28	23	26	31	40*
U Rio	56	63	61	52	61	40	36	34	43	49	49*
V Sidney	38	45	47	36	47	28	28	26	31	33	42*
W Singapore	39	46	46	39	46	27	32	27	32	39	46*
X Tokyo	27	32	32	27	32	27	27	27	27	27	32*

*These percentages do not include housing.

Figure 8 : 3

object of this is to allow expatriates to adopt their own spending patterns and to force them to adapt to the assigned country over a period of time: the adaptation allowance remains constant for three years and is then reduced annually by 20 per cent although it is never reduced by more than the annual salary increase. The percentages of base salary range from a minimum of 10 per cent for an intracontinental transfer and of 20 per cent for an intercontinental transfer to 56 per cent (plus housing). Certain cities have an additional element for housing, since these costs are already high and rising fast.

L	M	N	O	P	Q	R	S	T	U	V	W	X
20	15	23	25	25	23*	20	25	20*	25	21	27*	39*
15	13	23	25	25	23*	25	25	20*	25	21	27*	32*
17	17	21	23	23	25*	23	23	21*	23	23	27*	32*
18	20	23	25	25	23*	21	25	20*	25	24	27*	39*
17	14	21	23	23	25*	23	21	23*	23	23	27*	32*
34	27	35	25	37	33*	20	30	29*	30	31	39*	53*
31	24	26	21	29	30*	23	21	28*	20	33	32*	46*
41	34	36	20	31	37*	23	24	35*	26	38	39*	53*
34	25	26	21	28	30*	23	23	26*	23	31	32*	46*
20	22	26	25	25	23*	21	25	20*	25	26	27*	39*
19	17	21	23	23	25*	23	23	21*	23	23	27*	32*
—	20	23	25	25	23*	21	25	20*	25	24	27*	39*
32	—	28	25	30	23*	21	25	24*	25	29	32*	46*
40	33	—	25	30	32*	23	23	28*	23	33	32*	46*
59	52	47	—	27	44*	33	34	42*	34	52	46*	60*
42	35	31	17	—	30*	25	24	26*	17	35	32*	46*
35	28	30	25	30	—	23	25	28*	25	28	28*	42*
55	48	49	33	49	42*	—	40	40*	40	48	46*	60*
52	45	40	22	34	37*	28	—	33*	27	45	39*	53*
31	24	28	23	28	28*	21	28	—	23	24	32*	44*
52	45	40	20	34	37*	28	27	35*	—	45	39*	53*
36	29	30	25	30	28*	21	25	24*	25	—	30*	44*
39	32	32	27	32	28*	27	27	32*	27	30	—	44*
27	27	27	27	27	23*	27	27	25*	27	25	25*	—

The matrix shown in Figure 8 : 3 includes both qualitative and quantitative aspects of living costs and adaptation required to take on a foreign assignment. The costs for both US expatriates and third-country nationals can be readily calculated. This is unusual: in the authors' 1973 survey 42 per cent of companies applied the State Department indices directly to their third-country nationals. It is also the only system that allows for a reduction in allowances and in this sense shows a more advanced stage of thinking in expatriate remuneration.

Housing allowance

It is becoming increasingly difficult to assess the cost of adequate expatriate housing overseas. Not only is the cost, compared to America, substantially greater, it is increasing at an unprecedented rate. This particular problem makes the US State Department index (as well as figures supplied by some outside consultants) somewhat unrealistic. The survey on which State Department figures are based dates back to 1961, and subsequent inflation has not been fully considered. Companies have to rely on their subsidiary companies or published surveys to update information on actual local housing costs.

There are several ways to calculate expatriates' housing allowances. The State Department favours paying a flat allowance according to location, while external consultants often recommend a graduated allowance, which rises with income. Some companies (those with a more colonial tradition, or based in remote places) provide the expatriate with free housing. Others still have no fixed policy, negotiating each executive's case as it occurs. An increasingly popular option is to assess what portion of an expatriate's salary would normally be housing costs (either deducting direct or allowing him to pay this percentage), the company paying all or part of costs in excess of this percentage. In this case, the allowance is tailored to the housing situation in the location. It is easy to administer, and the burden is on local management to approve the housing selected by the expatriate, since they will be footing the bill. If there is no ceiling, and the company pays all the excess, there is not much incentive for the executive to select appropriate housing: he may be tempted to rent his family a palace. If, however, there is a total percentage limit, or the expatriate pays a proportion of the excess cost over the basic housing percentage, an element of restraint is effectively introduced, at least for lower-income executives. The percentage of salary chosen to represent average US housing costs varies: it can be a flat percentage (most often 15 per cent, though 12 per cent and 10 per cent figure in the surveys) or a sliding scale, whereby the lower-paid executive is expected to pay a higher proportion of his income in housing than the senior executive. This policy is based on the fact that housing costs decrease (relatively) as incomes increase.

Companies usually take the overseas cost of utilities (such as gas and electricity) into account when calculating housing allowances; but in the *Business International* survey, at least 14 per cent disregarded utilities completely in their calculations. It is rare for companies to encourage home purchase abroad and this is one reason why housing allowances are not always as generous as they appear. If the executive owned a home – in the US for example – commensurate with his status, it was probably a spacious house and garden for 10–15 per cent of salary. He goes overseas and finds that an apartment with three or four rooms in the city centre costs 20–25 per cent of his income, even before paying for all utilities. Buying accommodation in crowded Europe and Japan can be very expensive indeed.

In Figure 8 : 1, Company A has fixed a low ceiling of $4 500 annually, which amounts to 15 per cent of a $30 000 base salary; while Company B pays 80 per cent of costs over 15 per cent of base salary, with a maximum 25 per cent of salary. Company C operates the sliding scale previously mentioned: 12 per cent of salary is considered as average US housing costs for salaries up to $20 000, plus 6 per cent of the portion above $20 000; and the foreign-service employee is reimbursed for 75 per cent of his rent and utilities which exceed the US norm. For temporary transfers, Company D pays 90 per cent of housing costs exceeding 15 per cent of base salary; for the indefinite assignment, housing is included in the adaptation allowance (except for a few cities with rapid inflation in accommodation). In the latter case, outside consultants calculate the housing costs. Details of the adaptation allowance have already been covered above under cost-of-living.

Tax equalization

By adopting the balance-sheet approach to remuneration, many more companies have become involved in the complexities of offering their expatriates tax equalization. The principle is that the expatriate should not be obliged to pay more or less tax when resident overseas than he would have done had he stayed in domestic operations. The company determines his domestic liability, his hypothetical tax as an expatriate, and then includes this amount as a debit in the balance-sheet package. The company then pays the expatriate's full income tax (or reimburses him), both at home and overseas. When the overseas liability is lower than in his home country, the company lets him keep the excess, but protects him from paying any excess tax should the situation be reversed. What companies consider to be taxable income can vary considerably: base salary alone; salary plus foreign-service premium; all allowances as well as salary. Any bonus is usually included. Although a lot of companies calculate the hypothetical tax for federal taxes only, there is a marked trend towards including state taxes.

Companies follow the local rules in paying the tax due to any foreign government, although they are not always obliged to make a declaration of the expatriate's income. If the employee withholds information about his total revenues (salary, allowances, etc.), the foreign government may ask his home-country government for the relevant information, if a bilateral tax treaty exists. This is more likely when the foreign country is nationalistic and where it is evident that the expatriate is receiving a split salary. The legality of this practice depends very much on the attitude of the host-country government. Some have no interest in global income, and the expatriate is only liable for income earned in the assigned country. In some cases, a company can alleviate the expatriate's tax burden by assigning him to projects outside the assigned country, where he would work directly for the parent corporation, but on the whole companies prefer to avoid involvement in his tax problems. Nevertheless, most companies want to be sure that the expatriate is not evading his host-country taxes and that their reputation is clean within the assigned country. Some expatriates would prefer not to have their tax liabilities protected, because they may be able to take advantage of tax laws, so that they pay less while overseas than the hypothetical tax calculation. This may be a mixed blessing, particularly when point-of-purchase taxes are not taken into account. For instance, in France, as a deliberate instrument of fiscal policy, income taxes are relatively low, while VAT is high. The reverse is true in Britain. So for an expatriate, his total tax burden could be the same in the two countries, but he might lose under a tax equalization policy.

Company A reimburses excess tax burden on 60 per cent salary and allowances received in the assigned country: its policy is to pay 60 per cent of the expatriate's income in the host country; this is only feasible when the latter does not insist on worldwide income being reported. When total income is reported, the company pays actual tax liability rising in the assigned and home countries, like Company C. But while Company C withholds hypothetical federal tax on initial base salary, Company A reimburses excess costs, that is, protects rather than equalizes. Company B washes its hands completely of its expatriate's affairs. The expatriate is paid fully in the assigned country. Company A intends the transfer premium, cost-of-living housing and education allowances to be after-tax amounts, and reimburses taxes and contributions paid to compulsory benefit plans in the assigned country which exceed what the expatriate would normally pay on his home salary and bonus. In both the latter, for temporary transfer and the indefinite transfer, the company makes deductions for the US expatriates, and also deducts compulsory benefit plan contributions; but the individual is responsible for filing his own tax declaration. The foreign-service employee on a temporary assignment is paid, whenever possible, 100 per cent in his home country. The situation when he is on an indefinite assignment is slightly different. The policy of the company being to make him adapt to his new environment, every effort is made to loosen his ties with the home country. Instead of receiving a split salary, which helps cover financial obligations still existing in his home country, he receives 100 per cent salary and allowances in the assigned country. The company calculates hypothetical tax and compulsory contributions on salary, bonus and position allowance (if applicable) in his base country; runs through the same calculation for the assigned country (but including adaptation allowance and education allowance), and the difference between the two sets of calculations becomes his tax allowance. This is simpler to administer, since no modifications are made after the first calculations, which increase or decrease proportionately the adaptation allowance. The allowance remains the same for the rest of the assignment.

Other benefits

Two other major benefits that the majority of companies allow their expatriates are an education allowance and home leave. Companies usually expect the expatriate's dependent children to be educated in the assigned country, in state schools if possible. If local private schools only are deemed adequate by the company, they usually pay education costs incurred, including uniforms, books, laboratory fees, etc. If local private schools, in turn, are inadequate, the company pays for education (with board and lodging) in the home country: sometimes they fix a maximum amount (for example, whatever would have been paid for the best comparable school in the assigned country). The child is usually granted one trip a year to the assigned country, in addition to the home leave. The readiness with which companies pay this allowance indicates their fundamental belief that an expatraite's children should not suffer in the quality of their education because of the mobility of his job.

Most companies grant annual home leave to the expatriate and his eligible dependants (usually wife and children up to university age, though sometimes over). Round-trip economy air fares are usually provided, but some companies give the expatriate the equivalent amount, leaving him free to choose where to spend his vacation. It is preferred, however, that the family will return to their home country, allowing them to get up to date with social and professional developments.

Benefits coverage is a far more delicate subject and not all companies have solved the problems. It is relatively simple to keep US expatriates in US company benefit plans for as long as they are overseas. Although they do not always remain in the private benefit plans, this is no great hardship, since nearly every industrialized nation has better social security benefits than the US, even if they are more expensive. In addition, US expatriates tend to have slightly less need for security than many other nationalities. French managers are a good example of this security-consciousness: they know that by going abroad they are leaving a complex and bureaucratic but excellent system of benefits. Special arrangements can be made to keep them in companies' private benefit plans, which have the advantage of being portable (that is, transferable from one country to another). Other foreign-service employees, however, are not so lucky. They may only be allowed to remain in their home-country benefit plans (either social security or private) for a limited period. This is particularly significant for pension rights: an employee may become an international expatriate, after several assignments overseas, never returning to his base country and therefore losing all eligibility for benefits there. In this case, many companies make the employee a promise to maintain at least the standard of benefits he would have received had he remained in his home country. He can contribute to assigned-country plans, but the company covers him by an umbrella policy and meets the difference between the latter and the amount of the assigned country's benefits. For examples of a medical plan, and a disability, death and retirement plan, see Appendix B (Exhibit 17, pp. 403–6). This applies to retirement, accident, widows' benefits and medical plans.

8.2   Evaluating exchange rates

Most companies have at times had to face the problem of fluctuating exchange rates. The problem arose through the custom of US multi-nationals linking the major elements of the remuneration system to the dollar standard. Even if the expatriate receives all his income in local currency, for administrative purposes the headquarters personnel department maintains a record in dollars. If the employee is paid in a strong local currency, there is a risk that his total financial rewards, after some time, will compare unfavourably with home-country executives (in dollar terms) and will become a disincentive to return. Companies often choose to protect the remuneration received in local currency (which, in effect, is what Companies A and D do in Figure 8 : 1). It can be a fixed amount actually received, or an estimated spendable income, although the latter leads to all sorts of problems of definition: for instance, over clothing and holidays, which are often paid for in home-country (although they are part of the spendable income). A few companies continue a policy of equalization, and for every adjustment made to the local currency portion, the dollar part is proportionately reduced. Most companies do not, however, reduce the dollar amount.

Even when the company is prepared to compensate for exchange-rate losses, there are certain problems. How quickly should they make the necessary adjustments: monthly, semi-annually, yearly; or should the expatriate provide evidence of *actual* losses incurred in transferring income to the host country on his expense account, and have it reimbursed under usual expense-account procedures? When should the changes be made, on a dollar figure ($50 per month) or when the fluctuation exceeds two or five per cent? Whether to adjust spendable income, or income paid in local currency, or income transferred into local currency is another decision to be made; and whether to make the adjustment by an identifiable currency-adjustment allowance, or cost-of-living adjustment, or expense-account reimbursement (to avoid the problem of income tax, gross amount, etc.). Company personnel departments should, under these circumstances, make a special effort to communicate the company's remuneration policy and administrative procedures.

Although these are the principal benefits a foreign-service employee most commonly receives, there are many others, which vary from company to company: for example, cars, clubs, relocation; clothing, foreign household improvements, key money, emergency evacuation, etc. The significance of these to any company will depend on its own particular needs and philosophy.

8.3   Third-country nationals

There are special problems, over third-country nationals, who have customarily been treated somewhat differently by the multinational than expatriates from the home country. Their remuneration used to be calculated on an *ad hoc* basis: now there is a trend towards greater consistency. They now receive a total package comparable to that of a home-based expatriate; and salary scales are closer to those of other expatriates, reflecting the rapidly evolving management salary structures in many industrialized countries, particularly in Western Europe. This is specially true of third-country nationals working in regional or inter-national headquarters. Although most components of the package, including education allowances, are given to third-country nationals, tax equalization is less common, because they are rarely liable for home-country as well as assigned-country taxes. There is some indication that companies are experimenting with an elimination of the extra allowance package for intra-European transfers, giving a big boost to a manager's salary if he is transferred to a lower-salary country, or a position allowance if moved to a higher-salary country. Even Europeans feel, however, that there are certain cultural and educational differences which always warrant some reward for a European transfer.

Many companies apply US expatriate allowance calculations to the third-country national's base salary (which may be somewhat lower than the American executive's). In the survey of international remuneration practices conducted by the authors in 1973, 42 per cent were adopting this approach. Some others attempt to adjust their allowances to the different living patterns and consequent costs of the third-country nationals. Company D in Figure 8 : 1 has opted for this policy. Others ensure that the foreign-service employee, whether expatriate or third-country, has the same allowance, based on his home-country salary. Although this approach can be very expensive, from the point of view of paying higher allowances to TCNs, and from the administrative angle (trying to develop and keep up to date housing, education and tax information from the many different third countries), there are some advantages. It is internally consistent and flexible: it makes the expatriate less conscious of his exceptional and negotiable status, and allows a gradual move towards a more equitable rule of equal salaries for the same work in different company locations. It facilitates transfers and makes local managers feel that they can become respected members of the company's top management team, instead of remaining second-class executives.

A major problem in third-country-national remuneration is determining the country salary scale on which his salary will be based. The *Business International* survey referred to earlier showed that 25 per cent of companies use the home-country salary ranges, 25 per cent calculated on a case-by-case basis, while 22 per cent used the assigned-country ranges: there is obviously no current consensus. Foreign-service premium is paid by 49 per cent on the same basis as to US expatriates, while 30 per cent do not pay it. Cost-of-living and housing allowances are more consistently applied. Tax equalization is unusual, but some 80 per cent of companies practise some form of tax protection, usually based on a hypothetical home-country income tax. Where the third-country national is transferred to the US, lack of accurate and comparative statistics for cost-of-living and housing has led to very diverse practices in extra allowances. Of course, every company has to formulate its plans for financial rewards to suit its own particular needs; the examples only provide some ideas for someone wishing to evolve a new policy. A specimen letter of assignment for a third-country national is shown as Exhibit 16 in Appendix B (pages 399–402); Exhibit 17 (pages 403–6) shows specimen letters to those participating in special benefit plans.

8.4 Formulating a package of financial rewards to suit a company's own needs

Every company should bear in mind certain considerations when planning its own remuneration package. For those companies without extended overseas operations staffed by expatriates, the task will be easier, since there will be less resistance to change. Figure 8 : 4 outlines the action steps in determining what a future policy should be and how it should be handled, together with the issues which the company should examine before finalizing its programme.

Figure 8 : 4

**PLANNING AN INTERNATIONAL COMPENSATION PROGRAMME
PRIORITY ACTIONS/FACTORS FOR CONSIDERATION**

1 Outline policy guidelines

What should be degree of unification of policy between different
 countries?
Which are key external market reference points?
Which are key internal equity points which should be maintained?
What is level of incentives to be provided?

2 Identify the company's specific needs

Project company requirements for international executives for next 10–15
 years:
      Mix of home-country expatriates, third-country nationals, local
      nationals.

Figure 8 : 4 (cont.)

    Mix of senior, middle and lower management.

    Overall numbers, by function, age.

    Focus on needs to withdraw foreign-service employees or recruitment, development, retention or motivation.

    Quality of executive manpower, current and future.

Estimate impact of compensation programme costs on profitability and need to relate it to financial resources.

Decide if need exists for separate compensation policies and practices for expatriate (2—5 assignments) and careerist (5 years plus).

3 Define administrative procedures and techniques

Review domestic and international base salary structures and their effects on:

    Budgets.

    Executive motivation.

    Attitudes to relocation.

Review techniques in calculating allowances and previous assumptions:

    Abolish allowances and pay base salaries?

    Eliminate, phase out or reduce foreign-service premium?

    Modify or abolish selectively cost-of-living allowance?

    Reduce cost-of-living allowance, on the basis that expatriates must adjust?

    How do housing allowances tally with actual housing costs?

    How carefully should tax windfalls be controlled?

Examine compensation policies for third-country nationals:

    What currency of payment?

    Should their compensation be linked to their home country?

    What (if any) split-salary arrangements should be made?

    Will key executives leave because they are not protected against dollar losses?

    On what basis should third-country nationals' allowances be calculated?

Examine benefit programmes (especially for third-country nationals).

Determine what effect the dollar devaluations have (and will have) on:

    Pay — tie back to US or not?

    Benefit planning (particularly TCNs) — consolidate worldwide or not?

    Capital accumulation?

    Salary split?

Figure 8 : 4 (cont.)

Assess use of exchange rate in converting salaries and allowances:
    End-of-month spot rate?
    End-of-quarter rate?
    Daily average?
    Intercompany transactions?
    Range of rates?
Determine frequency of updating on compensation practices and subsequent adjustment of compensation:
    More frequently for allowances?
    Annually for salaries?
    Minimize administration or adjustments quarterly?
Make provision for modifying allowances in assignment letters to expatriates.

The first step is to ensure that there exist good corporate policy guidelines. These will enable the decentralized operations to develop, with subsidiaries making their own recommendations, thus ensuring that top management only has to take a decision exceptionally, where local practices are a long way off desired corporate policy. A parallel step with this is to identify the company's needs, in the short and long term, regarding manpower, policies for temporary/indefinite assignments, mix of people, new emphasis of personnel policies, costs, and new technologies impacting on the organization.

Having set the guidelines and determined its requirements, the company should spend a considerable amount of time considering the sheer routine of running such a complex set of policies. Often in all good faith, companies decide they want to position themselves in the upper echelon of their industry, or of a national remuneration survey. But they never think of how they are going to implement this policy, and still less about how much it would cost to bring all their underpaid executives up to the minimum requirements. Even buying the expertise to administer the programme is costly. The programme also needs to be communicated and kept up to date as and when required. Whilst companies usually go outside for occasional assistance with accounting, and tax and legal matters in other countries; and expertise is needed over salary, bonus, and expatriate- and foreign-pay practices (including tax/legal knowledge); there should be a strong executive controlling the sensitive area of internal administration, where special interpersonal skills are required. The techniques involved in running such a programme have already been treated in some depth, and

Figure 8 : 4 offers some ideas which might help a company to launch its own programme: for instance does the company want an executive to remain tied to his home country; how does it want to use split salaries (if at all)?

Although all these steps are time-consuming, they will be beneficial, not only in terms of better short-term manpower management, but in allowing the company's top management to focus on all the elements required in multinational human resource management and to evaluate its own long-term strategies in the light of its human resources.

9
International management development

The transnational corporations are no longer paying mere lip service to the development of globally-minded managers, although there still is and will continue to be a critical shortage of internationally-minded executives. The increasing emphasis on developing international managers is partially the result of too many failures — both of individuals and of companies. These failures have led to unrealized profit expectations and resultant ill will from host countries. Additionally, many of the mega-companies have had to turn down potentially sound mergers and acquisitions through a dearth of management talent to integrate the potential acquisition into its parent corporation. Also, expansion plans have been thwarted through lack of strong leaders to provide direction. New concepts in the organization of international operations have produced a growing need for globally-minded executives to manage regional and international operations. More decentralization has become necessary.

There is a dearth of management sophistication among local nationals who are managing foreign subsidiaries. This problem is aggravated by demands from foreign governments, particularly in developing countries, to prepare local nationals quickly for all local management positions. Proper preparation of local nationals to assume their full responsibilities as policy makers in a large complex organization necessitates more emphasis on management development. Local nationals must be given opportunities to learn to function fully as senior executives of a geographically distant corporation.

There is also the increased complexity of management itself. To function effectively as a senior executive in an international environment requires both the awareness of and the ability to cope with, rapidly changing conditions in labour, society, government, production, technology, currency transactions, and the world economy and its impact on the local subsidiary. Uncertainty is the rule, and not the exception. These conditions require well-trained, well-informed general managers, who are able to size up a situation quickly and to use modern management principles and methods in dealing with it.

Then there are demands from a new generation of managers actively seeking new authority and autonomy in local decision-making. They seek recognition through opportunities to develop their managerial skills and potential. Many national governments, both in developed and developing countries, have introduced payroll taxes, ranging from 0.5–2.0 per cent of the total payroll, to encourage training and development at all levels within the company. They give rebates to companies who take advantage of opportunities to build a well-educated workforce. These government schemes apply equally to management personnel. In most instances, a formal plan must be approved in advance by the appropriate government ministry. This development by itself has forced employers to pay more attention to manpower forecasting, planning and career opportunities at all levels.

All these factors have given rise to a rapid increase in the number and variety of consultants and outside educational institutions (public and private), to build up the level of professional management: national governments are encouraging and financially supporting these institutions. These forces have also served to highlight the status and professionalism of the human resource function within a company. Payroll taxes for training and development represent a substantial investment, and business organization seek to measure and improve their return on this investment in human capital.

There are many points of view, often conflicting, as to the best way to develop senior managers for the international environment. Indeed, it is still not clearly understood just what management development itself involves. Perhaps the most helpful approach is the systems concept illustrated in Figure 9 : 1. The diagram shows the close relationships between the essential business activities and the management development process. It is designed to portray the inescapable fact that one of the manager's key responsibilities is to provide a qualified replacement for himself. The model further recognizes that manager development is synergistic. The emphasis must be upon maintaining the present vitality of the organization, while systematically relating individual development activities to business plans which produce immediate improvement in present job performance while providing for future growth.

The systems approach to manager development has no real ending; it is a continuous process. It is a closed loop of vitality and continuity which flows and eventually recycles to provide capable managers. Sound business and manpower plans produce good men to work the plans and make the plans work. If we accept this concept of management development, then

Figure 9 : 1

A SYSTEMS APPROACH TO DEVELOPING MANAGERIAL RESOURCES
BASED ON VITALITY AND GROWTH

1.   Business planning

Business charter.
Management philosophy.
Company policy.
Business needs and constraints.
Position descriptions.

Guide to selection.
Corporate objectives.
Division goals.
Organization planning.
Limits of authority and responsibility.

2.   Knowledge of what is expected

The individual job to be done

A job well done: quantitative and qualitative

Goals planning.
Challenges.
Opportunities.
Projects.
Action plans.
Timetables.
Systems and procedures.
Applicable policies.

Achievement measures.
Key indicators.
Yardsticks.
Performance standards.
Results expected.
Anticipation of obstacles.

3.   Feedback of results

Review of achievement

Measures of accomplishment against goals

Critical check points.
Monthly reports.
Quarterly audits.
Semi annual performance appraisal.

Quantitative and qualitative appraisal of each man's accomplishment.
Identification and solution of problems.
Review and readjust goals as necessary.
Coaching and assistance as needed.

4.   Individual action plans

Early identification of strengths, ,
   limitations and developmental needs.
Pay in relation to performance.

Determine individual career interests,
   plans and timetables.
Assess potential for future development.

5.   Manager development

Manpower inventories, quantitative and
   qualitative.

Manager's attitude and leadership style.
General principles and practices for a

Figure 9 : 1 (cont.)

Manager development:
    Job enlargement.
    Job enrichment.
    Job rotation.
    Job specialization.
    Special assignments.
    Task force.
	successful programme: large, medium
	and small organizations.

6.   Promotion decisions

Accomplishment.
Development.
Outside activities.
Physical stamina.
Age.
	Job responsibilities *vs.* individual
	    qualifications.
	Outside hiring *vs.* inside promotion.
	Use of reference checking in manager
	    development.

the question of implementation arises. This is particularly difficult in developing multinational managers. It is not a question of in-company development against attendance at outside institutions and courses: rather it is a question of how much of each and when. It is not an overnight process. It is broader in scope and dimension becaue it reaches beyond national borders.

9.1   The Omega company approach

The company in the case study cited in Chapter 3 (pages 37—48) expounded the thesis that the development and proper utilization of all management potential within its far-flung, worldwide organization was not only a policy and a moral duty, but essential to survival. Accordingly, an exhaustive study of this organization's human resources was planned, to include recommendations of management development programmes suitable to its needs. The obvious shortage of adequately trained managers did not preclude or permit relaxation of the company's efforts to strengthen, through new recruiting, the existing management cadre, pending completion of the study. Quite the contrary, immediate action was taken in this area, and several executives were hired.

Each regional vice-president was requested to list, for the manpower inventory, all general managers of all operating companies and branches under his control, plus the senior members of his regional staff who were deemed to be of general-management calibre. The listing included ages of the incumbents and how many years each individual was expected to remain in his then position. A second step was to list each individual who would be a designated replacement for the individuals on the first list, under each of the two following conditions:

If the present incumbent manager or staff member were to be removed immediately.

If the present manager were to vacate the position in the next three to five years.

The third step was to appraise the qualifications of each man on each list in relation to the functions he should be performing (existing incumbents), or would be expected to perform under the stated conditions (for the back-ups who were identified). The results of each appraisal included a list of functions for which the candidate's qualifications and development were adequate, and another for which his qualifications were inadequate. The final step in the appraisal process included a statement as to whether the individual's deficiencies as identified could be rectified or not; and if they could be, by what means: job rotation, special training within OMEGA, outside institution courses, etc. This was accompanied by a timetable to accomplish the development objectives.

Organization and manpower reviews were conducted by the international director of human resources, and verified and compared against his own management assessments with the regional vice-presidents. The final document constituted the general management resources inventory. After the reviews, each regional vice-president was expected to have a planned schedule for the development of future management resources and for the correction of deficiencies in the human resources immediately available. The development schedules were quite specific, in writing, and included organization back-up charts. They were supplemented by specifying the developmental activities to be performed, the beginning and ending dates for training, and the men involved. If training courses outside the company were recommended, the name of the institution, total costs, type of training, duration and location were given.

The idea was quickly to develop a reasonably complete, practical plan for assuring the availability of executive manpower when needed. It had the effect of indicating both the needs of the region which could be met from within the total company and those for which new recruiting was required. The schedules took into account the operating needs of the regions and the duration of time high-level managers could reasonably devote to development activities and be absent from their jobs. This, in turn, forced replacement planning and more delegation to the lower levels of management and, in itself, served as a management development tool. The extent to which intracompany training (among different OMEGA locations) could benefit the individual was carefully considered in relation to comparability of markets, products, culture, languages and social patterns. It was considered to be a waste of time and money to attempt to develop managers who were lacking in interpersonal skills, flexibility, and other qualities cited in Chapter 6 (see pages 141–50). Unfortunately no quantitative method can measure these qualities: thus heavy reliance was placed upon the individual's past and present performance, and the subjective impressions of two or three senior executives who were best qualified to make this delicate assessment.

It was recognized that on-the-job experience is the best teacher as well as the best management development method. Because modern management is so complex, it is not possible for an individual to work in seven or eight major functional areas of the business for any length of time. Hence, to overcome part of this deficiency, when a man's general management potential was recognized at an early stage in his career, and as time and individual circumstances permitted, he was given job-rotation assignments in other functional areas, to give him practical experience. These assignments included temporary jobs, to observe, to assist, and to do, as well as to receive instructions from general managers and managers with functional expertise in those areas where experience was lacking. These temporary assignments lasted from two to six weeks or more. They were on a *quid pro quo* basis, that is, the executive in training was expected to make a positive contribution to the host company.

OMEGA used outside management-development courses to remedy deficiencies stemming from lack of knowledge, provide basic general-management principles, and to broaden a man to meet the challenges of a complex sociopolitical economic environment. The courses selected were as specific as possible over the knowledge and theory to be gained; and a full report was submitted, with a plan showing how and when the knowledge gained would be used. For example, an outstanding salesman as a management candidate: his previous education and experience showed a gap in accounting principles and financial management; so he was sent on a course about the fundamentals of accounting and financial management analysis. Courses in general subjects were usually avoided if they were deemed to be of little or no value in overcoming an individual's specific deficiencies at the time he was being considered for promotion. But select ones were included when they were part of a longer-range plan aimed at preparing a person for general-management responsibility. The advanced management courses, such as those offered by Harvard, Columbia and Stanford universities, were limited to those experienced and competent managers who were already high up in the organization hierarchy and were destined for general management.

This, generally speaking, was the manager development pattern followed by the OMEGA company. It was deliberately kept simple and practical. It utilized resources within the total company as well as those outside of the company. It included special one-week seminars, at selected locations, for financial directors, managing directors, sales managers, factory managers, and service and field managers. A similar plan was formulated and implemented for personnel managers. A training programme of 15 weeks for a general manager in a developing country was conducted in three developed countries. The plan included the following:

Three weeks

Construction methods: tooling, route organization, efficiency and cost control, trouble reports, reporting system.

Production organization: contract control, methods, tooling, material handling, factory cost accounting, quality assurance, production reporting system.

Two weeks

Engineering organization and administration: product data, lead time, project budgets, material lists, specifying.

New sales: estimating, price lists, promotional literature, selling methods, market development, customer relations.

Product service: estimating, maintenance contracts, price policies, contract processing, reporting system.

Branch management: profit centre concepts, organization, head-office (line/staff) relationships, administration, cost and expense control, budgets.

One week

Regional and international offices: financial reporting and control, management meetings, performance standards, management-by-objectives, overall organization, systems, controls, working relationships.

The executive trainee had to submit a monthly report on what he had learned, how he planned to apply it within his cultural framework, and what criticism he had of the training received. These reports were discussed at length by the trainee with the appropriate regional vice-president and the international director of human resources, who personally guided the man during his training.

9.2   What other companies do

Because of the added dimension of multinational management, transnational corporations have approached this aspect of management in a variety of ways. Here are a few representative examples.

Siemens

Siemens AG has more than 300 000 employees. This company constructed a special centre for management training south of Munich. Roughly 20 000 national and international management trainees receive training here in modern management over periods of one to four weeks. The objective is to increase by threefold the intensity and variety of training and development activities needed to meet the special requirements of their industry. This German multinational recognizes that they cannot continue to recruit approximately 2000 management trainees per annum (which they must do to fulfil growth needs and gaps within management ranks) without this training. One of their aims is to launch a vigorous attack against over-specialization, inflexibility, and lack of positive initiative. There are two basic seminars:

Young managers under 40 years of age. These are qualified people, who are judged to be capable of advancing and able to assume broader responsibilities. The participants, in general, have several years of company experience, have completed legal, economic and technical studies, and have had successful departmental responsibility. The course length is two weeks.

Senior managers. Approximately 20 participants in a two-and-a-half week course. This seminar deals with the problems and goals of the company, its function, role and priorities in society. A variety of additional subjects are covered, such as planning, finance, organization and decision-making, personnel, social and educational policies, and motivation through obtaining cooperation and support from subordinates. A full week is spent by the participants in managing three imaginary companies within the electronics industry. This gives the participants an opportunity to evaluate their decisions. Different experiences are exchanged, and the seminar concludes with a full day's discussion with the top corporate managers.

Royal Dutch Shell Group

This group of more than 500 companies, operating in more than 100 countries, with businesses in oil, gas and chemicals, has had a strong management development programme for many years. They recognized the revolutionary changes in both technology and management, and are coping well by keeping their managers up to date. They have the philosophy of decentralization, and the managers of the countries where they are established are for the most part local nationals. They are responsible for achieving both short- and long-term objectives. However, because their business decisions often require knowledge of affairs outside of their home countries and affect the welfare of the other operating companies, the total business requires a high degree of cooperation and coordination, both functionally and geographically. This entails developing managers with both multifunctional and multinational experience. For the young 'high potentials', a number of changes in job assignments and environments are planned and executed, to broaden experience and outlook and to condition them to accept change as a way of life. Because of the large size of the company, there is both the opportunity and the flexibility to plan careers far into the future.

They recognize local requirements and barriers in staffing national, regional service and international operations. This group believes in and practices mobility of its managers. By using 'foreigners' in select management positions, local managers receive stimulation and new ideas, and the foreign manager is prepared for a more senior job at home or at group headquarters. The nationals must take their full share in the management responsibility and conduct of the business at the national level. The group staff is by design multinational in character and composition.

The recruitment process is done both at national and group level, and from numerous academic disciplines. Personality and scholastic achievement are stressed. More and more graduates from the best business schools are sought out. The group believes that the best preparation for managers of the future begins with an integrated approach to business studies.

Early identification of young 'high potentials' is an important part of the manager development process. The higher dimensions of skill and ability for managerial jobs include the power of synthesis: that is, the ability to view problems with a broad perspective, based on a man's personal vision. Next is the power of analysis: that is, the ability to break down a complicated problem into its component parts, and make it manageable so as to detect immediately any weakness or error in an argument or proposal. Thirdly imagination: to be able to produce new and promising ideas which will shape or change the course of the business.

Mental vitality is deemed to be of equal importance: the ability to cope with complex situations, without adverse effect on the quality of a man's work, and without his losing perspective. A sense of reality is also of importance: to select the right course of action, without either over-estimating or understanding his own capabilities or those of his organization. Finally, the group value those personal traits and characteristics that allow the individual to motivate and stimulate the organization to new heights of achievement.

By the time young managers, in their thirties, have demonstrated through achievement and promotions to responsible positions, their potential for general management, they are sent on a five or six week, in-company course, to correct tendencies toward over-specialization, and to study thoroughly the group's objectives, policies and management techniques, particularly financial analysis.

Senior managers must also be kept up to date, to avoid obsolescence in their thinking and management practice. Special-purpose training programmes are developed, in such areas as computer appreciation. The most important aspect of this training is the element of self-development. Unless a man is himself enthusiastic to learn and to keep up, any formal training has severe limitations. A great deal of emphasis is placed upon technological innovation, information technology and man/management relationships: hence upon the social and behavioural sciences.

Manpower planning and forecasting and systematic manager development plans permit the company to suit its individual development actions to the needs of the individuals themselves, and the businesses of which they are a part. The practices are constantly reviewed and adjusted in the light of rapidly changing business conditions in the global environment.

Unilever

This is a large, transnational corporation, with approximately 500 companies and factories and a total of 300 000 employees throughout the world. Their many products include foods, household items, toiletry and sundries. It is of Dutch/British origin, with its operating units guided and controlled from the central office, but enjoying considerable independence in their local decision-making. The senior members of the board concern themselves with policy matters and final decisions, in such areas as capital investments, annual budgets, research expenditures, and the appointment of senior managers. Overall management planning takes place in London and Rotterdam, the two major centres of the corporation. There is a personnel policy committee, composed of the chairman of the various geographical groups, assisted by the personnel directors. They assist and make recommendations to the special senior policy committee with regard to senior management.

The top officers recognize that management is a scarce commodity, and it cannot be left to chance to rely on having the required numbers of senior managers of the right quality and experience at a chosen time. Because shortage of managers at any given time can hamper the growth of the company, and a surplus of managers results in frustration and wastage, management manpower planning and forecasting were undertaken in a serious manner after 1960. This necessitated a systematic approach to attain manager development objectives, which consisted of three major points.

1 A continually updated inventory of its present position, that is:

Job descriptions, salary structures, job evaluations.

Inventory of present management, including performance and promotability appraisals.

Yearly organization and manpower reviews at all management levels of the company.

Back-up lists of managers available for promotion.

2 A clear insight into the future organization of the company. This is projected five years into the future:

The planning is done at the operating centres and progressively goes upward to the top of the organization, that is, company management, national management, directors, group management. These groups are assisted by the central advisory services. All planning includes expansion in new directions.

The business plan is translated into organization charts, which indicate the organization and managerial manpower required in order to achieve its objectives.

3 The third requirement is the system of communication channels and its organization to execute the placement and development procedures for the staffing of the future organization from presently available managers.

The company makes every effort possible to promote from within the organization. The idea is to build loyalty and a cadre of managers who are willing to work and grow within the company over a long period of time. Loyalty and experience represent a considerable investment. The vitally needed human assets can best be developed within the establishment.

Internationalization is also a very important principle because this worldwide concern requires internationally-minded managers. Coupled with the principle of international flexibility, the best use is made of available managerial resources on a worldwide basis, which helps to overcome the limitations caused by the scarcity of managerial talent. Local operating units, in principle, are manned by local managers. Local circumstances require specific local know-how and experience. Unilever makes every effort to avoid the image of a foreign company, dominated by foreigners.

There is a special organization throughout the company, equipped to handle all problems connected with the development of managers throughout their careers with Unilever. This group takes care of all training activities, trainee development during the first two years with the company, organizing courses, advising on outside participation in manager development programmes, etc. Within each product group, there is a management development department, with a training adviser and training officers in the various geographic centres. Courses are organized within the company, with a view to further development based on frequent visitations of central staff personnel directors, who conduct management reviews in the various local operating companies. The recruiting effort is well planned, systematic and continuous. It is based on future organization and manpower planning. This regular intake establishes excellent ongoing relationships with recruiting sources such as universities.

Manager development is well established as an integral part of the total corporate planning process in this mega-company.

Exxon Corporation

Exxon is in the oil or energy business. It is a US corporation, with 140 000 employees encircling the globe. It is the world's largest industrial corporation by sales volume. The company has a top-level committee for compensation and executive development which meets weekly. Exxon develops people, as well as producing, refining and marketing oil. It is no secret why the world's largest industrial corporations continually appear on the Fortune 500 list, with minor shifting of their relative positions. All have well-established policies, objectives, plans and programmes for developing managers. This is an integral part of each company's total investment planning. Otherwise, they could not survive.

The Exxon committee for compensation and manager development concerns itself with pay, movements and appointments to the top 500 corporate jobs worldwide. This committee has its counterparts in each of Exxon's 12 regional and operating companies and national affiliates. Every manager around the world, beginning at the field operations level, has the responsibility to prepare a succession plan for the long-range replacement needs of his company. He also prepares and implements individual development plans for each executive identified as having high potential. Plans include a five-year advancement schedule, together with his best estimate of how high in the company the man is capable of advancing. The high-fliers are identified early, moved around and helped to grow and develop. The basis system includes a hierarchy and classification of all executive positions. This helps to determine the relative importance of jobs.

The total remuneration system is aimed at rewarding the best people and encouraging them to build their careers within the company. A planned attrition is built into the organization. Not everyone can reach a top position, and this is determined by a formal appraisal system which discriminates between the good and marginal performers at all levels. It provides essentially for the continuing upward mobility of the top 10 per cent and the elimination of the bottom 10 per cent. Every effort is made in this system to ensure that the people with high potential are not buried or overlooked. There is an annual development appraisal, which each manager has to complete for each of his subordinates. It includes 25 performance factors, which are rated on a scale ranging from (1) outstanding to (5) inadequate. Performance and promotability evaluations are cross-checked for consensus with several key executives: at least the next two-higher levels of management must concern themselves with the evaluation of a man by his manager, particularly among the senior-level positions within a big company.

Great emphasis is placed upon the annual executive development review. For example, the chief executive of the national subsidiary in Germany reviews his executive development plans with the European manager. This review includes detailed tabulations of replacement plans for key executives, and incorporates first, second and third possible replacement candidates. Development opportunities are created as necessary, to move executives across functional and regional lines. Mobility is paramount; and although the high-fliers are not told they have been selected as such, it becomes obvious through their very rapid movement, from job to job, all over the world. By the time a man has reached the age of 35, he should already be moving up rapidly in the hierarchy. For Exxon, life without its system of management development would be unthinkable.

Others

There are numerous other companies that work hard at developing management talent. Their growth rates in volume and profits reflect this effort. IBM, General Electric, Xerox, all continually stay on or near the top because they recruit the best and then train, develop, broaden and advance them as rapidly as their abilities will permit. Many have separate management schools, wherein courses vary from two to sixteen weeks to train all levels of managers. The levels are grouped: young high-potentials, middle managers, and senior executives.

When a small- or medium-sized company has to recruit a senior manager, they inevitably go to the large company, which has developed a professional cadre of managers. The large companies, in turn, go to larger companies, through executive search firms, looking for greater professionalism in their managers. Most small- and medium-sized companies do too little in developing their managers, so they do not grow. The corporate giants seldom, if ever, seek top managers from the latter, since these firms do not develop management talent.

9.3   Outside institutions

There are hundreds of consultants, universities, non-profit-making institutions, government-owned education facilities, that provide an unending variety of specialized and general courses to prepare an individual for international management. They offer many advantages, the chief of which is exposure to other managers from other companies and other countries at the same organization levels. This allows an exchange of ideas and experiences necessary for managers going on foreign assignments. It gets them away from a totally company-minded outlook and imparts multinational management concepts.

The institutions have as faculty members, specialists in each functional area, who have had broad, international experience and often general-management experience. They have usually acted as consultants to a variety of transnational corporations from several nations. The length of the courses ranges from one week to eight months; in some cases, a master's degree is granted over an extended period of one to two years. The most popular institutions include:

The American Management Association and its affiliates worldwide

Courses/Studies
    Course for presidents:
        Principles and practices of a chief executive.
        Multinational management.
        International collective bargaining.
        Preparing to go abroad: for wives.

Methodology
> Lecture and informal discussion groups, led by experts, successful
> businessmen.
> Use of audiovisual aids and handout materials, case-study method.

Centre of Industrial Studies (CEI), Geneva, Switzerland

Courses/Studies
> International executive course:
>> Special studies related exclusively to international business.
>> French.
>> Marketing, finance, investments.
>> Impact of changing environment in business and on its executives.
>> Studies in specific international business problems.

Methodology
> Formal and informal.
> Frequent meetings: students and faculty.
> Industry studies and field trips.
> Visual aids and case studies.

Centre for Exchange of International Technology (CEIT), Cahors, France

Courses
> Cultural, social, political and economic studies of all areas of the
> world.
> Society, international politics, culture and civilization.
> The individual in international service.
> Language options.
> Specific international business problems.
> Programme for wives.

Methodology
> Similar to Centre of Industrial Studies.

Columbia University, New York City, USA

Courses/Studies
> Executive programme for international managers:
>> The manager in the international economy.
>> General management.
>> Quantitative controls and management techniques.
>> Impact of and on the international businessman in a foreign
>> environment.

Methodology

Extensive use of international business problems.

Outstanding businessmen as guest lecturers.

Field trips, company visitations.

Institute for Study of Methods of Management of the Enterprise (IMEDE), Lausanne, Switzerland

Courses/Studies

Annual programme leading to the MBA degree.

Advanced management seminars.

General management business. International orientation: all areas of the world. Harvard case-study method.

Managing the international company, corporate committee.

Environmental influences on international business.

Methodology

Case studies from real-life international experiences.

Audiovisual aids, discussion groups: formal and informal.

Extensive use of field trips, guest speakers and a variety of real international business management problems.

Courses in English and in French.

Institute of Superior Studies of the Business (IESE), Barcelona, Spain

Courses/Studies

International programme on national management of multinational firms.

Analyses and studies of multinational firms, specific problems and solutions.

Operation of multinational enterprises.

Methodology

Similar to IMEDE.

Institute of European Business Administration (INSEAD), Fontainebleau, France

Courses/Studies

Similar to Stanford advanced management programme.

Annual programme and courses of shorter duration.

Offers master's degree, with a focus on Europe and North America; uses Harvard case-study method.

Direction and operation of business in Europe and North America.

Multinational management.
Organization development.
Exposure to foreign business cultures.
Quantitative methods.
Behavioural sciences in multinational environment.
Methodology
Similar to IMEDE.

International Marketing Institute (in conjuction with Harvard Business School), Cambridge, Massachusetts, USA

Courses/Studies
Market development, management and research in foreign areas.
Major emphasis on international marketing.
Study of US multinational companies.
Methodology
Harvard case-study method, and study of specific marketing problems.

Northwestern University Graduate School of Business Administration, Burgenstock, Switzerland

Courses/Studies
Institute for international management.
Role of the multinational enterprise, operation, methods, policies, and effects on environment.
The effect of a foreign environment on the enterprise's economic, social, political goals and means of implementation.
Methodology
Lecture, discussion, case study, problems.

For more comprehensive information on institutions which provide services and courses in international management development, please refer to: N. G. McNulty, *Training Managers – The International Guide* (New York 1969). This is the only complete reference guide to mid-career-management and executive-development programmes throughout the world. It is cross-indexed for easy reference, and provides information for evaluation and selection of programmes, giving data on:

Programme character and description.
Geographic location.
Class schedules, costs and dates.

Typical job titles of participants.

Teaching methods.

Curriculum syllabus and faculty.

Graduate degree programmes in modern management.

The only drawback is the fact that it was published in 1969, and hence information may be out of date, particularly with regard to curriculum and costs, but it is still a useful guide.

A number of developing and developed countries have their own organizations and institutions to teach general business management. They often recruit from, and establish close relationships with, outstanding universities: for example, the New Centre for Management Studies in Iran makes liberal use of Harvard faculty members for its MBA programme. The growth of such centres shows that many people are now concerned with the development of professional managers.

International manager development is a total programme; a process designed to raise the managerial abilities, both of local nationals and all those concerned with the parent company's nondomestic markets. The future managers of transnational corporations must be in tune with all parts of the world they service: this can affect the ways they manage their businesses. Moreover, companies are beginning to recognize that a sharp and complete division between their domestic and international operations can split the company down the middle. A number of firms have overreacted and dissolved the international headquarters as such, placing the product responsibility for international operations under the domestic division or product head. This is just as bad as, if not worse than, keeping the international activities totally separate from the domestic ones. The interchange of products, ideas, technology and services is absolutely necessary if a mega-company is to utilize all its global resources fully.

A growing number of corporations are moving in the direction of appointing to the board individuals from within and outside the company, who have had years of personal experience in a foreign country. This makes good sense inasmuch as overall corporate policy in allocation of resources needs perspective and balance.

9.4   Conclusion

Despite the high costs, the uncertainty, and the difficulty of measuring accurately international management development efforts, more and more companies are adopting plans and programmes to develop their managers.

Many enterprises which have been active in this endeavour continue to expand. The company is very rare which, once having started a manager-development effort, abandons it. Once a corporation has a system, they try, not always successfully, to improve it, to achieve their aim: to have available promotable executives and back-ups as and when needed.

Because the survival of any business is dependent on the present and future performance of its managers, management development is a vital issue which is receiving a great deal of the time and attention of the most senior executives – the small handful at the top. Highly sophisticated programmes are not necessary, provided that the chief executive officer and his staff are committed to excellence in short-term performance and are insistent on being prepared for tomorrow. Even the small- and medium-sized multinational can begin with a sound business scheme. This will, by definition, include:

Business, organization and manpower plans.

An estimation of which positions will need to be added or created within the next three to five years.

A knowledge of who might fill the positions within the company, including anticipated vacancies because of death, retirement and resignations.

A simple performance appraisal system, which identifies strengths and weaknesses of present incumbent managers.

Plans to correct underachievement and deficiencies.

Plans to broaden existing managers.

Select, outside, advance recruitment and training, to fill anticipated voids in advance.

Simple techniques of job rotation, task-force assignments, temporary or special assignments, supplemented by select, short-term outside education.

Making each manager responsible to develop a back-up for himself and including this responsibility in the man's appraisal of performance.

Conducting informal organization and manpower reviews with all senior managers.

Getting rid of deadwood.

Providing the climate and remuneration system to attract and retain the highest quality management.

Ensuring that the corporate human resource manager is a professional, who is able and willing to invest a significant portion of his time to the tasks of:

Identifying young, high-potential performers.

Teaching and counselling executives on how to develop people: management-by-objectives, delegation, discussing performance.

Providing methods and techniques for developing executives, by conducting in-house seminars, to raise the level of professionalism within the company and simultaneously to help to improve business results.

When the line executives, starting at the top, accept as one of their most important goals and responsibilities the development of capable managers under their direction, the process will spread very rapidly. The techniques are considerably less important than the attitude and the climate for development.

If a company has to go outside to hire an executive more than once in filling five vacancies, it will come to the grim realization that there is little long-term prospect of its growth and prosperity.

PART FOUR
THE FUTURE

Introduction

In the world business environment a growing number of forces are emerging which significantly influence the employer/employee relationship, and hence necessitate a more professional approach to human resource management. Some of the more important influences, together with their implications for professional human resource management, are as follows:

The world business environment

Implications for human resource management

Increasing government influence in business:
    Further growth, before
      decline, of nationalism.

Preparing managers to cope with the sociopolitical dimensions of jobs.
Policies for repatriation of expatriates.
Training and development of local nationals for senior management responsibility.

Imbalances in population and economic growth:
    Polarization of developing
    and developed countries.

Reallocation of human as well as technical resources.

Increasing demands for social reform:
    Individualism *vs.* pluralism.

Living with industrial democracy:
    The social audit.
    Social accounting and accountability.

Interdependence of the transnational corporation and the world society:
    The disappearance of the transnational's independence.

A new role in society:
    Social costs *vs.* opportunity costs *vs.* profit optimization.

The world business environment (cont.)

The monetary crisis:
    Continuing inflation.
    Individual tax burdens.
    Effects on search for new
        markets.

Inability to predict the volatile
    business situation:
    Impact on present-day
        budgeting and forecasting.
    Reduction in short-term
        profitability.

Decreasing role of international
    trade unions:
    More government legislation.
    More local autonomy.
    Public intolerance for strikes.
    Emergence of works councils.

A new role for the chief executive
    officer of the transnational
    corporation:
    The leadership crisis.
    Disappearance of the
        technocrat.

New dimensions in human resource
    management:
    Policy level considerations.

Implications for human resource management (cont.)

Executive remuneration.
Social implications of shifting
    profits.
The management audit in joint
    ventures.

Forecasting the sociopolitical
    climate.
New forms of organization:
    Increasing decentralization.
    Restructuring management
        jobs.
Management-by-objectives for
    quick action *vs.* delayed
    reaction.

Collective bargaining strategy at the
    local level.
Retention of management
    initiative.

New concepts in organization
    design.
Preparation of industry's future
    leaders.

First a businessman, then a
    personnel manager:
    Human engineering at all
        levels.
A blend of business
    sophistication and social
    science.
Problems of executive
    mobility.

Implications for human resource management (cont.)

Career planning as part of the
    employment contract.
The general managers of the
    future?

This final Part is intended to stimulate thought, and action, among chief executives of transnational corporations who, in the quest for new profits and market opportunities, too often neglect the human element — the most important factor in any business venture. It is intended to encourage a realistic reappraisal of the international business environment a reappraisal that has profound implications for human resource management.

While there are some stabilizing elements in world society, there are also many disquieting trends, which, if ignored, will quickly lead to new patterns of control which will make future international business expansion impossible.

The stabilizing elements include a move towards a single world society which will ultimately be superimposed on the many national units which exist today. This will lead perhaps to the removal of trade barriers, economic sanctions and restrictions, protective tariffs and limitations on intercontinental communications, work and travel. There is also a growing economic interdependence among nations, which may eventually make political boundaries and ideological differences obsolete. That will foster a world economic, monetary and social system, and ultimately the end of war, which no nation will be able to afford. However, until mankind matures and assumes its rightful posture as one human family, it is the businessman who must accept responsibility for social change and progress. Governments are slow to react, except nationalistically. The world lacks the political leadership to bring about the *almost* visionary reforms suggested here. But it is business, with its vast resources, which can and must take the initiative in making the world a better place in which to live and work.

10

Towards social reform

Demand for social reform is becoming one of the greatest challenges to management's ingenuity. This chapter explores the most significant elements in that demand.

10.1 Industrial democracy

One development which is having a major impact on the management of human resources is the movement for employee participation. European governments have enacted far more legislation in this area than has the US; but even where employees are not by law given participation rights, their expectations of how employers should fulfil their social responsibilities have increased. Employee action to thwart corporate decisions which impinge on their personnel is often tacitly favoured by government. This alliance circumscribes even further the right of management to make unilateral decisions. The trend seems set to continue and to be reinforced by external and internal pressures on top management.

Industrial democracy varies in its application

Loosely defined, industrial democracy is the participation of company employees in the decision-making process. The use of the term varies between European countries. In West Germany it covers the legal requirements for worker representation or supervisory boards (*Mitbestimmung*). In Sweden, Norway and Denmark 'company democracy' is a term for decentralizing and diffusing decision-making, stemming either from statutory requirements or from management initiative. The term 'industrial democracy' in Britain is usually limited to worker representation on boards of directors. '*Auto-gestion*' and '*gestion démocratique*' in France have become the objectives of certain political parties and labour unions, and are closer to the Yugoslav model of worker control. These interpretations may differ, but they all require a readiness on the part of management to share with their employees some of the decision-making, particularly in the areas directly affecting their working lives. Linked to the imprecise definition of industrial democracy is the wide range of participative practices in different countries. These extend from the full self-management by Yugoslavian workers of all companies with more than five employees, to the spreading use of flexible working hours. It is evident that the degree of employee participation depends not only on the political, economic and social environment, but on the history of labour/management relations.

Although the Swedish model of participation is extolled by many observers, any attempt to graft it, without modification, on to another country's labour relations system would be unsuccessful. It depends to a great degree on the unusual cooperation that exists between LO (the manual workers' central organization) and SAF (the employers' federation). This shared normative system results, in part, from the centralization of the union and employee federations, and realization, over thirty years ago, that their internecine conflict, if uncontrolled, could only be harmful to their interests. In addition, there has been a close relationship between LO and the Social Democratic Party, which has long been committed to social reform. The Social Democrats have been (except briefly in 1936) in power since 1932: this means that Sweden has benefited from an unmatched social stability, with a government pledged to social improvements. Although this explanation of Swedish labour relations is simplistic, it highlights major differences with other European countries, such as France, Italy or Britain. In Britain, attitudes of unions and employers, Socialists and Conservatives, have, in recent years, hardened into the 'them' and 'us' positions, leaving little room for amicable cooperation in achieving common goals. In fact, there seem to be no common goals. So each country has to evolve its own philosophy and processes, those best suited to its background, while drawing on other countries' experience; and hope for that one 'moment's insight (which) is sometimes worth a life's experience'.

The different types of industrial democracy currently existing in certain European countries are shown in Figure 10 : 1. They are divided into major categories, such as financial participation, works councils, participation in management or in organizational change. It is clear that countries are by no means at the same level of development: trends are moving in the same direction, but not at the same speed. The countries shown have been chosen to demonstrate the diverse approaches. Yugoslavia is, of course, the extreme example of an economy controlled mainly by the workers. This has been so since the end of World War II, when President

Figure 10 : 1

INDUSTRIAL DEMOCRACY IN SELECTED EUROPEAN COUNTRIES

Country	Participation in management	Profit-sharing	Works councils	Participation through organizational change
Yugoslavia	All decisions made by workers, either through referendum or the workers' council. Managers elected by workers' council, which delegates to them necessary authority.	All companies with more than five employees are owned 100 per cent by workers (nationalization by which *workers* not state have control). No shares or capital gains.	Introduced permanently in 1952. Central Workers' Council controls an Operating Co-ordination Board (workers holding managerial jobs). President runs different profit centres.	Workers' council makes all decisions.
Germany	Worker representatives have equal power on supervisory board, in coal and steel industries, a third of place elsewhere. (Mandatory: all stock and limited-liability companies with more than 500 employees.) Law proposed to give workers	Remuneration levels and profit-sharing distribution set through collective agreements. Proposed 'asset formation' legislation: firms will have to contribute shares to central fund, frozen for employee accounts for seven years.	Established in 1952, strengthened in 1971. Powerful councils, supported by employers and unions. Each unit has workers' council with voting power on personnel matters and advisory capacity on others. Obligatory for all companies	Experiments in job design and flexible working hours, e.g., Bosch, Klöckner—Möller, Daimler—Benz and Siemens. Government now subsidizing some experiments.

parity in all stock and limited-liability companies with more than 2000 employees in 1975.

with more than five employees.

Netherlands Works councils (with shareholders and management) can nominate candidates for supervisory-board vacancies. Works councils and shareholders can veto actual selection. No direct worker membership.

No interest.

Created by law in 1950. 1971 amendments gave councils greater powers. Unions and employees consider councils to be very important. Workers' representatives tend to take company point of view. Workers' council can veto board selection, codecides on personnel matters and has advisory capacity on others.

Employers' groups and unions support participative experiments. Major example: Philips.

Sweden Employees elect two members to the board of directors.

Union proposal expected in 1976.

Collective agreements in 1946 created councils and they were given more power in 1970. Employers support them and have often voluntarily expanded their role.

Most advanced country. Employers and unions have gained main experience since 1969, when the results of Norwegian experiments in participation published. Companies conducting projects, include Granges, Saab-Scania, Volvo, Scan-Väst, Kockums.

Figure 10 : 1 (cont.)

Country	Participation in management	Profit-sharing	Works councils	Participation through organizational change
France	Worker directors have two non-voting seats on boards. Employers and unions hostile to worker-director voting power.	1967 law: companies must contribute small part of annual profits to employee funds, frozen for five years (plans afoot to alter or abolish 'frozen' period). 1973: tax benefits for employee share-purchase plans.	Created by law in 1945. Not usually a powerful body. Runs social programme. Cooperates on improving working conditions. Advises on training programme. Is informed and consulted on organizational/economic matters.	Growing interest, but union hostility frequent. Projects: BSN, General Foods, Faiveley, Leroy-Somer, Télémécanique.

Tito won the loyalty of the population. The system has a positive impact on social values, since manual work is more highly rated than managerial skill. This, in turn, dampens any incentive to take on managerial responsibilities. Collective decision-making tends to slow up the speed of a company's reactions (a criticism, incidentally, levelled at the German *Mitbestimmung*), and there is too great an orientation towards short-term planning and towards production. Economic growth has been satisfactory (in Communist terms), but the system certainly needs a higher standard of worker education and of awareness of the interdependence of capital and labour that exists in most Western European countries. Such maturity exists in Sweden and to some extent in the US and Germany (where the Union DGB is one of the largest employers), since employers and employees share the same value system. It is interesting to note that Germany has moved a long way towards codecision-making (at least in theory), virtually ignoring financial participation, while France, under President de Gaulle's leadership, launched a profit-sharing scheme, but with ineffective real participation in management. Until now, French unions, like British ones, have been loth to take on the responsibilities of management. Ostensibly they fear that their elected representatives would adopt the management viewpoint, thus becoming isolated from their base. For advanced systems of codetermination to work well, in the interests of both employers and employees, a high standard of living seems to be a prerequisite. There is otherwise a tendency for meetings to become forums for airing grievances and attempting negotiations.

Until now we have been considering those aspects of industrial democracy which have been the subject of legislation: board representation, works councils and financial participation. There are, however, other forms of participative activity which are more readily accepted and implemented by management. There is an unfortunate tendency nowadays to label as 'industrial democracy' every system which is even vaguely participative in nature, such as job enrichment or flexible working hours. We say 'unfortunate' because the term itself may to some managers, more particularly in the US, be synonymous with abdication to Communist militants and/or to psychiatrists, and therefore incompatible with the self-imposed task of every good manager, which is to make a profit. Without delving too deeply into the motives of those who first experimented with job enrichment, it can be said that it has resulted very often in increased productivity. lower absenteeism, and other benefits to all parties. If this were not the case, it is doubtful whether participative management (from management-by-objectives downwards) would be half so popular. There are basically, two unlegislated approaches to industrial democracy or participative management: flexible job design, and changing the power structure. The first involves job rotation, already practised often in the motor industry, and job enlargement; also the worker changes jobs to increase the variety of tasks he performs. In the second, the number of tasks making up one job is expanded; and in job enrichment, the variety of tasks and the need for judgement increases. These changes are not in themselves participative, since they can be ordained by management. The second approach, involving a change in the power structure, means that management allows workers more decision-making power, since they are in many cases better able to handle certain facets of their jobs than their supervisors. The workers often in fact design their own autonomous work groups, setting their own standards, controlling workflow, etc. Progress in these concrete areas is likely to have more impact than increased worker representation at board level. These groups appeal more to the basic human need to belong to a social group, since the routine, boring jobs created by automation become even more frustrating when the individual feels isolated, and cannot relate his work to a final product. This alienation has increased more rapidly in recent years due to higher educational levels, increased affluence and decreased adherence to the Puritan work ethic. Until recently, the economic boom in most Western countries meant that there were enough jobs available for nearly everybody (this was truer of Europe than the US), and the menial tasks were performed by immigrant workers — Turks, Jamaicans, Portuguese, Algerians. This contributed to the mental rebellion of indigent workers, who were then able to focus on obtaining job satisfaction as well as financial rewards. It is likely that certain expectations have been built up, and will continue, helped by Government legislation, in spite of the recession.

There is an increasing number of experiments in participation taking place, and Sweden is by far the most advanced country in this area. The major impetus to their efforts came after the results of Norwegian experiments were published in 1969. Although Swedish unions had been antagonistic in the 1960s, when they recognized the value of these experiments they cooperated with employers in launching many new types of participation. These trials have been astonishingly successful, both in terms of worker satisfaction and productivity.

Volvo–Sweden. Volvo is the best-known of these experiments, particularly after their construction of a factory at Kalmar based on the principles of work groups.

The high educational level of Swedish youth led them to rebel against the classic mode of automobile production; turnover and absenteeism were high. This caused Volvo to start up a massive programme for improving working conditions (Kr.150–200 million by 1974). The objective was to allow each individual to achieve self-realization in his work; but the success was limited by the traditional assembly line, as the worker still felt isolated, with no sense of personal satisfaction in his work. Volvo did not rely on their extensive recreational facilities and restrooms to improve worker morale; the workers were integrated into groups, which were to a large extent organized by themselves, and the immediate supervisors were given systematic training to help them adjust to their new roles. Encouraged by the success of these new modes of work organization, Volvo conceived and constructed a new factory at Kalmar (encouraged by the government), which would be based on these concepts. The initial study took two years (the same time as for usual plants) and Volvo consulted national and local unionists and representatives of their existing factories, incorporating many of their suggested changes. Volvo's basic desire was to make the factory more human: where everyone could know each other (therefore not more than 600–700 people); most of the factory where assembly work took place would give on the landscape outside, with material stocks, some maintenance operations and the final product existing in the centre; working groups of 15 to 25 people, who would be responsible for all activities necessary to assemble the cars, including division of tasks, method of assembly, working speed, etc.; each group would work in a separate unit, with their own stock of materials readily available; the unit would have its own entrance, lobby WCs, restroom and sauna. Volvo was prepared to pay approximately 10 per cent above the normal costs of factory construction, estimating tha the easier working conditions and greater latitude for the workers would make the investment worthwhile.

Saab-Scania, Sweden. When Saab-Scania commissioned a new plan for manufacturing and assembly of petrol engines, a new design approach was used for the assembly department. Groups of three to four are responsible for assembling the whole engine (minor preassembly work is completed elsewhere). There is a high level of individual and group freedom; materials are handled smoothly, being sent to the group only when one engine is completed. There is no mechanical control of the assembly workflow. Of the seven work groups, one is a training group. Each group can determine its own work distribution, and the maximum cycle time is now 30 minutes, compared with the traditional assembly time of 1.8 minutes. Although with this design more floor space is needed, and at any one moment there is more material tied up than in conventional factories, there are substantial advantages. The autonomy of the units makes them less vulnerable to external disturbances, more flexible, while productivity is of the same order as classic assembly lines.

Olivetti, Italy. In 1971, Olivetti signed a labour agreement, committing itself to a programme (to embrace 2000 workers) of job restructuring, skills expansion by greater job rotation, new production techniques, and a change in job specifications. These activities were specifically geared to the Italian perception of job enrichment as a means to increase the qualifications of workers to enable upward mobility. The changes involved the cooperation of workers and unions.

A major project was conducted at Ivrea, in northern Italy. It involved the production of a complex accounting machine, assembled on a long line, with 50–60 works stations and task time-cycles of one to five minutes. The line was broken into eight shorter ones, containing 4–6 work stations, while the time-cycles were usually 20 to 40 minutes, often 50 minutes. The worker was now able to have a more significant idea of his total contribution, particularly when given additional training in order to rotate jobs. The workers were given the opportunity to test their own work, and foremen could now leave more of the details to each worker, freeing them for high-level supervision.

Product quality increased noticeably, morale was higher and labour conflicts became less frequent and manageable. This form of work design would be particularly appropriate to modern products with a short life span.

ICI, UK. The company (100 000 employees) initiated a series of programmes to involve its employees more in the running of the company. ICI and the unions agreed that a worker should be employed to the best of his ability and be paid in recognition of his contribution.

At the Gloucester nylon-filament plant (2500 persons) discussion groups were formed, to include foremen, shop stewards and workers. Meetings were held regularly and memberships rotated, while management tried to persuade the suspicious shop stewards that they genuinely wanted dialogue. Eventually the groups started a job assessment study, with employees becoming involved in assessing their own jobs. They started to manage their own jobs and make concrete improvement suggestions. By the end of 1973, the plant had a 20 per cent saving in employee numbers, pay gains up 15 per cent, and grievances diminished.

In another division of ICI, the organization was changed to give design engineers more satisfaction, by increasing their responsibilities. Senior engineers were given complete independence in their projects; others were given as much independence as they could handle. Each engineer could choose outside consultants himself, spend the money on a project that was required, and select his own junior staff. This resulted in less need for supervision, decisions of a higher quality, increased job satisfaction, ability to handle an increased workload, and greater ease in external recruitment.

Philips Lamps, Netherlands. Philips started its organizational change programme in the early 1960s, relying largely on the theories of Herzberg, McGregor and Likert. They now use the methods propounded by the London Tavistock Institute, which see the people and the technical systems in the organization as an entity, whose potential can be realized in favourable conditions for group working (what they call 'sociotechnical systems').

Philips approached this at three levels, the first two simultaneously and the third later in 1970. The most radical idea in work structuring was the design of a television-set assembly unit. Work groups of seven assembled complete TV sets, instead of on a continuous assembly line. Groups were responsible for a large part of organizing their work, giving the members a sense of shared purpose and a more challenging job. Profitability increased 12 per cent and worker satisfaction also increased. Similar methods are being used in the manufacture of colour TV sets. There seems to have been an overall improvement in 12 projects, from the point of view of quality, quantity, turnover, absenteeism, although some were less successful than others.

At the same time Philips was moving towards the improvement of white-collar and blue-collar working conditions, on such matters as hours, monthly pay, pension eligibility, etc. Both sets of workers now benefit from a participative target-setting process, and performance evaluation.

By 1970 Philips launched another project on work consultation, in an attempt to get workers more involved in management. Like ICI, discussion groups were organized at local plants, to discuss plans for their units and existing problems. Headquarters advised units on how to run discussion groups. In spite of resistance from middle managers, afraid of losing their control of employees, these groups have expanded in 35 out of Philips' 85 units. These activities are often strengthened by the works councils, which wield considerably more power than their legal powers would suggest.

Management must analyze the consequences of greater company democracy

These few examples illustrate the different forms participation can take in different companies and countries. What are the implications for the management of companies which have not yet explored these new forms of work structuring, and employer/employee dialogue? One obvious result, of course, is the necessity for managers to adapt their attitudes to the changing expectations of their employees. Having the will to manage does not necessarily mean using an authoritarian approach to problem-solving: employees will no longer tolerate being treated as non-persons. Although the ability of management to manoeuvre will be more limited, they will be able to exercise greater creativity in their planning and daily administration. They will benefit from more involvement by workers in managing their own work. There is evidence to show that a more participative management style can unleash reserves of interest and energy in employees which were previously unsuspected. The majority of documented studies show increases in employee satisfaction and in productivity. It requires flexible behaviour and emotional maturity for a manager (particularly first-line supervision) not to feel threatened by these changes. Although at first sight managers appear to have lost the initiative, this is not necessarily the case. Statutory requirements require management to accept and implement the brand of industrial democracy decreed. But in countries where there is no legislation to date, companies would do well to keep ahead by lobbying governments to adopt the system most appropriate to them.

The 1975 Green Paper from the EEC on 'Employee participation and company structure in the European Community', will, in the longer term, affect British and Swedish companies operating in the EEC. Very briefly, the European company will have a two-tier board, with employee representatives. Provision has been made for the employees of a European company to influence decision-making:

Conditions of employment may be regulated by European collective agreements.

European works councils are to be formed in every European company having establishments in more than one member state. (Such a council is informed of company affairs and has a veto right on certain aspects of personnel policy.)

Employees will have the right to participate in the appointment of a third of the members of the company's supervisory board.

These proposals are still under discussion in Brussels, but something along their lines is likely to be agreed, since the Community is committed to integrated social policies. The EEC has also issued a report on asset formation, whose objective is 'to contribute positive suggestions towards the formulation of a clear policy aimed at a fairer distribution of wealth throughout the Community'. This policy seems further from realization than the European company proposals, but it is mirrored by recent Swedish union demands.

Figure 10 : 2 shows the various degrees of industrial democracy that

Figure 10 : 2

DIFFERENT FORMS OF INDUSTRIAL DEMOCRACY

	Board representation	Works councils	Financial participation
Full industrial democracy	Worker directors with voting rights: Minority or parity board membership (Germany). 100 per cent ownership by workers and of board membership (Yugoslavia).	Legislated councils which take decisions, while management implements (Yugoslavia).	100 per cent ownership by workers of company assets and of profits (Yugoslavia).
	Minority number of non-voting worker directors, representing either specific company personnel or labour in general (France).	Legislated councils with voting rights on most major issues (Germany).	Partial but major ownership by workers of company.
	Some board members may be nominated by personnel, but no direct worker membership (Netherlands).	Works councils, with right of access to wide range of information, and voting power on certain matters (Netherlands).	Minor participation through gift of shares, based on profitability or asset formation, unrelated to individual performance (France). Opportunity for employees to purchase stock (France, USA).

Figure 10 : 2 (cont.)

	Board representation	Works councils	Financial participation
Minimal industrial democracy	Board members represent outside share-holders or minority pressure groups only (USA, UK). No worker directors.	No works councils (UK unlegislated). Infrequent, non-legislated councils, with limited role (France): Information or minimal consultation on minor issues. Token responsibilities (e.g., canteen, health and safety).	No participation by workers in either assets or profits. Top executives and share-holders only benefit from company's *profitable* operation (USA, UK).

can exist in the major areas. Just as it is unnecessary to rush into a situation of workers' control, it is also unnecessary to adopt *all* measures of industrial democracy at the *same* level: that is, it would be perfectly feasible to have parity of worker directors, while workers only had limited financial participation.

A more prosaic level of participation, but one which is likely to have more impact on the employees, is shown in Figure 10 : 3. The major areas involving human resources are outlined, with different levels of possible action over industrial democracy for each. Thus the management of a multinational corporation can compare the current stage of development of each of their subsidiaries in *each area*, and estimate what actions are most appropriate for each company. Hence, they might be prepared to have full participation, for instance, in training and performance evaluation, while reserving the right to take the final decision on plant locations, etc. It is in fact like the sort of 'shopping-basket' approach often used in remuneration packages. A world of caution: once experiments of this nature are initiated, it is virtually impossible to withdraw and, in fact, the demand for participation will probably increase. At the outset, therefore, it is difficult to foresee how far the company will have to go.

The immediate future will bring an increase in industrial democracy, particularly in Europe, in spite of the ambivalent attitude of unions and some management. In mid-1974, the UK Labour government issued a Green Paper, proposing a company law to institute a two-tier system, which would be even more extreme than the EEC's Fifth Directive. (Interestingly enough, liabilities usually carried by directors in cases of breach of duty, etc., will continue to apply to shareholders' representatives, but the worker directors will not be subject to these obligations, only to the fees.) If the employers' federation, the CBI, had attempted to influence government and public opinion earlier, instead of setting its face against the whole idea, perhaps the extremism could have been averted. The Fifth Directive of the EEC came in for a good deal of criticism in proposing supervisory boards, but it is likely to become effective, at least in the longer term, as it is linked to the EEC's European Company Statute. Another element of EEC policy which could eventually be approved by the Council of Ministers is a directive which proposes improvements in employees' protection against corporate concentrations. The provisions would apply to all mergers, acquisitions, or link-ups involving EEC-based companies (even if a non-EEC firm is involved). To protect employees' rights previously acquired in one of the companies, there will be an automatic transfer of a contractual employment relationship from the previous to the new employer. Mergers will not be considered adequate grounds for a reduction of the labour force: other solutions will have to be

Figure 10 : 3a

DEGREES OF PARTICIPATION AFFECTING HUMAN RESOURCE MANAGEMENT

	Company/Factory change	Organization	Personnel planning	Environment and the workplace	Safety and health
Full industrial democracy	Works councils must approve any changes which affect personnel, such as mergers, acquisitions, plant closedowns or re-locations.	Personnel representatives decide which changes should take place. Personnel representatives have right of veto on any organizational change which they deem to be a disadvantage to em-ployees.	Personnel representatives have right of veto on overall manpower plan prepared by manage-ment.	Management proposes changes in construction, technical installations, work processes/methods, workplaces, working hours. Personnel representatives/works councils have final approval.	Personnel control safety committee and agreed budget. Personnel initiate im-provements in safety programmes and medical facilities within budget.
	Works councils are consulted about pro-posed major changes. Works council has voting power on minor changes involv-ing indirect re-locations.	Management and person-nel representatives work together, defining organization needs and outlining final changes. Personnel representatives decide on employee groupings.	Staff specialists work with personnel repre-sentatives on manpower plan. Management has final approval of overall plan.	Management and em-ployees determine together new processes, construction, etc. Personnel allowed flexibility in choosing working hours, making minor changes in work-place conditions.	Management and employees cooperate on safety and medical projects. Personnel responsible for implementation on proposed safety programmes.

| Works councils are informed in advance of major changes affecting personnel employment. | Management informs personnel representatives of proposed organizational structure, justifies its actions and solicits their opinions and suggestions for change. | Manpower plan prepared by management staff specialists. Works council informed of overall plan and its suggestions solicited. | Works council or individuals are consulted by management on working hours, working conditions, installations, methods, etc. | Management runs safety committee, with consultation/participation by employees. Management takes final decision on safety and medical matters. |
| Management has unilateral decision-making power to approve mergers, acquisitions, plant closedowns, plant relocations, without prior information to personnel. | Management imposes organization structure, departmental layout, grouping of employees. | Manpower plan prepared by management staff specialists. Plan implemented without reference to works council. | Management carries out any changes in installations, work methods, without prior consultation with works council. | Management responsible for initiating all improvements in safety procedures and medical facilities. |

Minimal industrial democracy

Figure 10 : 3b

	Selection, hiring and transfer	Dismissal	Training and education	Salary administration
Full industrial democracy	Employees' representatives have final approval of all hirings and transfers.	Personnel representatives/works council have right of veto on dismissals proposed by management, either individual or collective.	Works council prepare annual training plans. Council approves expenditures within agreed budgets. Council assists in implementation of programmes.	Works council/personnel representatives decide salary procedures and policies. Council approves individual and collective salary-increase application.
	Personnel representatives must be consulted before hiring or transferring key personnel.	Management consults with personnel representatives on its intention to dismiss individuals or groups of employees. Management has final approval.	Management formulates annual training and education plans. Works council's suggestions for change incorporated into plan and they assist in implementation.	Management and personnel representatives negotiate policies, procedures, annual increase for *all* employees.
	Management consults personnel representatives on policies and procedures, man and job specifications. Management has final approval in implementation.	Management informs works council of its intention to dismiss group of workers. Final decision rests with management.	Management outlines training plans to works council for information purposes. Management implements programmes and consults with individuals on their training needs and wishes.	Management decides policy and procedures. Personnel representatives negotiate with management annual salary increases for certain sections of employees.

Minimal industrial democracy	Management determines man and job specifications and policies/procedures for use in selection, hiring and transfer. Management has final approval.	Management has unilateral decision-making power to dismiss individuals without referring to works council.	Management formulates annual training and development plans. Management implements programmes without informing works council or consulting individuals.	Management decrees salary administration procedures and policies. Management sets remuneration unilaterally.

Figure 10 : 3c

	Performance appraisal	Job posting	Individual rights
Full industrial democracy	Works council approves questionnaires and principles of appraisal to be used. Works council acts as court of appeal to individuals who disagree with performance rating. Works council and management discuss questionnaires and appraisal principles. Management approves final form.	Works council has final say on which jobs should be advertised internally and the contents of the notice (usually all jobs must be posted). Works council consulted on which jobs should be posted and contents of advertisements.	Employee allowed to see his own file and add his own comments to contents. Employee's performance discussed with him; he can keep copy of it and can include for the files appraisal on his superior. Personal grievances settled through union hierarchy or works council members only. Individual's salary increases can be dealt with through works council or union without discussion with superior. Employee allowed to see his own file in-company with works council member. Individual's performance discussed with him and he can see the written appraisal.

Figure 10 : 3c (cont.)

	Selection, hiring and transfer	Dismissal	Training and education	Salary administration
	Performance appraisal discussed with individual.			Employee's personal grievances settled with the help of a works council or union member. Salary grievances handled by works council after discussion with superior.
	Management informs personnel representatives and individuals of principles used. Individual informed of his rating.		Management informs works council of type of jobs to be advertised. Works council suggests contents of job notices.	Employee not allowed to see his personal file, but can add comments on performance appraisal, supervisors, etc. Individual's performance appraisal discussed with him. Individual can settle personal grievance through hierarchy. Employee can negotiate salary increases.
Minimal industial democracy	Management sets appraisal principles. Principles and application not communicated to individual appraised.		Management not required to advertise jobs internally. The contents of any job notices decided by management.	Employee has no right to see his own file. Employee's performance ratings nonexistent or not discussed with him. Individual has no right of appeal in the case of personal grievance. Salary increases unilaterally decided: no negotiation.

found first. Workers' representatives will have to receive prior notice of the reasons for the proposed concentration and of the legal, social and economic consequences. The terms are here greatly simplified, but they illustrate some of the constraints likely to be facing management.

Government can also hinder company mobility, in its effort to maintain regional employment levels, by tacitly supporting worker action. An example is the workers' sit-in after Litton Industries proposed closing down two typewriter plants at Hull and Leicester, with the loss of 3200 jobs: the government was asked to provide financial support for the workers' action committee. The standards of logical assessment of financial investment no longer apply. Other companies threatened by closure have recently been taken over by the employees: Lip in France was one of the first.

Employees are, in fact, looking for more security, and an integral part of this is seen to be increased employee access to financial information and participation in decision-making. Managements will need to become more adaptive to change, sponsoring new ideas in work organization: for example, flexible working hours; and new products, for example, the design of a tractor factory (by UK University of Manchester Institute of Science and Technology), especially for autonomous work groups, with great potential for use in developing countries. Openness of mind (not weakness) on the part of management cannot help but be profitable for their companies. And companies should provide their shareholders with an annual report, showing what actions they are undertaking in the social area.

10.2   Social responsibility

An adjunct to industrial democracy is the increasing pressure on corporations to temper their pursuit of profits with a sense of social responsibility. This concept goes far beyond any paternalistic activities some companies developed to a high degree in the early part of the twentieth century, for example, Bournville in the UK. Although the welfare of employees is still of major importance, it is no longer enough. Indeed, employees now often expect to have a part in deciding the range, type and mixture of benefits that a company concedes to them. They are not prepared to accept the company's right to ordain what benefits will be available: particularly those like company houses and company shops, which led to such abuse of workers earlier this century. Some companies have adopted less visible fetters, such as low-rate loans, preferential mortgages, discounts: however, the employees, in principle, have certain discretion over their employment and use of income.

Nowadays, a company is expected to extend this concern for employee welfare to concern for the local community and the public at large. The two often overlap: when a plant produces noxious fumes and dust, which cause disease in the workforce, this affects the community, physically and psychologically. Companies have often taken advantage of a site in a high-unemployment area, or of being the major employer in the area, to slacken safety standards, to minimize pollution controls. Local inhabitants may have tolerated this for many years, constrained by the need to earn their living. More and more, however, employees, consumers and the general public are questioning the right of large corporations to manufacture unsafe products, to continue with unsafe working conditions, to produce pollution, to discriminate against various employee groups, to make false claims when marketing their products. Probably one of the major advances was Ralph Nader's indictment of General Motors. Even more important, psychologically, than the gains he made in automobile safety, is that David took on Goliath — and won. This has given new heart to pressure groups of all kinds, including consumers, with a resulting increase in legislation to combat what they consider to be corporations' abuse of the public trust.

While the US companies may have done little in the field of industrial democracy, they have been more progressive in the area of social responsibility. US consumer protection laws are still less well developed than, say, France, but they have improved. Since the end of the 1960s, the rising tide of federal, state and local laws has taken the initiative out of companies' hands, by instituting pollution controls, allowing equal opportunity to minority groups, etc. The Equal Employment Opportunity Commission has launched several lawsuits to force companies to comply with the antidiscrimination laws. The 1972 Federal Water Pollution Control Act has meant that many companies have been obliged to close down plants that did not meet the act's requirements. Companies will be compelled to meet a series of progressively, stiffer goals in the fight against water pollution, until they attain the 'zero discharge' goal by 1985.

Many American companies, when faced with the need to shoulder their social responsibilities, have spent money in a haphazard way, trying to meet only the minimum statutory standards, and not even making the best use of their expenditure. Others laid out a specific plan: defined their strengths and weaknesses in major areas (safety of design, ecological impact, employment practices, occupational health and safety, selling and advertising, consumer affairs, general employee welfare); pinpointed the opportunities and the problems; and outlined their subsequent action plans. Their approach is systematic: using either a range of analyses (Figure 10 : 4), which should enable them to come up with a precise audit of their current/projected social actions; or at the least, a brief checklist of items, showing areas needing the company's most urgent attention (Figure 10 : 5)

Figure 10 : 4

ANALYSING VARIOUS ASPECTS OF A COMPANY'S SOCIAL RESPONSIBILITIES

1 Compensation

Technique

Average salary increase per employee.
Percentage of employees participating in increase.
Percentage increase in revenues per employee.

Purpose

Shows increases in *per capita* market value, reflecting increases in productivity.
Define scope of productivity increases.
Reflects *per capita* productivity increase.

2 Fringe benefits

Technique

Survey of employee benefit preferences.
Actual and expected insurance payments for medical, life, disability and employment coverage.
Costs of in-company and external company-sponsored education courses: number, access.
Number of employees successfully completing courses: level and degree.
Costs of family benefits, such as subsidized housing, commercial centres.
Costs (in equipment, space, man-hours) of company parties, outings, athletic programmes.
Costs (in equipment, space, man-hours, R & D) of day-care services.
Costs and savings to staff of subsidized lunches, snacks, coffee, etc., and cost of employee time.
Cost of holidays, vacations, shorter working weeks.
Employee usage patterns of benefits.

Figure 10 : 4 (cont.)

Fixed and variable costs of programmes relative to optimum employee usage, e.g., day care.

Purpose

Enables comparison of costs of individual benefit programmes, with different programme mixtures which could be devised to employees' expressed preferences.

Highlights areas where company expenditure can bring highest level of employee satisfaction at lower cost.

Measures efficiency of social programmes (actual *vs.* optimum use).

Pinpoints employees *not* benefiting from training courses, for later action.

3   Quality of life

Technique

Survey of employee preferences.

Working space (square feet) per employee and cost differences between sites.

Costs of company premises *vs.* neighbourhood average, and of architects.

Cost of air conditioning, ventilation, dust extraction.

Cost of increased safety measures to meet/exceed legal requirements.

Cost of added partitions, carpeting, curtains.

Cost of trees, shrubs, grass, gardening.

Total daily parking cost (if paid by staff).

Cost of introducing job enrichment, enlargement (autonomous working groups, etc.) in productivity, salary increases, number/skill level of employees.

Purpose

Highlights areas where company expenditure can bring highest level of employee satisfaction at lowest cost.

4   Career advancement

Technique

Number, percentage of total, salary and fringe benefit costs of pro-

Figure 10 : 4 (cont.)

motions to positions of greater responsibility (minus demotion costs, where applicable).

Number of reduced voluntary resignations and the money value.

Number, increase, and equivalent cost of publications, awards and mention of company staff at public meetings, etc.

Purpose

Identifies any problems of stagnant organization.

Indicates degree of satisfaction on the part of employees.

Shows degree of exposure and type of reputation company has externally.

Measures public's image of company employees' competence.

5 Employment

Technique

Number and type of jobs created.

Percentage increase in total payroll.

Number and type of employees laid off.

Percentage of total employees and of total payroll decrease.

Cost of layoff provisions.

Number, percentage and type of employees leaving voluntarily.

Reasons for voluntary turnover.

Cost of voluntary turnover.

Number and percentage of times, and cost of company using employees' free time.

Purpose

Identifies whether and where company is creating new jobs or destroying them, particularly in high-unemployment areas.

Indicates whether business plans adequately forecast manpower utilization and identifies areas for improvement.

Highlights incidence of and reasons for voluntary turnover, and impact on total employee-skills profile.

Enables a more adequate manpower plan.

Pinpoints uneconomic use of manpower (through overtime or extra hours) and areas for improvement.

Figure 10 : 4 (cont.)

6 Equality of opportunity

Technique

Employment

Number and percentage of hourly-paid workers promoted to salaried positions.

Number and percentage of clerical employees promoted to managerial levels.

Number and percentage of minority groups employed.

Cost of salary and fringe benefits for minority groups, hourly-paid and clerical employees promoted.

Ratio of minority employees to total staff by percentage and by percentage of total salary.

Minority advancement Number, percentage, total increased salary and fringe benefit costs.

Women and non-whites given salary increases.

Women and non-whites promoted in management positions.

Total minority given salary increases and/or promoted in management positions.

Ratio of *minority salary increases* to total salary increases.

Ratio of *minority promotions* to total promotions.

Ratio of *minority managers* to total managers.

Purpose

Enables comparison of company's progress *vis-à-vis* other companies, in areas of environment, pollution, structural improvements.

Ensures sound basis for planning company's rate of progress towards defined targets and emphasizing projects falling behind schedule.

Assists company in making effective contribution to proposed government and state laws.

7 Environment

Technique

Number, percentage cost of improving environments (buildings, landscape).

Figure 10 : 4 (cont.)

Amount of paper for recycling, and cost of it being recycled.

Incidence of water, air and chemical pollution and costs of correction (calculated individually).

Cost and incidence of modifying completed or uncompleted structures, to comply with federal or state regulations.

Cost of improving packaging and product-design safety.

Purpose

Enables comparison of company's progress *vis-à-vis* other companies, in areas of environment, pollution, structural improvements.

Ensures sound basis for planning company's rate of progress towards defined targets and emphasizing projects falling behind schedule.

Assists company in making effective contribution to proposed government and state laws.

8   Public responsibility

Technique

Number, percentage, type, value of contracts having social impact.

Number, percentage, type, value of company's contribution to knowledge (patents, lectures, sabbatical leaves).

Number, type, percentage, value of awards (charities, foundations).

Number, percentage, type, value of contributions (in time or money) to public education or other institutions.

Use of local educational institutions and cost to community.

Purpose

Ensures firm basis for improving company's public image.

Enables company to refine criteria for choosing charitable projects and thereby choose those of optimum value.

Highlights contracts where company can make positive contribution (e.g., using minority suppliers, carrying out contract in high-unemployment area).

Figure 10 : 5

SOCIAL RESPONSIBILITY CHECKLIST

Social issue	Strength	Weakness	Improvement opportunities	Improvement difficulties	Possible action steps
Company policy and organization					
External environment					
Government relations.					
Community relations.					
Consumer relations.					
Pollution.					
Packaging.					
Product design safety.					
Investment relations.					
Environment.					
Company contracts.					
Business opportunities.					
Internal environment					
Organization structure and management style.					
Physical working conditions (quality of life).					

Minority groups.
Communications.
Industrial relations.
Education and training.
Compensation.
Fringe benefits.
Career advancement.
Employment.

Note to chief executive officer
Rate your company on a scale 0 (poor) to 5 (excellent): e.g., compensation practice clearly above local and/or national standards = 5.

Companies which have been prominent in this area, and have received awards, are in very different industries, and concentrate on very diverse issues:

Owens-Illinois, US. Company commitment in 1966. But in 1954 adopted new approach to paper-mill construction, which reduces pollution by 95 per cent. First company to install recovery boilers for cooking odours. Uses 50 per cent of water, and 20 per cent of chemicals needed by competitors. OI believes it will easily meet 1985 'zero discharge' goal. In 1968 OI were the first to appeal publicly to recycle glass bottles, and is actively participating in the National Centre for Resource Recovery.

Levi-Strauss & Co., US. Managers accountable for social-policy decisions as well as production and financial goals. Allocates 3 per cent of net profits to community projects (hospitals, unemployment, etc.) The community relations teams are run by local employees. Plants were integrated before the advent of the Equal Employment Opportunity Commission. In 1972 nearly 14 per cent of the company's managers and officials were women, and 10.1 per cent were classified as minority employees. A minority purchasing programme has been set up, requiring general contractors to obtain bids from minority businesses for each subcontract.

Polaroid Corp., US. 6.4 per cent of the company's 12 per cent black employees are salaried; another 3 per cent are disadvantaged. Only two out of 150 ex-convicts hired, as part of the programme, returned to prison. A subsidiary in Boston's Roxbury district is expanding, assisting 'unemployable' workers to move to other plants. The company is heavily involved in community projects in Massachusetts, including prison reform. It conducts a wideranging internal education programme, from which 20 per cent of employees have benefited. Employees working for doctorate degrees are given generous financial aid.

Coca-Cola Co., US. Were the first to sign a contract in Florida with Cesar Chavez' United Farm Workers. This abolished the crew-chief system of hiring, raised the wages, instituted fringe benefits, and allowed the workers to help set the piecework rates. They have developed permanent employees: in 1973, 300 were on hourly rates on an annual basis. 350 piecerate fruit pickers are used on maintenance work when not picking. The company has helped employees buy their own homes, and has built them subsidized houses.

Hallmark Cards Inc., US. Started a city renewal scheme in Kansas City. Crown Centre comprises the Hallmark building, a 730-room hotel, 5 office buildings, landscaped terraces, a central square, a bank and an underground parking lot. A three-level retail complex of 160 shops and an audio-visual communications centre, apartments and condominiums to house 8,000 residents and 50,000 daytime population are all due for completion in 1974. These activities are to complement the central business district where Hallmark is located.

Boussois-Souchon Neuvesel (BSN)., France. Employs 20 per cent of the workforce at Evian, managing many of the town's activities, including thermal station, two first-class hotels, the golf course and the casino. Recognizing the impact that it had on the quality of life in Evian, BSN helped to finance a study by outside consultants, to define a medium- and long-term development plan for the town. BSN and the municipal government are working together to implement the consultants' recommended action plan; and BSN has founded the Association Progrés et Développement, to study the problems of pollution caused by packaging (removal, treatment, recycling, recuperating, etc.).

Whatever their differences, none of these corporations has sacrificed either profitability or initiative in their acceptance of their public role. So how does a company launch a social programme?

Even if the president or the chairman has committed himself to a policy of public responsibility, it will probably not be easy to start from scratch. Several problems will arise at the outset. If this is a new field for the company, there is unlikely to be the necessary in-company expertise to make effective recommendations, particularly in technical, financial and operational areas. There may be confusion in implementation: who does what? Normally, in a decentralized organization, a divisional manager would be responsible for decisions involving capital expenditure, product policy, locations; this highlights another difficulty: how will the commitment to social responsibility affect their profit performance objectives? As social issues are difficult to define and quantify, the delegation practised in attaining good results, involving tight budgetary control and financial planning, will, in this case, be inappropriate. The chief executive officer's initial reaction will probably be to centralize the responsibility for corporate social involvement. A major difficulty is to identify the organization's problem areas, what progress has been made in correcting the problem, and how much it has, and will, cost to rectify. As social issues are not normally included in a company's financial or economic analyses, any study conducted will only portray a static situation. A prerequisite for successful social planning is to initiate a continuous survey and analysis of the company's position; it is for this reason that companies sometimes draw up a social balance-sheet, or indulge in human-asset accounting; it does not need to be over-complex.

From studies carried out in major US corporations, it would appear that companies go through three stages in their commitment to social issues. In the first, the chief executive officer publishes his intentions, then runs over the problems outlined above; and the policy, therefore, is often not implemented by line managers; whereupon outside pressure groups attack the company for the disparity between practice and declared policy. In addition (and this is true for all three stages), middle managers may not agree with the proposed programmes, and they may be unable to change their system of values rapidly enough to cope with the new environment. They themselves may become victims of a rapidly changing society. This is a human cost which every chief executive officer should be prepared to face.

In the second stage, the president brings in a specialist. His function is to keep up to date with relevant external events, to forecast the likely pressures the company will encounter, to recommend technical solutions, to assist line management in implementing policy, and to set up control systems to monitor progress. Often the corporate specialist does not have the support of line managers, because he usually lacks technical knowledge of the business, and seems to present a threat to divisional autonomy. This attitude is manifested by the tendency to leave the staff specialist out of the planning process, informing him only when the project has the investment committee's final approval.

The third stage, when the chief executive officer's original commitment is really implemented, is when the divisions or subsidiaries accept full responsibility for carrying out the policy. The active steps by the division involved are not far removed from the more usual planning of objectives:

Outline divisional plans for tackling social issues.
Agree on expected performance levels.
Monitor progress through a specially developed system.
Appraise individual manager, based on his success in meeting financial targets *and* social targets.

Having stated his position, the chief executive officer must stand firm: for some time operating managers will continue to think that the sole criterion of their performance will be financial success.

In the initial phases, a chief executive officer can make a random assessment of his company's problem areas by using a checklist (as in

Figure 10 : 5), grading performance from 0 (poor) to 5 (excellen
specific weaknesses and strengths which come immediately to mind. He
can compare notes with his senior executives, to reach a consensus on
priority areas. This will permit the company to concentrate immediately
on the priorities, whilst at the same time undertaking a more comprehensive study. Figure 10 : 4 outlines the fuller type of analyses that a
company should undertake, if they are to continue to meet their social
responsibilities. A major reason for carrying out these analyses is to ensure
optimum expenditure in the area: and from this stems the proposal to
undertake a survey of employee preferences: for instance, a day-care
centre may be preferred to a subsidized shopping centre.

The treatment of social responsibility as an emerging trend needs no
apologia, since it has become a part of corporate life in the US through
legislation and is coming under increased scrutiny in other countries. When
local governments really swing into action on companies' public responsibilities, the multinationals will be the first targets.

11
Emerging trends

11.1 Increasing government influence on business

Nationalism will grow further before it declines and disappears. One manifestation of nationalism is the gradual disappearance of the international executive, even in the developed countries. No nation, rich or poor, developed or underdeveloped, wants its resources, economy and industries to be dominated and controlled by foreign managers. Expatriate senior managers are disliked: the day is coming when all key management positions in a country may well be staffed with local nationals. Already local legislation in at least 20 countries restricts the entry and length of stay of foreign executives. Even where such restrictions have been shown to be detrimental to the efficient and profitable operation of a country's businesses and industries, foreign ownership and control has still been forbidden. Hence the need to re-examine a transnational's foreign policies, to comply with or anticipate government regulation in such areas as:

Training and development of local nationals.
Choosing a foreign partner for 'joint ventures' or 'joint ownership', instead of trying to go it alone.
Providing for some form of employee equity or participation in the business.
Establishing policies of repatriation for foreign executives.
Hiring local nationals who can quickly establish excellent relations with local governments.
Preparation of both local nationals and present expatriate management in matters of dealing with governmental relations.

In addition, any business plan which does not include a sociopolitical forecast and evaluation is not worth the paper it is written on.

Many foreign nations are also busily engaged in the expropriation of foreign properties, often without equitable compensation. This tends to discourage foreigners from investing capital. This hurts the local economy, but is yet another expression of nationalistic disapproval of the influential role played by foreign businessmen. Foreign subsidiaries of transnational corporations, with high measurable impact on a nation's economy, are particularly vulnerable.

The drive towards local management is deliberately aimed at getting rid of foreign management and control. Those foreign executives permitted to remain may well be relegated to the status of advisers. They will be stripped of line responsibility and authority, and their positions will no longer be as attractive to the expatriate manager in terms of career development. This poses a serious problem in developing globally-minded professional managers. The creative human-resource senior executive will have to find other ways and means of broadening senior managers in international business affairs. These measures may include frequent and prolonged trips overseas on project or task-force assignments to assist, guide and train local managers. They may take the form of additional outside education in international business, or temporary relocation to a foreign headquarters' operation. All this implies major changes in a company's organization structure.

Expatriate executives in a foreign country are sometimes subject to unusually high income tax, which include worldwide income, regardless of its source, as long as they have resident status in the country. This is another way of saying 'get out'. Some host countries, however, have recognized that their attempts to purge foreign managers from their countries were premature and disastrous: they had overreacted. Some have even recalled foreign managers; have liberalized restrictions on work permits, or quotas of foreign executives or advisers permitted to stay; and have recognized the need for foreign technological and managerial assistance. Nevertheless, the trend is still strong; and while it may take up to a generation to implement policies of local control completely, it will continue; and plans must be made to protect a company's physical assets, its personnel and its investment.

The areas discussed in 1.5 (pages 21–4) are all indicative of the increasing strength of nationalism: the form of investment, foreign partnership, local manufacturing, dividend policy, technical assistance agreements, currency transfers, the preparation of local nationals for top management positions. These must be reckoned with and dealt with at the policy level.

11.2 Imbalances in population and economic growth

Predictions are that world birth rates will start to fall. World population for the year 2000 is expected to be approximately 6.4 billion people. The problems will be with the less developed countries which will have to struggle even harder to increase per capita production and income. The facts are illustrated in the following table:

	Year 1965		Year 2000	
	% of world GNP	GNP per capita $	% of world GNP	GNP per capita $
Less developed countries	68	135	75	325
More highly developed countries	32	1675	25	5775

The less developed countries include those in South America, Asia and Africa. The more developed areas include North America, Europe, Japan and Australia. The gap between the 'haves' and the 'have nots' will widen. This could well lead to a north/south polarization of the world, because the per capita performance of the lesser developed nations, while more than doubling, will continue to fall further behind the level of the advanced economies.

As long as thousands of people continue to die each week of starvation, the world as a whole suffers, and this is intolerable. Despite the present crisis in the balance of payments of the non-oil-producing developed nations, they will have to share their wealth of technology and human resources through some form of transfer of their economic and educational expertise. This implies reallocation of human resources on a global basis. Until now two-thirds of the world's new business investment has been in the developed countries. Among the reasons are: quicker return on invested capital, more stable governments and safer investment, comparative ease of currency transfers, higher producitivity, better-educated workforces, and people preconditioned to industrialization because of cultural, educational and social values.

The biggest single problem to be solved in the transfer of managerial and technological expertise is the human problem: it can and must be solved. The professional human-resource manager has a key position because of his knowledge, experience, and application of the social and behavioural sciences. Corporations and the people who manage them can help to reverse the predicted trends in growing gaps between rich and poor nations. What is first required is a fundamental change in the very nature of the world's educational process: instead of the transmission of accumulated knowledge and the perpetuation of a culture, education must become — and start now — a process of preparation for change. The transnational corporations must make this investment in the human resources of the developing nations or else impede their own growth. The potential markets will never be tapped or developed until the standard of living is raised in those areas with the most rapid population growth.

Climatic factors can play an important part in the productivity of a nation's people; but advanced technology, preceded by training and pre-conditioning for changes in attitudes, can in large measure reduce the influence of a hot, humid climate. The investment will not produce a quick, short-term return — but neither does afforestation, also a necessary long-term investment.

11.3   Interdependence of the transnational corporation and the world society

The enlightened corporation recognizes that its former independence of action must yield to interdependence. There is no longer a clear distinction, for example, between the public and private sectors in a given economy. New government and business partnerships are rapidly being formed. More legislation is being added daily to restrict and/or to regulate foreign business transactions within a country's borders. On the one hand, ease of entry and departure are more closely governed; on the other, there is a proliferation of international cooperative agreements, in such areas as arms control, space exploration, exchange of scientific information, and regional economic groupings. These reflect a widespread belief in the value and the necessity for inclusiveness, mutual cooperation, and the fact that nations, as well as the foreign corporations within their borders, need each other. The appearance of the gradual breakdown of insularity and exclusiveness has begun to manifest itself.

There has been a shift away from the traditionally predominant profit/consumer-oriented production and marketing operations, and a movement toward the growth of non-profit institutions, in areas of education, research, health, welfare, and the professional disciplines. This is the real growth area because it truly meets the needs of developing societies at the core. The multinational corporations would do well to consider investments in these growing fields as a means of self-preservation and service to those economies which represent the markets of the future. This interdependence also translates itself into the obligations of the corporation to the individual. The concern for the individual and his quality of life, within and outside the corporation, necessitates a conscious attitude of responsibility toward society. It necessitates the linking of corporate goals to social goals. The action needed, particularly among the large industrial groups, is to plan, design, build and operate systems of total interrelationship between technology, man, nature and society. This, in turn, implies flexibility in the formation of consortia, join ventures, and inter-industry groups; and partnership with governments and institutions working in nonindustrial research and planning. In other words, the planned progression from national to world development.

Social cost vs. opportunity costs vs. optimum return on profit

The obstacles are primarily those of attitude. On the part of host governments, technology and expertise are indispensable for growth and development: yet many do everything they can to discourage foreign investment, particularly the developing countries. Their survival is largely dependent on their ability and flexibility to work with the transnationals. The challenge for the transnational involves a successful transition from a purely profit/product orientation to one of outcome. It involves a comprehension of the problems and peculiarities of each and every section of the world for the successful development of their own planning systems. A positive response to social needs is imperative, and, in fact, the future will witness a new form of profit measurement for the efficient and successful response to social demands. Maximum profit will have to yield to optimum return on profit, and social costs will be considered as a necessary investment in assessing opportunity costs. The present method of doing business internationally consists of multinational corporate interaction with fragmented markets and social systems, in pursuit of goals inherent to its own corporate system. This posture must soon give way to participation in, even a positive lead towards, a more fully integrated society.

The early chapters of this book deal primarily with successful operations in a fragmented system; for it seemed appropriate to deal first with achieving success in a segment of a foreign environment. Mastery of skills on this smaller scale will provide the groundwork for a global planning system, inasmuch as these experiences are translatable, particularly from a human viewpoint. The expected collision between the nation-state and the transnational corporation will not occur. Neither party would survive, even in the short-term. They need each other: thus the capacity and the creativity of the transnational to improve its ability to work with home- and host-country political leaders, regardless of the form of government, will improve. This will stem from better human resource management, both within and outside the individual company. One highly important step in this direction will be the development of better, more precise methods of measuring the utilization of human resources in world society. These measurements should encompass:

Social costs as an integral part of final net return on economic innovation.
Social sickness, such as disruption of living patterns, crime, pollution, mental and psychological stress.
Performance standards in the areas of social need, such as education, housing, welfare costs.
Social mobility *vs.* economic opportunity.

These costs will increase, and hence they should be viewed as opportunity costs and related to long-term, optimum return on profit.

The very role of multinationals may change: from one in which the transnational invests its capital to obtain fair profits, to one in which it provides a package of expertise (technological and managerial) to other firms and governments, in return for a consultancy or management fee.

11.4 The monetary crisis

The world monetary crisis is a long way from solution. The world is in fact faced with continuing 'stagflation' for a period of time: that is, simultaneous inflation and recession. A principal cause of the monetary crisis is that the major industrial nations have been committed to a policy of full employment. Although some measures are being taken to redress this situation, an increase in unemployment is an unacceptable political alternative. It has caused havoc with the relative value of currencies on the international exchange markets. Foreign-exchange speculation has resulted in near bankruptcies of some major banking institutions. While the problem will be partially solved eventually, the most optimistic estimate is for a gradual slowing down of the inflationary trend, which was aggravated, but not caused, by the oil crisis.

The implications for management include a consuming drive for exports: hence the need to develop ways and means of intensifying competition with overseas suppliers; and of coping with the drive for higher wages, salaries, and fringe benefits. It means more professional, top quality managers. The professional human resource manager's role must therefore be to anticipate, not just be aware of, these international forces which reach into the lives of all employees. Their net disposable income is affected and gradually brings about a reduced standard of living. When this is coupled with higher individual tax rates, new forms of indirect rewards must be devised and developed: motivation must be considered psychologically, as well as in tangible forms of remuneration.

The oil crisis intensified the already serious monetary and economic position of the industrialized world. This new concentration of foreign exchange in the hands of a few hitherto developing nations has led to international blackmail by the oil producers. It is yet another example of the need for a new dimension in international human relationships and understanding. Unless the oil producers can be persuaded to use their newly acquired wealth for productive purposes, and for the promotion of stability and welfare in the rest of the world, as well as for themselves, private enterprise in the free world will be seriously wounded – to everyone's detriment. Our society is now more vulnerable than ever before. Advances in communication and transportation mean that no place is remote, no violence is local: the entire world is affected. Interdependence is mandatory: a combination of the most advanced social and behavioural sciences in a marriage with the highest degree of business creativity and sophistication. A professional approach to human resource management is essential.

It is true that the multinationals merit a great deal of the criticism which has been levelled at them. Some of their practices stem from the old days of colonialism, when the host country was stripped of its natural resources, exploited without adequate compensation; at the same time profits were shifted from one country to another, to avoid local taxes, and little was done to upgrade the educational, technological and managerial expertise of the host-country citizens. Society no longer accepts this predatory type of behaviour; and the developing countries have justifiably reacted against these various forms of exploitation; their present aim is to get even. This is not the time to be vindictive, but to make new social contracts, which benefit both partners. As one progresses, the other must also gain, and not be penalized.

An arrangement which seems to work well in many countries is the joint-venture type of business. In fact, in a number of countries, this is the only means of entry for foreign investment: Indonesia is a typical example. The choice of the right partner helps to protect the mega-company's investment, and provides assurance of a fair return (in the long run) on invested capital. The management audit (Figure 6 : 1, pages 151–3) should be used, together with a self-reference criteria correction. The professional human resource manager, with his special skills in evaluation, can make a major contribution to the selection of the right partner. In both developed and developing countries wrong partners have been selected: this not only damaged the transnational's image, but resulted in a much lower return on invested capital than forecast.

In its enthusiastic search for new markets, the transnational corporation still pays too little attention to the human element – the cornerstone of any new company. Collapse is inevitable with the wrong partner, and this may shut off and shut out the foreign company for a number of years. Nevertheless, a partner must be given all the advantages of a stockholder in the multinational's home country: to do otherwise does a disservice to both partners.

The worst mistake which can be made by the transnational corporation is to regard the critical forces arrayed against it as impotent or disorganized. It took a great deal of public opinion and pressure from the United Nations to set up a study commission on multinationals. Insignificant concessions will not stop the tide of adverse public reaction. Preservation of the system, if this is deemed to be the most desirable alternative, will require fundamental, probably drastic, changes in policies, goals and organization.

11.5 Inability to predict the volatile business situation

The uncertainty which confronts every senior manager today requires new creative approaches to management. Most present-day business forecasting still concerns itself solely with economic and technological projections. Thus the business and financial analysts and the corporate planners look closely at national and international projections of the various components of gross national product, disposable income, market potentials, and the development of new materials, products, processes, machinery and equipment. Some lip service is given to the probable impact of social and political factors, but very little analysis actually takes place. Current planning processes must include the added dimensions of social and political trend analyses.

If this is done in a comprehensive and thorough manner, both in short- and long-term forecasts, a business is less likely to be taken unawares by events, and more able to react quickly to an impending revolution, the effect of major elections, tightening of credit, new and proposed legislation, and other environmental factors, such as reaction against pollution, more concern for worker health and safety, and a variety of social demands. Even with this four-dimensional forecasting, the element of surprise will never be removed completely. But the conditioning of managers in these two added dimensions will enable them to live more effectively with uncertainty, as they will be better prepared for it, and taught how to react quickly. A sudden shift in the sociopolitical environment, such as a new law prohibiting layoff or discharge of employees, or a provision for triple severance indemnities, can have as great a negative impact on profitability as the advent of a new competitor, with a better product which sells at a lower price.

The necessity to react quickly

A delayed reaction to a sudden change in the total business environment can produce disastrous profit consequences: the organization structure must become supple and efficient. Too often current budgeting and forecasting systems are completely invalidated within a few months of formal approval by the multinational corporate office. A government decree for a 30 per cent retroactive wage increase, a revolution, a sudden change in government fiscal policy, a devaluation, a nationalization, or the sudden presence of a strong competitor — the postulated figures become meaningless. How then can a company do a better job of financial forecasting, and avoid a liquidity crisis?

New organization structures and new forms of organization must quickly be devised and designed, to evolve with the maximum flexibility and decentralized authority. Larger companies are beginning to abandon the traditional functional structure and the top-heavy corporate staff in favour of divisional or regional ones: the basis is the creation of independent operating units, set up as profit centres: depending on the company size, and its products and geographic dispersion, the divisions or units are clearly defined by product, group, or market area.

The adaptive corporation

Survival will largely depend on the degree to which the multinational corporation can truly become adaptive. This necessitates charismatic and forceful leadership; strategic and contingency planning, and internal renewal as opposed to increased size. The needs are to identify clearly changing market trends, relative strengths and weaknesses of competitors, investment of time, money and goodwill, well-defined priorities and sense of direction, a succession plan, and willingness to modify organizational structure.

Diversifications and mergers are not necessarily the answers or solutions to problems: witness the failure of many so-called conglomerates. Neither is the indiscriminate application of conventional wisdom, such as decentralization, use of outside consultants, rapid introduction of management-by-objectives, sophisticated management information systems, industrial democracy, etc. There is no clear pathway to becoming an adaptive corporation, because each and every management tool or technique must be introduced and adapted to a company's individual situation. Poor timing, as well as the manner of introduction, can lead to failure.

Professionalism in all the functional disciplines is an absolutely essential element of the adaptive corporation. Professional managers must be given freedom to pursue creative solutions to complex problems, using an interdisciplinary approach. The organization cannot manage by numbers alone. A company will, at least partially, be measured in terms of the opportunities it provides for individual growth and development. It must provide opportunities for teamwork, flexibility and self-control, otherwise it will lose its good people and be unable to attract those with high potential. Communications must be easier in all directions: people must be able to go directly to the one person who can help solve their problems instead of climbing through cumbersome organization strata.

In brief, the adaptive corporation must develop and retain flexibility. It must avoid unwieldy top-heavy corporate management structures (more decentralization is a must); the headquarters operation must concentrate on business plans and allocation of resources. Strategic decision-making will concern the greater portion of headquarters executives, in contrast with current methods of solving operating problems of subsidiary units.

Disputes about definition of job responsibilities, personal rivalries, red tape, bureaucratic formalities and internal power politics will give way to more loosely defined responsibilities, common understandings of management principles, informal reciprocal exchanges of information and real teamwork. Those executives who manage the home market will be divorced from responsibility of multinational strategic management. The two must be kept separate, to avoid slow reaction to international problems when there are pressing domestic difficulties. Confusion is created when domestic executives attempt to inject themselves into the multinational communication and decision-making processes.

Finally, the present policy of many multinationals for 100 per cent control of the subsidiary company is out of date. This policy is increasingly at odds, in both developed and developing countries, because it lacks responsiveness to local and national conditions. The financial polycentrism which results partially from the instability of the currency situation is fostering the development of large regional units such as the EEC, LAFTA, The Andean Group. This makes the support of a strong joint-venture partner almost mandatory. Here again, the services of the corporate, internationally-minded human resources executive are indispensable. The right partner must be selected, which will help to ensure compatibility in the partnership.

11.6   Decreasing role of international trade unions

The influence of international trade unionism will lessen, and ultimately decline and disappear, in the form in which we know it today. The gains which these unions are achieving through legislative bodies, and the application of pressure on the local and national unions are laudatory. However, there are at least four factors which will dim the brightness of their ascending star.

Government legislation

In many countries, the employment contract has fewer and fewer areas left to the collective bargaining process. For example, wage scales are set by governments, including wage increases, hours of work, overtime and holidays; redundancies are being more closely regulated and limited; severance indemnities are provided for by law; discipline, discharge transfers and promotions are becoming fit subjects for legislative bodies; the actual working relationship between employer and employee is becoming defined by law, for example, worker participation on boards of directors, closure or cessation of operations. There are few traditional management rights which are not at least partially prescribed by law.

While unions have been largely responsible, through socialistic and communistic governments, for bringing about many of these improvements, they are, in effect, working themselves out of a job. The employer/employee relationship is rapidly becoming a matter of legal relationship, with precise laws and legally enforceable procedures for solving grievances, conditions, disputes, strikes and lockouts.

National government opposition

The legislative goals of the international trade unions, combined with their insistence on international solidarity, will be rejected by national governments and local unions, for the same reasons which make the mega-corporations vulnerable to criticism. The international unions seek economic power, domination over the destiny of millions of workers. Their strong stand against multinationals and capitalism, together with a blatant disregard for profits, will lead to alienation from governments, many of whom are currently seeking partnerships with business. The pressure the unions bring to bear today will diminish with time.

If one studies carefully the Socialist International declarations, they give world private industry and capitalism, especially international capitalism, only a limited existence. In Italy, for example, unionists, prompted by their international associates, are deliberately attempting to wreck capitalism by pushing foreign companies into bankruptcy. Some union leaders privately admit this.

Unwillingness of national unions to give up power

The national unions are unwilling, as are the national governments, to cede power to international bodies. Some governments, for example Austria, have enacted legislation prohibiting union members from being appointed to works councils in their official capacity as union leaders.

Such factors as strong political and ideological differences, as reflected in the parochialism of the British trade unionists, militate against the international confederations of trade unions. Indeed the numbers and variety of organizations which are attempting to restrict the further growth and development of the transnational corporations limit their own effectiveness. In Europe alone, for example, trade unions have some affiliation with the World Council of Labour, the International Confederation of the Trade Unions and the WFTU. Cultural, and linguistic differences, and lack of common interest, will eventually bring about the dissolution of these aims. It is hard to imagine a worker in Liverpool, England, going on strike to support the local demands of the Chinese in Hong Kong. The fact is that no one international union organization adequately represents or receives the support of a clear majority of employees on a worldwide basis.

National legislation with regard to the employer/employee relationship differs significantly from one country to another, and from one continent to another. What is deemed to be right, legislatively, for Germany is wrong in many respects for France: neither is valid for Japan or Australia. How then can the international trade unions possibly achieve a common denominator which applies across all world cultures?

The position of the transnational corporation is simple. It should refuse to short circuit national governments, local management, or national and local union leaders — all of which are unwilling to cede power to international trade secretaries. While the international trade union movement can set priorities and continue to push for more legislative action, in the final analysis they cannot enforce their codes or impose their will on local and national bodies. A worldwide policy system is neither a serious nor practical proposition. The shopfloor attitude of the local unions is one positive force militating against their species. The same workers who refuse to be pushed around and dictated to by management will soon refuse to be pushed around in the same way by the multinational union.

Public intolerance for strikes

The unions are going to lose, or at least witness severe restrictions on, their rights to call a strike — whether a sympathy strike, a strike for economic issues, or a strike for better employment conditions. The public everywhere is becoming increasingly intolerant of strikes, which disrupt public services, stop workers' pay-packets, and impose economic hardships on the community and the country. Legislation may eventually limit or eliminate the strike as the ultimate bargaining tool of unions.

A number of union leaders are privately opposing the formation of employees' works councils, which tend to function independently of the local and national union. If indeed workers do participate in management decisions, they will eventually become more responsible and responsive to the needs of the business as well as to those of the employees. They can, will, and in some cases already do effectively present the viewpoint of management to the workers. This is not true in the communist-dominated unions, whose object is to make trouble for management and stir up the workers. Union members are now better educated and are likely to become disenchanted with communist-affiliated unions. They are beginning to realize what really creates jobs, and the stability and wealth of nations: it is not government ownership and management of all industry. Italy is finding that national bankruptcy is the end result of government takeover of depressed businesses. In government ownership of industry, political considerations always predominate over sound business decisions. There are relatively few really healthy businesses, from a profit point of view, run entirely by government. One of the major reasons for the depressed conditions of Egypt and India is, without doubt, government ownership and regulation of the business sector of the economy.

The implications for human resource managers of globally-operating companies are that they must initiate positive action, by strengthening the local personnel manager and training him in collective bargaining strategy to retain management initiative. He can accomplish this by introducing various simple forms of participative management: by installing sound local personnel policies in accord with local needs, and through clear communication and sound administration of personnel policies, priorities and procedures. The best defence against the spectre of outside, unwanted interference from national as well as international trade union groups is the implementation of a sound, well-balanced personnel programme at the local level, which gives full recognition to all the elements described in Chapter 2 pages 29–34). The multinational employer who attempts to have uniformity in pay, benefits and working conditions, and actually physically conducts union negotiations at the international level, not only undermines the local company, but creates impossible conditions within that company.

11.7 A new role for the chief executive officer of the transnational corporation

The world is at present in a serious leadership crisis. That this crisis will continue is confirmed by the toppling of numerous governments, and the increased number of business failures within the past two years. Competence is all too scarce a commodity. The day of the technocrat is disappearing. There is an administrative and managerial sclerosis around the world, which breeds mass-suspicion and distrust: the casualties are the leaders themselves and their respective institutions, whether governmental or business.

There is a new role, particularly in the human dimension, for the chief executive officer. Instead of spending about 10 per cent of his time on matters external to his company, the complex needs of modern multinational management dictate that he spend 40 per cent or more of his time on these matters. He faces a double dilemma; if he shirks his responsibilities of running the business as a corporate manager, there is dire trouble; and if he shirks his role as a social arbiter, present-day assaults against the mega-company could become so intense that they could force a fundamental change in the corporation itself. He must become outcome-minded, whilst maintaining a healthy awareness of profit. Obviously, all the qualities of the expatriate executive (as cited in Chapter 6, pages 141–50 must apply in his new role.

The task of the professional human resource manager is to devise new standards of selection for filling the top position, new techniques of career planning and development, and new strategies in human resource management, designed to help him function effectively in his new role.

It is clear that the chief executive officer's role is changing. The job is too big for one man to handle. It is no longer sufficient to be trained in marketing, finance and/or production. Functional expertise is too limiting to provide the breadth and depth of experience, vision and ability to handle the top job. For one thing, he must be an effective communicator, with the ability to sell his ideas to his corporate owners or stockholders, or the general public; and he must take great pains to explain to them how he effects a proper balance between profits and social conscience. He must move out of the reactive stage of management and move into anticipatory planning in order that the company can more intelligently and more efficiently utilize its resources for the total needs of society. He must form partnerships with educational, governmental, research and service organizations, to maximize his capability to determine the right paths for his company, and to initiate and implement change. He must acquire the knowledge and the ability to adapt and apply concepts involving public and social accountability.

Thus, the search is on for new approaches to management, which will enable the chief executive officer to function properly and effectively in his dual role. This requires imagination and vision, new concepts of organization design, creation of task-force assignments, human engineering, more decentralization and delegation of operating decisions, and more time spent on allocation of scarce material and human resources to satisfy the needs of a world society. He must be thoroughly aware of, and in fact anticipate, world political/economic/social changes and plan his business to fulfil its rightful role in this newly evolving society. Above all, he must develop people: a cadre of globally-minded executives, upon whom he can rely as joint custodians of the welfare of his business, both in the short and long term.

12

New dimensions in human resource management

All the foregoing imply new dimensions in human resource management. This, in turn, makes a demand for the highest level of professionalism in the staff contribution of the human resource vice-president. He must first be a businessman, and then a socio-behavioural scientist. It is necessary to be able both to think and function at the policy level. This implies understanding the nature of the business, the reasons for its existence, and the products and services it provides to the public as consumers. Unless a human resource executive can put personal effort into raising the level of professionalism with a given company, he fails in his work. It is no longer sufficient to be a good union negotiator, to run a cafeteria, to keep good employee records, to develop a good scheme of wage and salary administration, or to be able to train foremen to manage more efficiently. His first and most important responsibility is the identification, selection, training and development of high-capacity, globally-minded professional managers, at the most senior management levels. To do this job requires experience in manpower planning and forecasting; skillful evaluation and assessment of management potential; determination of individual manager's strengths and weaknesses, and knowing how to teach methods of improving managerial performance through establishment of performance standards; introduction, implementation and follow-up in managing-by-objectives.

It is clear that attitudinal and behavioural change always begins at the top of an organization. Unless the professional human resource executive can obtain the respect and the attention of the chief executive officer, he is ineffective. We are already beginning to witness a new era in professional human resource management. To meet the challenges of the next two decades will require a blend of business sophistication and social science; and the persuasive ability to convince top management that social accountability is not a passing phase, but the reality of a new generation. The staff professional must be sufficiently well informed and imaginative to introduce human engineering at all levels of a company, and in a variety of cultures. To function as a senior adviser to the president, he must be able to introduce new concepts of organization design; to be sufficiently familiar with the profession of management to know when and how to advise on decentralization, and how to make it work from a human point of view. New methods of motivating executives to higher levels of achievement must be devised, developed and measured. They must include tangible and intangible rewards.

With the rapidly growing, worldwide trends in executive mobility, as witnessed by the proliferation of multinational and national executive search firms, a company must provide opportunities for growth, development and self-realization of its executives, or be faced with the wastage and/or erosion of its most precious asset: its managers. The human resource executive who foresees the immediate future will incorporate career planning as an integral part of the job offer to a new recruit. When selecting a senior executive of high calibre, the use of a reputable executive search firm is recommended. The criteria used to evaluate an executive search firm are included in Appendix B (Exhibit 10, pages 374–77).

Until five or ten years ago, the so-called traditional personnel function was avoided as a career by the brightest young university graduates. Hence, this talent is in short supply, and the shortage will become more and more acute as chief executive officers realize the need for professionals of the calibre required. The future will witness a growing number of general-management openings, which will be filled with professional human resource managers. After all, at present, about 60 per cent of a chief executive's job involves people and organization considerations.

European personnel managers are currently under fire because they have failed to anticipate the human problems which now plague their companies, at all levels of management. Corporations are beginning to view the management of their human resources, not as an administrative duty or conciliatory task, but as a major strategic business consideration, with long-term political implications, and as part and parcel of the corporate system of values. A new breed of personnel manager is needed, who can influence the organization and introduce purposeful change. More than half Europe's personnel managers have formal university education in law, business and economics, and the social sciences; they also tend to be mobile. While they are very interested in playing a significant role in shaping the strategy of their various companies, few are equipped to do so. Too many are still in the quagmire of labour/union relations, social legislation, low-level recruitment, and factory personnel practices. They are not generally accepted as senior management executives at the policy level. The situation is worse in Latin America and the Far East: most are only interested in the labour market, the cost of labour, and current and pending labour legislation; as yet they do not have the stature of senior executives, but this will change because necessity will demand it.

Professional human resource managers are not developed overnight; so many companies will continue to suffer the adverse effects of having non-professionals. Too often the personnel managers, both in the developed and developing countries, are limited to middle-management positions, by their education, training, experience and personal stature. A great deal more attention must be paid to hiring a top, professional human-resource executive, to report to the president in large- and medium-sized companies. One solution, frequently tried and seldom successful, is to appoint a senior, respected line executive to handle the human resource function. Too often, he is as successful as if top management had appointed the top marketing executive to head the financial department. Experience is a necessary ingredient for professionalism, and there is no substitute for ten or fifteen years of high-quality experience in professional human resource management. The future for the function is excellent; for the individual, it is an excellent career choice; for it may well become one of the main avenues for advancement into the highest level of management.

Conclusion

The transnational companies must develop a sensitivity to the legitimate goals of the societies and of the individuals in those countries in which they operate. This requires a fundamental change in the attitudes of chief executives and the policies which govern their businesses, particularly in the larger multinationals, whose significant strength can influence and help to shape the environment within which they operate. Citizens of both developed and developing countries will demand a greater voice and a participation in those decisions which affect their lives and their livelihood.

The most senior executives who are involved in building and developing true multinational business enterprises must recognize that they are fast becoming the most important social architects of this day and age. Our global society is now demanding a more equitable distribution of the benefits derived from the earth's resources.

A change will take place in the boardrooms of the transnationals, whereby the emphasis will shift from profit to outcomes. Social accountability will receive as much attention as net profits after taxes.

The transnationals will meet these challenges and adapt their organizations and allocation of resources — material and human — accordingly.

They will form new partnerships with governments, other businesses and educational, service and research organizations. And, finally, seated next to the chief operations officer, as one of his senior advisers, will be the professional director of human resources.

APPENDIX A
WORLDWIDE HUMAN
RESOURCE SURVEY

Exhibit 1

HUMAN RESOURCE SURVEY REPORT: A DEVELOPED COUNTRY

November 1974

Hourly-paid, clerical-salaried, managerial and professional

Rating guide:
(1) Excellent
(2) Good
(3) Needs improvement

Survey areas	Rating	Comments/Recommendations
1 Company personnel manager		
There is a manager of personnel, recently appointed. Function reports to managing director.	(1)	The newly appointed individual should stay in this position for at least two years, to give stability to the department and regain the credibility of the function.
2 Up-to-date organization charts		
Company organization charts exist for all levels of management.	(2)	Too many changes in organization and personnel. This situation needs to be made stable to avoid organization confusion.
3 Written personnel policies		
Some personnel policies and procedures are written.	(3)	Area needs an overhaul; clearly defined and communicated policies are needed for all areas of personnel, including recruitment, training, development, compensation, organization. Present plan is to have this project completed in six months.

4 Manpower planning and forecasting

Formal manpower planning and forecasting is good and plans are available and included in the annual budget for field and factory personnel. This is reviewed quarterly and annually.

(2) Formal manpower planning needs strengthening, particularly with regard to executive management back-ups.
Audit of management talent to identify high potentials has begun.
Performance appraisal system is extended to all management personnel and has been in effect for approximately three years.
Overall executive manpower plan is targeted for completion by year-end 1974.

5 Employment/recruitment

Recruitment of hourly and clerical personnel is planned at least three months in advance, and crisis hiring is avoided. There are overall guidelines. No pre-employment testing, although company is considering simple physical-skills testing of stenographers.

(2)

There are separate, well-done application forms for hourly, clerical and managerial personnel.
Reference investigations are conducted for all classes of employees, after interview, but before hiring. Content is good.
Disadvantaged personnel are employed by the company.

(1)

There is regular recruitment of university graduates: budgeted and effected; about 10 per year.

(1) Advance recruitment of high-level middle managers should be more formalized and specifically budgeted, utilizing inputs from all department heads (management committee).

There is a formal training plan. However, there are gaps with regard to formal recruitment of high-level middle managers. It is on a hit-and-miss basis.

(3)

Exhibit 1 (cont.)

Survey areas	Rating	Comments/Recommendations
There is a good formal procedure for requisitioning of new managerial personnel; it is tied into the annual budget and separately identified as such.	(1)	
The company's basic policy is to promote from within, but because of prior years' neglect, a great deal of outside hiring is still necessary.	(2)	It would be advisable to issue a report to be circulated *only* to management committee on numbers and percentage of job openings filled from within *vs.* outside hired — broken down by organizational and levels of responsibility.
6 Formal orientation and induction		
Orientation and induction procedures are rather informal in the factory for hourly-paid, and for clerical-salaried employees at headquarters' operation.		
There is no plan of follow-up on the part of the personnel department.	(3)	An orientation plan should be devised and implemented for clerical personnel. There is high turnover in this area. It is understood that there is a plan for improvement. It is hoped that this will become a high priority item in the management-by-objective of the personnel function.
An audiovisual approach is used in the district offices. There is a procedure for follow-up with newly hired managerial employees.		
Work has begun on a company orientation brochure, but this is a low priority item.	(3)	It was felt that the orientation and induction procedures for managerial employees could and should be strengthened.
7 Training and development		
Training programmes for factory, and service personnel, are well-defined, implemented and followed up; this is tied in with	(1)	

trade-union requirements and legal-minimum obligations. There is planned advancement in both field and factory operations. Hourly paid employees are trained and paid on company time.

Clerical training, with the exception of estimators, is on a hit-and-miss basis; virtually nonexistent.

(3) This may be one of the reasons for high clerical turnover, and it is reasonable that this becomes a high-priority item.

There is a policy, plan and procedure for tuition assistance, which is used to improve present job performance and/or prepare an employee for advancement. This applies to all classes of employees.

(1)

There are well-established plans for training of supervisors in field and factory. Both internal and external courses are conducted.

(2) Perhaps there could be made some special efforts more precisely to measure and evaluate directly the effects of this training in relation to costs incurred.

An attempt is being made to introduce MBO at the supervisory levels in both field and factory. Branch manager training is conducted regularly.

(2) This should be followed closely and personally implemented by the personnel function in conjunction with senior management.

There exists a system of professional appraisal to measure results of training, which is also used to develop individual objectives for the subsequent year. The participants are also asked to evaluate the course.

(1) Close involvement by the personnel and planning function, is recommended, from the viewpoint of coordination and counselling.

The early identification of young, high-potential managers is just beginning. There is some sales training now which requires improvement. Good audiovisual aids and programmes are being developed for new sales and service sales personnel. MBO started several years ago in this company. It was unsuccessful. Within the past three years, it was begun again: from top down.

(2) Early identification and strong follow-up, training, etc., for all high-potential managers should be considered a number one-priority item in the MBO plans of the personnel function.

Each senior manager sets his own objectives. More follow-up and appraisal is required.

(3) This should be considered as another high priority area.

Certain management-development methods, such as job enrichment, job enlargement, special assignment, and task-force approach have not been used for all practical purposes.

(3) This should, in the near future, become an important goal for each manager as a follow-up to the early identification of high-potential promotables.

Exhibit 1 (cont.)

Survey areas	Rating	Comments/Recommendations
There is a great deal of participation in outside seminars by management personnel. It is loosely administered, not followed up, and results of training are not systematically evaluated and measured.	(3)	Since this is a high-cost item in terms of managerial time and money, it should be centralized as soon as possible and more properly controlled.
Many key people do participate in training opportunities in other companies. The actual magnitude and impact is not known.	(3)	It is also planned to get a better management control over these activities, visits, meetings, etc. Many are called and scheduled by headquarters staff personnel.

8 Communications

Survey areas	Rating	Comments/Recommendations
Attitude surveys have not been conducted among hourly paid and clerical-salaried employees. There is no plant newspaper. Small group meetings are planned for factory and field employees by the new director of industrial relations. There are written shop rules which are administered in accordance with the law. There is some employee counselling in the area of social benefits, conducted by the plant personnel manager. Some exit interviews are conducted, but the programme is not well administered. Statistical data and reasons for leaving are not properly analysed and followed up.	(3)	The entire area of employee communications in all forms needs to be carefully studied, defined, added to and improved. This is recommended as a high priority area for the personnel manager and the exit interview programme needs to be more closely coordinated and followed up.
There is no managerial attitude survey. Performance appraisals exist for the majority (about 90 per cent) of managerial employees. There are job descriptions and performance standards for most positions. These are closely linked with MBO.	(3)	All management personnel should receive an annual performance appraisal and review. This point mentioned should be corrected and used as a basis for goal-setting and performance improvement.

There is very little career planning and counselling. It is generally limited to poor performers. Executive problem-solving procedures are limited to individual discussions between the man and his manager.

Management staff does meet regularly, at least once a month, as a group, plus many special committees.

(3) This should be corrected as soon as possible; another high-priority item.

These committees meet as necessary to determine policy matters and approaches for recommendation to managing director.

There are also branch managers' meetings, regular regional managers' meetings, budgetary control meetings, etc. Each department head appears to hold regular staff informative and problem-solving meetings.

(1) Management communication overall is good, based on factual data and personal observations over a period of time. Managers do feel free to discuss their problems with each other and the managing director.

Management exit interviews are conducted for those who leave the company.

(2) Perhaps the respective roles of the manager (who had received a resignation from one of his people) and the personnel department could be more clearly defined, although there does not seem to be much of a problem with voluntary resignations among managerial personnel.

9 Compensation

Compensation for hourly paid employees is the direct result of industry-wide negotiations. There are no job descriptions as such for hourly rated personnel. There are wage escalation clauses in the union contracts.

There are job descriptions, salary schedules and annual salary surveys for clerical employees. A number of clerical employees, primarily draftsmen, are represented by trade unions.

(1)

Exhibit 1 (cont.)

Survey areas	Rating	Comments/Recommendations
It is planned by the personnel department to overhaul the salary administrative programme for clerical employees.	(2)	
There are position descriptions, job evaluations and salary schedules for managerial personnel, down through the first line of supervision. It is planned to update the evaluations.	(2)	This should be implemented as soon as possible.
There is a bonus system for senior executives. Salary reviews are conducted once annually and the salary structure is updated annually.	(2)	
Club memberships are limited to a few executives, for business purposes only.	(1)	
The use of company cars is limited to a few senior-level managers.	(1)	This is a common practice.

10 Fringe and social benefits

Government schemes provide ample medical, life insurance and pension benefits to employees.	(1)	
There are additional benefits for management staff, in accordance with local practice, e.g., additional pension scheme, with cost-of-living increases built in, and additional life insurance benefits, over and above government provisions.	(1)	
Vacations are regulated both by law and local practice. This covers all categories of employees.	(1)	
Vacation time off with pay (no additional bonus) is 20 working days for more than one year's service.	(1)	
There are no employee loans as such.	(1)	

There is a company recreation fund which makes nominal funds available to help support group recreational and social activity. (1)

Local well-done benefits surveys are available from outside groups and purchased by the company. These reports are produced annually. Fringe benefit costs are between 15–20 per cent. (1)

A gold watch is awarded after 25 years' service.

11   Employee incentives and awards

There is no formal suggestion system or plan for employees. A weak attempt was made to start one. (3)

There are no special awards for submitted ideas to any category of employees.

There are group recognitions, in the form of safety awards, but no special efforts made to obtain employee support on improvement of quality, costs, productivity, etc. (3)   This is another area which needs some attention in the future.

Promotions are announced through the local publication system, but only if managers remember to do so. (2)   Some thought should be given as to whether to formalize this procedure or discontinue it altogether.

12   Labour and/or union relations

All factory and field workers belong to trade unions. Some clerical people, and first-line supervisors, are union members. (3)   Union situation in the factory is difficult — hampering management efforts to improve productivity, quality and costs. Special attention seems to be required in this area, and we understand that appropriate plans are being formulated.

The company has to negotiate with five different unions. Personnel manager and branch personnel officers participate in negotiations with employee unions.

There are formal grievance procedures to resolve employee dissatisfactions. These are prescribed in union contracts. (1)

Exhibit 1 (cont.)

Survey areas	Rating	Comments/Recommendations
The company strike record is not bad. In the past two years, there was one major strike. The *estimated* cost to the local company was in excess of $500 000.		
There are no shop councils or workers' committees in the local company.	(1)	
A shop stewards' council does exist.		
There is an intensive amount of local labour legislation, dealing with mandatory hours, workmen's unemployment compensation, conditions of employment, dismissal procedures, severance indemnities, factory location, etc.		
Generally, the interpretation, in the event of a dispute, favours the worker. There is no compulsory arbitration. The general rule in dismissals is one week's pay for every year of completed service with the company.		
There are no restrictions on management rights, other than those given up by management as a result of contract negotiations.		
Uniforms, protective clothing, are provided to field employees at company expense.		
Cafeteria for factory employees is largely subsidized by the company.	(2)	Is this a negotiable item or good will?
As previously mentioned, some first-line supervisors belong to unions.	(3)	A potentially dangerous practice, to be avoided, if at all possible, because of implications of divided loyalty.
Regular meetings are held with representatives of supervisors' unions.		

13 Working conditions and housekeeping

Working conditions and housekeeping are generally good.
The company has received safety awards. There are safety
officers for both field and factory, plus safety committees.
Locker facilities are provided for both factory and field
employees.
No special provisions for transportation, other than car
allowances for salesmen who must use personal cars to
conduct company business.

14 Employee statistics

Employee statistics are presently accumulated, but have little
meaning for improving analyses and control. For example,
statistics on employee turnover are accumulated monthly on
a manual basis, but actual full-time employment at any specific
time is not known.

There is no running cumulative total by department for
turnover or absenteeism. There is no attempt to tie present
data in with exit interviews for analysis and control.

Overtime hours are analysed for both field and factory, and
efforts are made to control excessive overtime.
There is good statistical data on wages and average hourly
earnings.

(3) The company has high clerical turnover, but *perhaps* in line with
other companies because of tight labour market, particularly
for clerical and stenographic help.

(1) Personnel manager is acutely aware of the problem, and places a
relatively high priority for total improvement in this area,
including computerization, if at all possible.

Exhibit 1 (cont.)

Survey areas	Rating	Comments/Recommendations
Improvements are needed in: Factory employment for better control of ratio of direct to indirect. Management and clerical employee statistics, salaries, hours, etc.		
Total recruitment and training expenses need to be isolated for better budgeting and control.	(3)	Management aware of the situation, with plans to improve same.
Data on severance indemnity is lacking.		
Management turnover not available. There are no pre-employment physical examinations.	(1)	This is common practice in the country.
Activity per employee data is regularly maintained and closely followed.		See annual detailed, financial reports and management reports.
15 Safety and security		
There are many legal mandatory requirements in the safety area which are fully complied with.		
Company has a variety of memberships in safety organizations. It employs full-time safety engineers, has safety committees and close follow-up on accident statistics.	(1)	
There does not appear to be a problem in the area of accident-prone employees.		
The top management group takes an active interest and participates in the company's overall safety programme.	(1)	
There are regular safety inspections, full-time nurse and part-time doctor. A good safety programme which appears to be well implemented.		

16 Community relations

Company has a summer employment programme for students.

Individuals hold memberships in various local management organizations.

Top management is actively involved in outside professional organizations.

17 Other

The personnel function has a total of 20 people, of which 8 are professionals. The remainder are clerical employees.

Summary of conclusions and recommendations

Because of frequent changes in the personnel department staff within the past two years, the department has lost some credibility. While many excellent programmes were begun, the lack of continuity has resulted in a fragmented approach to a total well-balanced programme.

Most legitimate activities are being performed at the present time. The key to success is to avoid any other major changes of people within the personnel function for at least one full year.

With a consolidated approach, completion of personnel function staffing, and well-defined goals which meet company needs, the department should be able to re-establish its credibility.

The high priority goals as we see them, should include:

1 Completion, communication and circulation of all necessary personnel policies, practices and procedures.

Exhibit 1 (cont.)

2 Strengthening of formal manpower planning, particularly at the executive level.

3 Further formalization and budgeting for advancement recruitment of people to fill back-up slots for senior management positions.

4 Formalize and strengthen employee orientation, induction and training plans, particularly for clerical, salaried employees.

5 More accurate measurement, evaluation and consolidation of all training, within and outside the company, to derive more benefit and closer control of the significant amounts of time, effort and money which are being expanded.

6 Intensify management development efforts within house for all high-potential, talented managerial personnel.

7 Careful study, definition and revision of company's total communication programme.

8 Reduce turnover of clerical, salaried employees by improving selection, recruitment, orientation and exit interviewing processes and procedures.

9 Update the job description, job evaluation plan, and salary administration systems, for all managerial employees.

10 Seriously consider the proper introduction and professional implementation of an employee suggestion system.

11 Special efforts should be made to improve union cooperation and attitudinal change to support management's efforts in the areas of productivity, cost and quality improvement.

12 Complete overhaul of total employee statistics, improve and follow up, and effectively use the data obtained.

Respectfully submitted,
Staff Director of Human Resources

Exhibit 2

STATISTICAL RATING SUMMARY OF 17 COMPANIES, USING 15 CATEGORIES PER HUMAN RESOURCE SURVEY (all companies, except G, have a personnel manager)

Rating guide:
1 Excellent
2 Good
3 Needs improvement

Category	A	B	C	D	E	F	G	H	I	J	K	L	M	N	O	P	Q
Organization charts	1	2	2	1	1	3	3	1	3	2	3	3	1	1	1	1	2
Personnel policies	1	3	3	2	3	3	3	3	3	3	3	3	2	3	2	2	3
Manpower planning	2	3	2	2	3	3	3	1	3	3	3	2	3	3	3	3	3
Recruitment	1	2	2	2	3	3	3	1	2	3	3	3	3	3	3	2	3
Orientation	1	3	3	3	3	3	3	1	3	3	3	3	2	3	2	2	3
Training and development	1	2	2	3	3	2	3	2	3	3	3	3	3	3	3	1	3
Communications	1	2	3	2	3	3	3	1	3	2	3	2	3	2	2	2	2
Compensation system	1	3	2	2	3	3	3	1	2	3	3	3	2	3	2	2	3
Fringe benefits	1	2	1	1	1	3	2	2	2	1	2	2	2	2	2	2	1
Employee awards	3	3	3	1	3	3	3	3	3	3	3	3	3	3	3	3	3
Labour relations	1	1	2	3	2	2	1	1	3	2	2	2	3	2	2	3	2
Working conditions	1	2	2	2	2	2	2	1	2	2	3	2	2	2	1	3	2
Employee statistics	2	3	3	3	3	3	3	2	3	3	3	3	3	3	2	3	3
Safety	1	1	1	2	3	2	3	3	3	2	2	2	2	3	1	2	2
Community relations	2	3	1	2	3	2	3	3	3	2	2	3	3	3	2	2	3

Exhibit 3

RATING OF COMPANIES, SOLELY ACCORDING TO THE STRENGTH OF THE PERSONNEL PROGRAMME*

Companies	
A	20
B	23
C	30
D	31
E	32
F	33
G	35
H	36
I	36
J	38
K	38
L	39
M	39
N	40
O	40
P	40
Q	42

*No weighting, either according to size of company, nor the relative importance of each category.

Exhibit 4

SUMMARY, BY CATEGORY, OF 17 COMPANIES

Category	Rating 1	2	3
Organization charts	9	4	4
Personnel policies	2	4	(11)
Manpower planning	1	4	(12)
Recruitment	2	6	(9)
Orientation	1	4	(12)
Training and development	3	3	(11)
Communications	2	10	5
Compensation system	1	6	(9)
Fringe benefits	6	10	1
Employee awards	1	4	(12)
Labour relations	4	8	5
Working conditions	3	12	2
Employee statistics	0	4	(13)
Safety	5	10	2
Community relations	1	6	(10)

Rating guide:
1 Excellent
2 Good
3 Need improvement

Priorities for improvement

Out of 17 companies

(13) Employee statistics
(12) Employee awards...............Low priority
(12) Employee orientation
(12) Manpower planning
(11) Personnel policies
(11) Training and development
(10) Community relations............Low priority
(9) Compensation system
(9) Recruitment

Exhibit 5

RECOMMENDED INTERNATIONAL PERSONNEL POLICIES

Manpower planning and forecasting

As part of the business planning process, the total manpower budget for the current year will be supplemented with a three-year manpower forecast and plan, which will include a breakdown of additions and replacements by job title, skill, education and experience requirements, as well as timing to meet present and projected business needs.

Recruitment

The company needs more highly qualified employees and managers to improve profitability and take advantage of growth opportunities. Accordingly, based on the manpower plan and forecast, recruiting needs will be aimed at selecting employees with growth potential, and programmed and budgeted in advance to avoid crisis-oriented hiring practices which result in high turnover, low productivity and failure to meet profit projections. This does not necessarily imply a total net addition to payroll costs.

Employee orientation and induction

All newly hired, transferred and promoted employees will be given sufficient orientation and induction into the company to enable them fully to understand: the nature, organization and special characteristics of the company; their job responsibilities, priorities and authority; all employment-related conditions, and the contributions they are expected to make to company growth and profitability.

Training and development

Every employee and manager will be provided opportunities to realize his full potential for professional growth and development. This requires precise performance appraisal and review; establishing high individual performance standards and objectives at all levels of organization; early indentification of both high-potential and marginal performers, and select career planning assignments to accelerate individual development. Qualified back-ups will be available for all *key* line and staff positions.

Exhibit 5 (cont.)

It is the personal responsibility of the senior line executive in each location to plan for and build a highly qualified mangement team, and to make people available for promotional opportunities within the company.

Compensation system

The company's wage, salary and benefit programmes will be designed and administered in such a manner as to attract and retain the most qualified people and encourage them to build their careers within the company. Through experience and meritorious performance, people will be able to attain a total compensation equal to or exceeding prevailing compensation levels for comparable work in their various geographical areas.

Employee statistics

Accurate, timely statistics will be maintained on all employees and managers, for the purpose of efficient utilization and control of total manpower costs and expenses, in such areas as turnover, absenteeism, training and development, accident frequency and severity, productivity, wages, salaries and fringe benefits.

Personnel policies

Appropriate local personnel policies will be developed, written and communicated to all employees and managers in regional and company locations. These policies will complement and supplement international personnel policy, with full allowance for local conditions and prevailing local legislation and practice. These local policies are to provide guidelines to managers and employees in the proper, consistent handling of all major personnel matters which affect more than one department or function in a given location.

Exhibit 6

SUGGESTED GUIDELINES FOR IMPLEMENTATION OF INTERNATIONAL PERSONNEL POLICIES AND IMPROVING THE RETURN ON HUMAN CAPITAL

Policies/Priorities for improvement	Small companies(1) (under 250 employees)	Medium-sized companies(2) (251—1000 employees)	Large companies(3) (over 1000 employees)
Manpower planning, forecasting and control	*Note.* On all priorities designated for improvement in these guidelines, the items under small companies represent the first priorities for all companies, regardless of size. This applies to all pages of this Exhibit. Consolidated manpower plan and forecast for all levels: separate budget item for next three years: To include additions and re-placements. Specific jobs to be identified, together with education and experience requirements. Timing for each new position to be added. Projected organization charts, all levels of management, one, two and three years.	Same as (1), plus: Plan for advanced recruitment, to allow time for proper training. Consolidated by the personnel department, for advance planning and control of manpower costs. Job description and personnel specification for all positions to be filled.	Same as (1) and (2), plus: Measurable contribution of each new employee to profits, growth, productivity, efficiency and customer satisfaction. Relationship, performance standards for each new management position. Analyses of projected employment costs in such areas as: Return on investment per employee. Sales per employee. Backlog per employee. Profitability per employee. Direct *vs.* indirect labour. Overtime. Fixed *vs.* variable employee costs Activity per employee.

Exhibit 6 (cont.)

Policies/Priorities for improvement	Small companies(1) (under 250 employees)	Medium-sized companies(2) (251–1000 employees)	Large companies(3) (over 1000 employees)
Recruitment	As a matter of principle, the company will make every effort to develop people and promote from within.	Same as (1), plus:	Same as (1) and (2), plus:
	We prefer not to hire senior executives from outside the company because of the high risk of failure and the adverse, psychological effect. Nevertheless in the event of a need to:	Position description, manpower specifications, and defined working relationships within the company, for all new jobs to be added or created.	Programmes of summer employment for outstanding college seniors.
	1 introduce a new concept;	Development of best sources for people in local environment, e.g., schools, employment agencies, government employment offices.	Building company image through active participation of executives in professional and community associations.
	2 reintroduce imagination into a faltering company;	All preliminary screening and reference investigation *prior to hire* by personnel department.	Open house, factory and offices to public.
	3 produce an overall, major change;	Ensure the establishment of a workplan and priorities for all newly hired supervisors and managers — to be available at time of hire.	Regular recruitment at schools and universities.
	We will not hesitate to go outside.	Hire .... college graduates per year.	Hire .... college graduates per year.
	The problem of back-ups in all companies, for the first and second levels of management, must be proposed to and solved in conjunction with the staff personnel director.	Establish a selection committee for management personnel.	
	It is partially a staff responsibility, working in close cooperation with line management, to assist in developing back-ups for the first two		
	Advance recruitment, based on manpower forecast and plan to allow adequate time for orientation and training.		
	Complete employment application, separate for workers, clerks and managers.		

Employee orientation and induction

Management directive policy

All employees and managers at all levels are completely free to consult with the next two higher levels of management on all matters pertaining to their jobs.

His manager must be informed, but the appointment will be only between the aggrieved individual and the most senior manager to whom he directed the appeal.

New employee's immediate manager is responsible for complete company and job orientation, including all employment conditions, privileges and responsibilities. He will be assisted by the managing director or his designated representative.

Working relationships, authority, and performance standards for the new employee to be defined in writing by his immediate manager.

In medium- and large-sized companies the personnel manager will have the overall responsibility for all orientation and induction of employees new to the company. Same as (1), plus:

Brochure on company history.

Written and oral explanation of all employment conditions, including shop rules, where applicable.

One to two days' company orientation and introduction for all supervisory and managerial hires, plus copy of personnel policies, organization charts, departmental projects, objectives and priorities.

Plant and field tours in operating companies for all newly hired and transferred personnel.

Total systems of communication within the company, written and oral.

Opportunities for education and development within the company.

Same as (1) and (2).

Exhibit 6 (cont.)

Policies/Priorities for improvement	Small companies(1) (under 250 employees)	Medium-sized companies(2) (251–1000 employees)	Large companies(3) (over 1000 employees)

Training and development
 	
Management directive policy
No training is to be provided which cannot be put to the company's productive use by the individual in the short or intermediate future.
	(A) Based on well-defined jobs and personnel specifications, provide appropriate training for all levels of present employees and new hires:
	  To update skills and knowledge.
	  To increase efficiency.
	  To accelerate productive usefulness of new employees and managers.
	  To prepare in advance for promotional opportunities.
	  To correct performance deficiencies.
	  To reduce waste and scrap, human and material.
	  To reduce controllable employee turnover.
	  To prevent, or at least, to recognize early, when a selection error has been made.
	  To clarify job responsibilities, work priorities and working relationships.
		Same as (1), plus:
		
		Formal first-line supervisory training in field and factory, to teach, measure and follow up, to ensure that supervisors are properly fulfilling their managerial roles, as methods and technical leaders, as well as motivators of people and controllers of costs and expenses — human and material.
		All supervisors and managers should gradually be given training in cost reduction techniques, while maintaining or improving the level of quality and service.
		All levels management personnel should gradually be given formal training in management-by-objectives, including delegation, to improve their own and subordinates' performance.
		Tuition assistance on a local basis, as appropriate, to improve
			Same as (1) and (2).

(B) Training is also an investment in human capital and, as such, it must be well planned, controlled, and audited to produce the desired results: improve the return on investment in human assets.

(C) Total training costs and expenses should be *limited* to 2 per cent of total payroll costs in a rapidly growing company; less in a company which is levelling off. This excludes productive time of trainees, which should *not* be charged to training expense. There should be a separate budget for all training costs and expenses, in-house and outside, and this should be monitored and controlled by the local personnel manager or individual responsible for the function.

present job performance and/or prepare for promotion.
Provide back-ups for first two levels of management, through in-company training and development of high-potential employees, as identified through superior performance of present jobs.
Provide opportunities within house for job enlargement, job enrichment, and task-force assignments.

Plus: provide back-ups for first three levels of management.

Plus: provide training opportunities for newly hired and present executives from other companies.

For all three categories

Take full advantage of all payroll taxes applied to companies for training and development. Criteria as outlined above must still apply.

Exhibit 6 (cont.)

Policies/Priorities for improvement	Small companies (1) (under 250 employees)	Medium-sized companies (2) (251–1000 employees)	Large companies (3) (over 1000 employees)
Compensation system	Local wage, salary fringe benefit surveys with comparable companies in same or related industries, to ensure equitable total compensation of company personnel at all levels.	Same as (1), plus:	Same as (1) and (2).
	Each manager to explain to each of his people reporting direct the bases for the computation of his total remuneration, including:	Job evaluation system for all jobs at all levels of management.	
	Internal relationships.	Participate and/or initiate local total remuneration surveys where these are not available commercially, on a current basis, for the immediate geographical area.	
	External relationships.		
	Cost-of-living/inflation.		
	Market trend data.		
	Performance/achievement.	Development of formal salary structures, with appropriate salary ranges, based on job evaluation and local survey data.	
	Separate annual performance and salary reviews for all salaried employees, not represented by a union, to be conducted by the manager to whom the individual reports.	Maintain and update local salary structures as often as necessary, dependent on local conditions, high inflation, etc.	
	Two levels of approval required for all salary adjustments.	Recommend to next higher level of management the necessary addition of indirect compensation programmes, in accord with *local competitive practice* based on carefully documented surveys. For example, certain additional benefits, such as insurance, pension schemes, cars, club memberships, bonus arrangements, etc.	

Employee statistics

The following applies to all three categories

Need for a centralized employee records system, with individual dossiers on each employee, to include:

Application form.

All positions, dates, salary history within company.

All in-company experience, regardless of where and when obtained.

Any event of significance during his past years:

Performance appraisals.

Special commendations.

Job-related discussions.

Certain minimum statistics, on a local-company-wide basis must be centralized within the personnel department and used by general management to control more effectively total manpower costs and expenses. This data should include:

Overtime worked, for each department and each employee.

All costs and expenses of training and development within and outside the company.

All recruitment costs: direct and indirect.

Productivity records of new personnel.

Employee turnover and exit-interview data:

By department.

By supervisor.

By employee.

By day of the week.

By length of time on the job.

Employee absenteeism data.

Accident frequency and severity rates, and all lost time associated therewith, by department and by individual.

Direct *vs.* indirect employees on a monthly basis, by department.

Activity, productivity, and profitability, per employee.

Special Note

While many companies do have a variety of employee statistics, these statistics are not used properly as a management tool, to gain more effective control over total manpower costs: direct and indirect, fixed and variable.

Most statistical data should be accumulated and acted upon monthly.

Exhibit 6 (cont.)

Policies/Priorities for improvement	Small companies (1) (under 250 employees)	Medium-sized companies (2) (251–1000 employees)	Large companies (3) (over 1000 employees)
Local personnel policies	*The following applies to all three categories*		

To be developed locally as needed, but to include written policies and simple workable, well-communicated procedures, in such areas as:

Manpower forecasting and planning.
Recruitment/selection.
Training and development.
Compensation.
Resolving employee dissatisfactions.
Performance appraisal and review.
Transfers/promotions.
Matters of a legal nature affecting employee/employer relationships.
Pre-employment physical examinations and reference investigations.
Accidents.
Employee communications at all levels.
Participation in outside professional and community organizations and clubs.

These policies are to complement and support international personnel policy, as local conditions, legislation and customs permit.

The main issue is to have written policies distributed and explained to all local management personnel, to ensure uniform, equitable treatment of all employees in matters of major importance, where consistency of action is both necessary and desirable.

| **Recommended size of local company personnel function to ensure proper implementation of** | No personnel manager. But function must be performed by manager of finance and administration, in | The total number of professional and clerical staff engaged in personnel function activity should be between 0.8–1.0 per | 1000–3000 employees: 0.70–0.90 per cent. Over 3000 employees: 0.50–0.60 per cent. |

foregoing policies and guidelines

conjunction with the managing director.

cent of the total payroll, excluding social services personnel, e.g., security guards, cafeteria employees, and payroll clerks, where applicable.

The following additional guidelines apply to all companies regardless of size:

Role of regional and international directors of human resources

To participate in annual organization and manpower reviews.

To conduct high-level executive searches.

To assist in the selection, training and counselling of local company personnel managers, properly to perform all aspects of their jobs in a professional manner.

Directive policy

Provide a solution to the problem of executive back-ups for the first and second levels of management, in close cooperation with the company's managing director and regional manager.

To coordinate all intercompany training for newly hired and developing managers.

To monitor and audit the implementation of international personnel policy and guidelines.

To design uniform systems and procedures, where necessary and desirable, e.g., manpower inventory, performance appraisal format, employee statistics format, computer applications for manpower planning, as appropriate.

To assist in the formulation and realization of local company human resource goals, as requested.

Role of managing director

Actively to support, with personal participation and involvement in the human resource function, the realization of policies, plans, programmes and personnel goals for his company.

To improve measurably the return on human capital.

Exhibit 7

EXAMPLE OF A PROFESSIONALLY DONE HUMAN RESOURCE PROGRAMME, BASED ON THE SURVEY RESULTS

September 1974

Human resources department: a developing country

Top priorities

1 Compensation plans.
2 Management development programme.
3 Reduction of yearly turnover rates from 32 per cent to 18 per cent.
4 Training and development programme.
5 Recruitment and selection programme.
6 Better employee communication.
7 Occupational health/safety programme.

PRIORITY ONE: COMPENSATION PLANS

Why?:

Alleged underpayment regarding hourly paid and FOD employees.

Absence of accurate salary surveys.

Lack of consolidated temporary compensation policies and procedures.

Our duties:

Human resources manager	Line management
1 Issue temporary, emergency policies and procedures to resolve present compensation problems.	1 Fill in questionnaire and other forms requested for job evaluation.
2 Establish sound and comprehensive compensation policies regarding, for instance:	2 Submit, in advance and confidentially, to human resources, all proposals of nonmandatory wage/salary increases, through appropriate hierarchical channels of approval.
Legal mandatory increases.	3 When requested, take part in job evaluation committees.
Cost-of-living increases.	
Promotion increases.	
Merit increases.	
3 Design and implementation of job evaluation systems.	
4 Audit the compensation plan, periodically.	
5 Issue and/or approve in advance all forms of employee communication regarding compensation matters.	

Exhibit 7 (cont.)

Results expected

1 Reduction of time lost in haphazard wage increases decision-making.
2 Improvement of employees' morale.
3 Best knowledge of salary market trends.
4 Reduction of turnover by relative underpayment.
5 Reduction of individual claims to the courts about compensation inequities, which are 80 per cent of employee claims.
6 Improved productivity in the first weeks of employment, because of provision for systematic training and personnel specifications.
7 Possibility to set up semiskilled and skilled advancement through upgrade of skills.

Phase	Action steps description	Starting date	Ending date
1	Hire an experienced wage and salary administrator.	Aug. 74	Aug. 74
2	Issue of temporary compensation policies, regulating legal mandatory increases; cost-of-living increases; merit increases and promotion increases; use of salary surveys.	Aug. 74	Aug. 74
3	Set up job analyses/job descriptions for hourly paid jobs.	Sept. 74	Jan. 75
4	Classify jobs by job families and occupational/skill groups.	Feb. 75	Mar. 75
5	Design job evaluation manual, suited to company needs.	Feb. 75	Mar. 75
6	Put evaluation committees into action.	Mar. 75	May 75
7	Prepare statistical tabulations on jobs evaluated.	May 75	June 75
8	Define job classification for factory employees.	June 75	June 75
9	Choose key jobs to compare with salary survey data.	June 75	June 75
10	Plot present wage structure *vs.* market-place wage **structure.**	July 75	July 75
11	Implement the new compensation plan according to a time schedule, paying attention to overpaid and underpaid employees. Revise temporary compensation policies. **Adopt new compensation plan.**	Aug. 75	Aug. 75
12	*Employee communication key-points:* during phase 1 and before phase 2; after phase 3; after phase 4; before phase 6; after phase 8; in phase 11.	—	—
13	Provide semiannual maintenance and review, by means of compensation audits.	—	—

PRIORITY TWO: MANAGEMENT DEVELOPMENT PROGRAMME

Why?:

Improvement of managerial ability.

Provision for further company growth and development.

Very few promotions from within.

Very scarce back-up personnel, at present.

Human resources department	Line management
1 Counsel senior management on management-by-objectives (MBO) methodology.	1 Develop, implement and follow up own and subordinates' MBO goals.
2 Coordinate MBO efforts on a company-wide basis, and follow up how departments are progressing towards their goals.	2 Implement individual performance appraisal systems, and coaching, as needed.
3 Consolidate and update back-up charts, on a company-wide basis.	3 Suggest individual development plans for their subordinates to human resources manager.
4 Develop company-wide manpower inventories.	4 Identify and develop back-ups for own and subordinates' positions.
5 Provide early identification and career planning for young, highly talented people.	
6 Approve and make recommendations on individuals' development plans suggested by line management.	

Results expected

1 Improve overall efficiency within the company.

2 Better contribution to future regional plans as regards the local company's role in developing business.

Exhibit 7 (cont.)

3 Meet high personal needs of management people.

4 Eliminate employee's distrust about management effectiveness. For instance, avoid losses, estimated at $40 000, in respect of resignations and dismissals concerning managers, section heads, sales representatives, and engineering trainees, in last seven months.

5 40/60 back-ups need to be prepared.

Phase	Action step description	Starting date	Ending date
1	Follow-up MBO evaluation of first 14 months of MBO implementation.	July 74	July 74
2	Stimulate top management team to express views about their organization plans till the end of 1976 (manpower plan and forecast also).	Sept. 74	Sept. 74
3	Update back-up charts and set up quarterly reviews.	Sept. 74	Sept. 74
4	Define, in a top-management staff meeting, quantifiable middle-management needs, from October 1974 to mid-1976. Provide semester review of plans. Ask for international director, human resources to help in conducting this meeting. Monthly follow-up during staff meetings.	Oct. 74	Aug. 75
5	Comprehensive manpower inventory from present middle management to clerical, sales representatives, FOD and factory supervisory personnel.	Oct. 74	Nov. 74
6	Early identification of high-potential employees. Build up quarterly performance appraisals.	Dec. 74	Feb. 75
7	Plan job rotation and special assignments for management, sales and engineering trainees. Direct recruiting of senior undergraduate university students. Hiring of high-potential ones. Follow up.	Mar. 75	Apr. 75
8	Develop specialists/middle management, as professional managers through individual development plans.	May 75	Aug. 75

PRIORITY THREE: REDUCTION OF YEARLY TURNOVER RATES FROM 32 PER CENT TO 18 PER CENT

Why?:

Affects company's image as employer.

Increases scrap losses, lowers productivity, physical output and employee morale.

Increase hiring, induction, orientation and training costs.

High turnover is a clear symptom of bad psychosocial climate within the company.

Our duties:

This goal affects recruitment/selection, training/development and employee communication goals.

Only as an example, let us examine the induction/orientation function.

Human resources manager	Line management
1 Set up a formal initial induction programme. Company's history; line of products; compensation policies; timeclock procedures; benefits package; cafeteria; internal-safety regulations, etc. 2 Follow-up along probationary period.	1 Introduce new employees to their peers and people they have to be related to. 2 Give employees orientation on shop rules, safety, workflow, workload, job methods.

Exhibit 7 (cont.)

Results expected

1 Direct costs saving nearly $130 000 yearly, as follows:

  Plus: Present turnover: 2.7 per cent monthly.
  Present payroll without charges: x dollars.
  Average (40 per cent) payroll social charges: x dollars.
  2.7 x y dollars = z dollars due to monthly turnover.
  y dollars x 12 months = y dollars due to yearly turnover.

2 Decrease scrap losses within the company.

3 Increase in quality of personnel selection, as a consequence of decreased personnel hiring for replacing people who have quit or have been dismissed.

4 Better company image as a fair employer in local communities.

Phase	Action steps description	Starting date	Ending date
1	Turnover statistics analysis (sex, age bands, length of service, job/position, wage and salary brackets, birthplace, department, supervisor).	Aug. 74	Aug. 74
2	Introduce and put exit interviews into action.	Sept. 74	Oct. 74
3	Writing of personnel specifications from job descriptions.	Oct. 74	Feb. 75
4	Introduction of visits to the workplace just before preliminary interviews.	Oct. 74	Oct. 74
5	Stimulate promotion-from-within policies.		
6	Identify new labour sources and use better recruitment media.	Oct. 74	Nov. 74
7	Develop pre-employment tests for hourly employees.	Dec. 74	Mar. 75
8	Develop pre-employment tests for clerical and supervisory people.	Jan. 75	Apr. 75
9	Intensive supervisory training in factory on employee counselling and interviewing, dissatisfactions compensation, transfers, interpersonal relationships problems, personal financial problems	Mar. 75	Mar. 75
10	Implement formal appraisal evaluation forms for monthly clerical employees.	May 75	June 75
11	Clerical supervisory training programme on appraising employees.	June 75	July 75
12	Implementation of merit appraisal and seniority criteria for hourly paid employee.	Aug. 75	Aug. 75

PRIORITY FOUR: TRAINING AND DEVELOPMENT PROGRAMME

Why?:

On the average, employees are lacking even minimum skills required for a good output.

Some vital line areas cannot get their problems solved without upgrading and/or updating employees skills.

Urgently needed to change some supervisory behavioural patterns.

Human resources manager

1 Identify broad overall training needs in the company.
2 Train line managers in on-the-job training techniques.
3 Suggest and implement training results evaluations and measurements.
4 Develop key training programmes.
5 Provide technical support and training for line managers concerning training programmes, lessons plans, instructional units and instructional aids.
6 Follow-up to ensure that outside training applies to company needs.

Line management

1 Identify short- and long-term problems within their department that can be adequately solved through training and submit them to human resources department.
2 On-the-job training.
3 Allow people to attend internal or outside course, according to individual training needs previously identified by human resources department expert.
4 Stimulate subordinates to self-improvement and to improve their formal education.
5 To facilitate application of training to job responsibility.
6 Measure the degree to which the training is applied on the job.

Results expected

1 Productivity increases in output and quality, as measured by 10 per cent increases in the 'activity per employee' index.
2 Improved company morale through decreasing veiled dissatisfaction in field and factory.
3 Good pilot-testing for training future supervisors.

Exhibit 7 (cont.)

Phase	Action steps definition	Starting date	Ending date
1	Hire a well-experienced training and development man.	Aug. 74	Aug. 74
2	Through face-to-face interviews with top line managers, bring about conditions to implement urgently needed training and development programmes, for instance as follows:		
	Supervisory training in factory.		
	Training for upgrading skills in building and maintenance jobs.		
3	Set up a training-needs identification, by means of operational and individual analysis.	Sept. 74	Oct. 74
4	Set up specific training goals.	Oct. 74	Oct. 74
5	Plan for results evaluations and measurements.	Oct. 74	Nov. 74
6	Choice of the best training mix to be applied to each case, concerning training methodology and instructional techniques.	Nov. 74	Nov. 74
7	Development of programme contents into instructional units.	Nov. 74	Nov. 74
8	Choice for best suitable training time schedule and split instructional units according to them.	Dec. 74	Jan. 75
9	Development of detailed lesson plans for each instructional unit.	Dec. 74	Jan. 75
10	Choice of the most appropriate instructional aids.	Jan. 75	Feb. 75
11	Provision for instructional facilities.	Feb. 75	Feb. 75
12	Previous communication to candidates and their supervisors.	Feb. 75	Feb. 75
13	Programme begin.	Mar. 75	Mar. 75
14	Planning for follow-up to evaluate effectiveness of the training programme by application of new skills on-the-job.		

PRIORITY FIVE: RECRUITMENT AND SELECTION PROGRAMME

Why?:

High turnover rates have been partially due to mistakes by the supervisory team in doing their own personnel selection.

Good recruitment/selection can ease and save money in training and development tasks.

Personnel selection procedures are, indeed, very poor.

Human resources manager		Line management	
1	According to approved manpower forecasts, recruit people using the best available sources, trying, first of all, to promote from within.	1	As much as possible, fill personnel requisitions in advance of job openings due to forecasted dismissals.
2	Set up personnel specifications, stemming from job descriptions.	2	Provide human resources department with all personnel specifications, detailed skills, educational and behavioural aspects concerning vacant jobs.
3	Design and/or administer pre-employment tests.	3	Before asking for headcount increase, be sure all other possible solutions have been carefully examined.
4	Use in-depth interviews, in order to assess abilities, past professional life history, interests, potential and personality traits in all prospective candidates to job vacancies.	4	Administer on-the-job pre-employment achievement tests.
5	Train line managers in improving their interviewing skills.	5	Interview candidates previously screened by human resources department, as regarding technical/professional aspects.
6	Analyse applicants' résumés, jointly with line managers.	6	Analyse applicants' résumés, jointly with human resources department.
7	Validate pre-employment selection procedures, periodically.	7	Give human resources department immediate feedback when misunderstandings occur in preliminary selection process.
8	Make reference investigations prior to employment.		

Exhibit 7 (cont.)

Results expected
1 Reduce turnover.
2 Better placement.
3 Improve quality of people hired, including people who have potential to grow.
4 Easier and quicker matching of line managers' needs to personnel requisitions.
5 In medium-range terms, it will be easier to find back-ups from within.

Phase	Action steps descriptions	Starting date	Ending date
1	Hire a well-experienced personnel recruitment/selection man.	Aug. 74	Aug. 74
2	At a minimum delay, try to hire the best key people immediately necessary to the several departments.	Aug. 74	Sept. 74
3	Set up personnel recruitment and selection flow charts and controls at human resources department.	Aug. 74	Sept. 74
4	Build up sound personnel specifications, from job descriptions.	Oct. 74	Feb. 75
5	Set up a sound promotion-from-within policy.	Oct. 74	Oct. 74
6	Develop adequate recruitment sources fitted to each kind of skills need.	Oct. 74	Nov. 74
7	Develop pre-employment tests for hourly paid and FOD people.	Dec. 74	Mar. 75
8	Develop pre-employment tests for clerical and supervisory personnel.	Jan. 75	Apr. 75
9	Train line managers, supervisors, and local branches administrative assistants, in test administering and interviewing skills.	May 75	July 75

PRIORITY SIX: BETTER EMPLOYEE COMMUNICATION

Why?:

Psychosocial climate has not been good in recent times.

We can foster employee morale: and thus improve output by means of simple, costless measures.

This will strengthen our company's image.

Human resources manager

1 Train line managers in employee counselling.
2 Issue guidelines to line managers for administration of disciplinary action.
3 Conduct exit interviews with all employees who leave the company.
4 Use bulletin boards effectively as employees' communication media.
5 Deal with labour claims at the courts.
6 Implement a suggestion plan.

Additional comments on personnel daily work

1 Revise, reissue, and permanently update, personnel procedures, forms and controls.
2 Provide that all payroll and related legal and social security's data are always provided on due time.

Line management

1 Counsel employees about personal dissatisfactions:
   Interpersonal relationships.
   Benefits.
   Compensations.
   Personal finance problems.
2 Ensure compliance with shop rules and disciplinary procedures.
3 Conduct exit interviews with employees who quit voluntarily.
4 Obtain prior clearance from human resources department before dismissing an employee.
5 Deal with labour claims at the courts only upon human resources department's delegation.

1 Neither transfer nor promote without prior consultation to human resources department.
2 Strictly comply with all personnel policies and procedures.
3 Give requested information to payroll on due time.

Exhibit 7 (cont.)

Results expected

1 $48 000 yearly in cost savings from suggestions.
2 Change positively our present psychosocial climate.
3 Strengthen *esprit de corps*, and thus heighten employee retention rates.
4 30 per cent decrease in unjustified absences from work.

Phase	Action steps description	Starting date	Ending date
1	Introduction of exit interviews.	Sept. 74	Oct. 74
2	Issue of quarterly two-page 'letter from the president'.	Oct. 74	ongoing
3	Middle-management intensive training in conference leadership.	Nov. 74	Dec. 74
4	Manager/subordinate fortnightly meetings. Follow-up of their agendas.	Mar. 75	Apr. 75
5	Planning effective use of bulletins boards: training courses, safety contests, new shop rules.	May 75	May 75
6	Suggestions plan and its cash awards.	June 75	Aug. 75
7	Intensive short-term supervisory training in written and face-to-face communication.	July 75	Aug. 75
8	Lay-out of a monthly, four-page, low-cost house organ.	Aug. 75	Dec. 75

PRIORITY SEVEN: OCCUPATIONAL HEALTH/SAFETY PROGRAMME

Why?:

We can lower our social-security insurance rate.

Humane consideration of human beings.

Compliance with new Occupational Health and Industrial Safety regulations, to be enforced after 1 January 1975.

Human resources manager

1   Try to reduce overall accident rates, mainly severance rates (frequency and severity).

2   Maintain mandatory and non-mandatory accident statistics.

Line management

1   Develop attitude of safety-conciousness.

2   Strongly support internal safety committee's recommendations on their area.

Results expected

1   Avoid any death-by-accident in mid-74/mid-76 period.

2   Reduce by 10 per cent our frequency rate.

3   Reduce by 20 per cent our severance rate.

4   Social security insurance savings of $ .... yearly.

Exhibit 7 (cont.)

Phase	Action steps description	Starting date	Ending date
1	Update accident statistics, in order to comply with legal regulations.	Aug. 74	Sept. 74
2	Accurate study of reasons for accidents by department: supervisor; exact time when the accident happens; the day of the week the accident happens.	Oct. 74	Nov. 74
3	Provision for compliance with federal regulations, which will be enacted on 1 January 1975.	Dec. 74	Dec. 74
4	Study about prevention measures to be taken in order to decrease possibility of accidents.	Jan. 75	Feb. 75
5	Put internal safety committees into action.	Mar. 75	Apr. 75
6	Ask for a reduction in social-security charges and accident-insurance costs.	May 75	ongoing

APPENDIX B
SPECIMEN DOCUMENTS

Exhibit 8

DEVELOPING COUNTRY: TWO-YEAR HUMAN RESOURCE GOALS

Objectives	Strategies and tactics	Date of imple-mentation	Required means	Expected results
1 Manpower planning and forecasting				
Establish and maintain an updated manpower forecast, with one year firm and two years estimated, with due regard for the need to reduce overall head-count in line with realistic workloads.	Introduce into the company new concepts of manpower utilization in order to alleviate traditional and cultural biases. Make better use of non-white labour in the field, both to cut costs and remedy short-ages. Line management, with specialist personnel department assistance, specify periodically the numbers of different types of employees needed. Consistent implementation of manpower controls.	Apr. 1975 to Jan. 1976	In consultation with line management, preparation by personnel department of re-education/work study programmes aimed at re-moving barriers to better utilization of all levels of staff, in order to lay foundations for restructuring of the service, construction and factory operations (Sept. 1975). Personnel department set up data collection procedures, to provide information required on which to base manpower projections (June 1975).	Managers are becoming more skilled in relating manpower requirements to workloads in a realistic way.

Exhibit 8 (cont.)

Objectives	Strategies and tactics	Date of implementation	Required means	Expected results
2 Recruitment				
To increase, by appropriate recruitment from inside and outside the company, the number of highly qualified employees, black and white and managers in the company in order to improve profitability and take advantage of growth opportunities.	Based on manpower plan and forecast, recruit only employees with growth potential. Ensure that the full potential labour supply available on labour market is being tapped at minimum cost. Internal recruitment to reduce overall number of heads. External recruitment only for selective replacement of key personnel not available from inside. Draw up proposals for intake of selected graduates.	Oct. 1975	Appointment of professionally trained recruitment/training officer (June 1975). Preparation of position descriptions manpower specifications and defined working relationships for all new and key jobs (Sept. 1975). System of internal advertising, so that staff may nominate themselves for promotionary positions (Sept. 1975). Personnel department to set up system of selection panels on which line managers will serve (Sept. 1975). Training of line supervisory staff in better selection interviewing, exit interviewing and assessment procedures (Oct. 1975).	Crisis-orientated hire situations are reduced in numbers. Improvement in speed with which we fill key vacancies. Drop in turnover. Assessed potential of available manpower shows progressive improvement.

3 Employee orientation and induction To provide all newly hired, transferred and promoted employees with an adequate company induction, so that their integration into their respective job areas may be speeded up.	Aug. 1975	Personnel department has responsibility for developing, in conjunction with line specialists, orientation and induction programmes (both general and technical) for various levels of staff. In decentralized operations, an employee's immediate manager, using provided materials, to be responsible for complete company and job orientation. Working relationships, authorities and performance standards are to be defined in writing to all new employees by own manager.	Preparation of brochure on company history, conditions of service, etc., to be prepared by personnel department. Additional induction training materials to be developed, in conjunction with line specialists and supervisory staff given training in effective use of this (Jan. 1976). Model one- to two-day induction programmes, to be set up for supervisory and management appointees (Mar. 1976). Factory and field visits, where possible.	High turnover, particularly in early part of service, low productivity and failure to meet profit projections, due to poor definition of responsibility and inadequate integration of new staff members, are being progressively reduced.
4 Manpower mix Optimize the manpower mix in the company, in terms of present and	Jan./Feb. 1976	Identify any inadequate spread of talent which may be causing particular branches,	Explore work on and present statistical analyses of the company's and departments'	An improvement in the spread of talent, at different managerial levels, between

Exhibit 8 (cont.)

Objectives	Strategies and tactics	Date of implementation	Required means	Expected results
expected future business demands.	sections or departments of the company to be contributing less than they should to achievement of company objectives. Reduce vulnerability to unexpected deletions by increasing the mobility and flexibility of management and supervisory resources. Start work towards a skills and experience register, in line with future business plans.		manpower inventories which clearly illustrate significant differences in the talent mix (Jan. 1976). Management committee has had these problems and demonstrated to them and plans and implements action to correct any inequitable spread of talent (Feb. 1976).	departments, sections, branches, functions, etc., in the company. An increase in the ratio of persons available, and prepared to fill or be promoted to a number of positions inside and outside their present department/branches, to those in respect of whom the possibilities are more limited.
5 Training and development				
To improve productivity and profitability by increasing employee effectiveness at all levels.	Identify and develop back-up personnel for all key positions. Based on well-defined job and personnel specifications, provide appropriate training for all levels of employees, with both in-company and external training courses being catered for.	Apr. 1975 to Sept. 1976	Development of precise performance appraisal standards and review procedures, and training of supervisory and management staff in the use of these (Sept. 1975). Set up programmes and procedures for early identification and subsequent develop-	Possible successors for predicted vacancies have been identified. Assessment of on-the-job performance at each level in the company is showing progressive improvement.

| | | May. 1975 to Oct. 1975 | ment of those that show supervisory and management potential for specialist development (Jan. 1976). Gain secondment of appropriate line specialists to work on development of technical training materials required (June 1975). Appoint and train suitable full-/part-time trainers in all major branch or factory areas (Sept. 1975 onwards). |

Introduce procedures and standards in terms of which training results can be measured. Establish a total training budget to be monitored centrally by the personnel department. Establish and equip a technical training centre, to be used flexibly for apprentice, artisan and non-white training. Full advantage to be taken of all tax rebates available.

6 Compensation system

To set up a reward policy, which is competitive, results-orientated and, where possible, based on profit objectives.

Rationalize conditions of service and remuneration policies, in order to ensure that they are competitive. Familiarize line management with system of job grading that has been introduced. Set up separate performance and salary reviews for all salaried and hourly paid employees.*

Training all line managers in criteria of job grading as a basis for job restructuring and work re-allocation exercises (May 1975). Continued participation in local- and national-salary surveys (Aug. 1976). Maintain and update current salary and wage structures (Oct. 1975).

Reduction in the number of cases and extent to which age/potential/market ratings are out of line with present salaries or wages paid.

Exhibit 8 (cont.)

Objectives	Strategies and tactics	Date of implementation	Required means	Expected results
7 Employee statistics				
To have available, for use by management, accurate, timely statistics, maintained on all employees, for the purpose of efficient utilization and control of total manpower costs and expenses.	Personnel department set up appropriate reporting and measurement procedures, in order to produce meaningful reports in the areas listed in the objective. A centralized record system with individual dossiers on each employee. Centralization within the personnel department of certain minimum statistics, on a company-wide basis in order to provide management with information to more effectively control manpower costs and expenses.	May 1975 to Dec. 1975	Procedures to be set up for routine collection of data in areas such as: overtime worked, all costs and expenses of training, all recruitment costs, productivity records, employee turnover, absenteeism, accident frequency, direct vs. indirect employees and activity, productivity and profitability per employee.	The position is obtained where senior managers' actions reflect their belief and confidence in the manpower figures which are produced.

Exhibit 9

DEVELOPED COUNTRY: HUMAN RESOURCES IMPROVEMENT PLAN: TOP PRIORITIES

Area of improvement	Situation in need of improvement	Objective in terms of results wanted	Action steps to attain objective	Dates Starting	Ending	Responsibility
Manpower planning and recruitment	At present we are projecting our manpower requirements for the year ahead only, and the basis we are using are the company historical growth trends, and other systems of a very limited forecasting period. On the other hand, our entry qualifications are not sufficiently well stated to specify the adequate kinds of people needed for the business.	(a) To have prepared by 15 Sept. 1975 a deep and valid assessment of anticipated manpower requirements, which should be geared to known causes of manpower reductions; and to clearly stated goals of corporate growth and expansion, expressed in terms of a three years' period including also the preparation of demanding entry standards and per-	1 Upon completing preparation of back-up tables, determine replacement needs for key positions.	1 Apr. 75	4 Apr. 75	
			2 Identify gaps which require immediate action.	7 Apr. 75	7 Apr. 75	
			3 Develop guidelines for sound recruiting practices.	24 Jan. 75	14 Feb. 75	
			4 Prepare performance standards for all key positions.	14 May 75	22 July 75	
			5 Determine the manpower needs, by departments, based on stated performance goals.	10 Apr. 75	5 June 75	

Exhibit 9 (cont.)

Area of improvement	Situation in need of improvement	Objective in terms of results wanted	Action steps to attain objective	Dates Starting	Ending	Responsibility
	Consequently, this entire situation results in a continuous 'firefighting' approach to our recruitment efforts and in a subsequent mediority of our staff services.	formance capability requirements, which will serve as the basis for a more effective recruitment programme.	6 Establish recruitment priorities and develop adequate programme for execution.	20 June 75	30 June 75	
			7 Develop a 'grass root' study to determine *actual* manning requirements.	3 Mar. 75	30 Apr. 75	
			8 Develop a manpower forecast for the next three years and present it to managing director.	30 July 75	15 Sept. 75	
Training and development	We do not have back-ups identified for most of our key jobs, and although **each manager could be** expected to have in mind a replacement for each key position there is no across-the-board planning to ensure sound	(b) To have back-up tables prepared by 30 March 1975, in order to know in advance who in the organization is or could be available, and qualified to substitute for whom, to fill the gap successfully. This also in-	1 Determine which are the key positions of the company.	20 Jan. 75	24 Jan. 75	
			2 Prepare tables to show key positions and incumbents, including age and coded data about performance rating, estimated potential and waiting period (tentatively).	27 Jan. 75	20 Feb. 75	

cludes the identification of key positions where ready or forward replacements are not available.

There are many managerial, professional and supervisory positions for which description is outdated or does not exist. Therefore, there are not accurate yardsticks for measuring individual performance against job requirements. The lack of this infor-

3	Meet with managers to identify possible ready or forward replacements in every key position.	3 Feb. 75	7 Feb. 75
4	Determine which are the key positions lacking ready or forward replacement and include them in the manpower planning and recruitment programme.	3 Feb 75	14 Feb. 75
5	Prepare tables and present them to managing director.	24 Mar. 75	28 Mar. 75

(c) To have described by May 1975 the properties of every managerial and professional position of the company to identify the competencies required to carry out designated responsibilities effectively. The descriptions are to be prepared in a clear and concise manner, in order to provide

1	Design a job description format, within the guidelines approved, and present it to managing director.	3 Feb. 75	7 Feb. 75
2	Discuss format with managers for acceptance and further implementation.	10 Feb. 75	13 Feb. 75
3	Arrange a series of meetings to provide guidance and assistance in the preparation of descriptions.	3 Mar. 75	7 Mar. 75

Exhibit 9 (cont.)

Area of improvement	Situation in need of improvement	Objective in terms of results wanted	Action steps to attain objective	Dates		Responsibility
				Starting	Ending	
	mation also represents a barrier for the preparation of a consistent salary structure.	the basis for organizing and correlating effort and for setting the type and quantity of work to be performed.	4 Set target dates for the receipt and checking of descriptions.	3 Mar. 75	7 Mar. 75	
			5 Present information to managing director.	10 Apr. 75	10 Apr. 75	
			6 Make distribution of descriptions to managers.	25 Apr. 75	25 Apr. 75	
			7 Prepare and issue a norm for reviewing and revising descriptions on an organized basis.	3 Mar. 75	30 Mar. 75	
	Our management and supervisory practices are, in general, in great need of improvement. There is a lack of knowledge in conducting effective job interviews, performance appraisals, handling of grievances, problem-solving and decision-making,	(d) To set up the basis by 30 Sept. 1975 for the gradual improvement of the managerial skills and effectiveness of our management and supervisory personnel by providing them with selective training and coaching for the adequate fulfilling of their day-to-day responsibilities in	1 Introduce and expedite preparation of an analysis programme, in order to detect weaknesses in the areas of supervisory responsibility and authority.	25 Jan 75	3 Mar. 75	
			2 Explain the programme to management and secure acceptance and commitment for implementation to lower managerial levels.	17 Mar. 75	21 Mar. 75	

training on-the-job, and counselling.

This situation, which is extensive to most of our management and supervisory levels, produces a great deal of 'upwards' delegation and impedes the improvement of our labour relations and personnel commitment.

managing subordinates.

3	Set target dates for completion.	17 Mar. 75	21 Mar. 75
4	Prepare a list of individual- or group-training needs detected through the analyses.	29 May 75	23 May 75
5	Prepare a training plan and present to management.	2 June 75	30 June 75
6	Prepare a plan for developing instructors from the supervisory group.	2 June 75	20 June 75
7	Study the advisability of conducting a second analyses programme in order to obtain feedback of progress achieved.		

Management development activities exist, but they are rather shallow and inconsequential and result in little improvement in the development of individual careers.

(e)	To establish the basis by 30 Sept. 1975 for a systematic review and identification of management people who can be expected to reach higher effectiveness more quickly through education and special assignments		
1	Prepare a management development policy for approval of managing director. This step considered essential for the preparation of the climate in management development activities.	18 Feb. 75	28 Feb. 75
2	Recommend managing director to establish a local management	10 Mar. 75	21 Mar. 75

Exhibit 9 (cont.)

Area of improvement	Situation in need of improvement	Objective in terms of results wanted	Action steps to attain objective	Dates		Responsibility
				Starting	Ending	
		than would be possible by job experience alone.	development committee, including an outline of authority and responsibilities of the committee members.			
			3 Recommend managing director the implementation of regular management development committee meetings, to decide on plans to be followed with regard to development needs.	21 Mar. 75	21 Mar. 75	
			4 Advise members on the techniques and methods to be used for estimating individual potential.	Apr. 75	Apr. 75	
			5 Prepare a presentation to management development committee members, in order to adopt the adequate tools and procedures to assure continuous and effective development activities.	19 May 75	23 May 75	

Compensation					
Due to lack of an organized system on compensation, practices are not consistent enough clearly to recognize individual differences in performance and contribution to company goals. We are operating mostly by intuition and rather timidly on the recognition of subject differences. Also, our salary levels have been somewhat unrelated to current salary levels of other local companies.	(f) To have set up by 30 Sept. 1975 an organized method to provide the basis for a more consistent and objective salary administration, including the preparation of an adequate salary structure, aimed to recruit, retain and reward effective people.	1 Prepare a salary administration policy and submit it for the approval of managing director.	Nov. 74	Nov. 74	
		2 Develop a salary structure, orienting the axis of the structure to median current salaries of other local companies, and submit it for the approval of the managing director.	Nov. 74	Nov. 74	
		3 Recommend managing director to establish a salary committee.	Done	Done	Not nominated yet.
		4 Specify the responsibilities and authority of subject committee and make recommendations to managing director.	Done	Done	
		5 Develop a 'classification chart' and allocate all monthly positions of the company.	Dec. 74	Dec. 74	
		6 Recommend managing director the committee nomination.	24 Jan. 75	24 Jan. 75	
		7 Discuss chart with the management group.	7 Feb. 75	7 Feb. 75	

Exhibit 9 (cont.)

8	Develop a 'classification standards' chart for all levels of salary structure.	3 Mar. 75	29 Mar. 75
9	Develop salary career curves by levels for all managerial and professional employees, in order to forecast individual salary progression, taking into account performance and potential.	14 Mar. 75	14 Apr. 75
10	Design a performance appraisal and review format, within the guidelines established, and discuss it with management for implementation.	3 Mar. 75	7 Mar. 75

11	Introduce the use of alternation ranking techniques, to identify the relative highest individual performance and potential.	12 May 75	23 May 75
12	Design a 'request for reclassification' format for effective maintenance of the 'classification chart'.	3 Mar. 75	5 Mar. 75
13	Provide guidance and indoctrination to salary committee members for effective use and interpretation of salary administration procedures.	8 July 75	11 July 75

Exhibit 10

CRITERIA FOR EVALUATING AN EXECUTIVE SEARCH FIRM

1 Questions they should ask

(A) *General background — industry and company*

Company position in industry: last five years:

(a) Market share, product innovation, strategy, price policy. All
    competitive advantages and disadvantages: price, service, delivery,
    quality, reliability, etc., diversification, plans, efforts.
(b) Company gaining or declining.
(c) Company growth and percentage of profit domestic *vs.* international:
    past five years.
(d) Investment in R & D as percentage of sales.

Overall company's major strengths and weaknesses: personality of
    company.
Written statements of company policies, objectives, goals, long-range plans.

(B) *Present company executives*

New candidates' peers (they may want to meet others):

Average age, education, competence, years of service.
How many recent hires among top group.
How many recent terminations? Reasons.
Describe present executives in terms of personal and professional traits and
    competences.
Chief executive's business philosophy: how communicated and
    implemented within the company?

(C) *Position itself*

Why open? New job, resignation (why?), reorganization, etc.
Characteristics of man in present job.
Position description.
Major challenges in job: problems to be solved.
Degree of support from president.

Relationship, formal and informal, to other executives above, same level
and below.
Major priorities, workplan, accountabilities, delegated authority, problems
to be solved (why problems to be solved exist today).

(D) *The ideal candidate*

Age, education, experience, personal characteristics, other professional
credentials.
Any restrictions: sex, colour, national origin, religion, etc.
Types of industries from which this man could come.
Types of industries where not to recruit.
Any 'non-raid' agreements with competitors?
What specific companies to stay away from.
Any preference of companies to recruit from.
Required intellectual capacity.

2 Conducting the search (*modus operandi*: search company)

Do they accept contingency assignments: no fees unless a candidate is
accepted? This is considered non-professional.
Do they insist on sending a batch of résumés to see if they are on or near
the target? Are candidates unemployed?
Have they actually interviewed candidates and found them tentatively
acceptable and willing to consider the position at the salary level
offered?
How frequently do they report on search progress?
Their estimate of how difficult to fill the assignment. If they *act* reluctantly,
bad sign.
Three months is adequate time to present acceptable candidate.

Do they compare candidates presented?

Comparative strengths and weaknesses of each man.
Their choice and why? Or do they ask your choice first?

How many candidates do they present?

Two or three should be maximum number.
All should be qualified: e.g., meet 65—70 per cent of job and man
specification.

Exhibit 10 (cont.)

Do they insist on regular client meetings?

Not good; we only want final candidates, not paperwork.

The search contract itself

Good firms 25—30 per cent of first year's total compensation, excluding
 fringe benefits.
    Plus up to one-third in expenses.
    Pay one-third right away.
    Then one-third at the end of first month.
    Final one-third upon conclusion of search.
    Guarantee candidate for one year or do job over again free, but
       charge additional out-of-pocket expenses.

3   Reference investigation

Extensive dossier on each man, including:

Complete description of what he has done.
His accomplishments: areas of underachievement, developmental needs.
Strengths and weaknesses as demonstrated through his on-the-job
   performance: emphasis on the last five years primarily.
Psychological testing bad: stay away from this.
Evidence of ability to get people to change, build loyalty, teamwork,
   commitment.
Credit, police, personal habits investigation; education verification.
Opinion of the candidate over the past two or three jobs, as given by his
   bosses, his peers, his subordinates.
Plus search consultant's own procedures to evaluate a candidate's
   professional, personal, technical and managerial competence. They
   should be able to ascertain in depth his functional ability.

4   Who will actually conduct the search?

Do not accept team effort: one man responsible.
Meet man personally responsible, to evaluate his capabilities to do the job.
   It takes a senior executive to entice another one. Often partner is good,
   consultant is mediocre.

Present workload of man doing the search.
> No more than five current assignments in varying stages of
> completion.

5 Search consultants almost inevitably try to get highest possible salary

This makes the job easier. If in this case they, say, base of $60 000, they
> do not know the calibre of man sought, or magnitude of job to be done.

6 Reputation of the executive search firm

Among other reputable search firms?
Among clients served?
Types of positions they have filled:
> Organization level, function, salary?

Record of successful placements:
> Still on the job after two years? Promotions?

Exhibit 11

MANAGERIAL OPINION SURVEY

1 Credibility

Degree to which he inspires trust and confidence in his subordinates.
Closely related to full delegation of responsibility, authority and
accountability for decision-making:

(1) Complete trust and confidence.
(2) Limited trust with some reservation.
(3) Lack of trust and confidence.

2 Charisma

Degree to which he makes one feel free to come in and discuss job-related
matters, i.e. his attitude, behaviour and receptivity. This is closely related
to motivation and loyalty:

(1) Individual feels free to initiate frank, open discussion on all matters,
including major problems, mistakes, bad news.
(2) Individual must speak in a guarded manner because of concern for
possible negative reaction from the boss.
(3) Individual witholds information because of fear for punitive or
negative reaction.

3 Communications

Degree to which there is a free flow of information within the management
team: upwards, downwards, and across. This also reflects clear
communication of International Department objectives and goals:

(1) Easily obtains ideas from his managers and uses them or clearly
explains why they cannot be implemented. Communicates all
matters of importance to individuals.
(2) Individuals are somewhat reluctant to come up with new ideas; they
also sometimes feel they do not get all the facts.
(3) He rarely gets ideas from his managers and seldom uses them when
received. Individuals feel they do not know what is going on.

4   Organization

Degree to which the organization is clearly defined, relatively stable, carefully planned, and results in clear work assignments through logical, orderly organization of the work to be done:

(1)   Organization is well defined, including individual relationships therein. It is well planned, clearly understood by all.
(2)   Organization changes frequently, causing some confusion in work assignments and relationships. Planning could be improved.
(3)   Organization is haphazard, poorly defined, changes too frequently, and individuals do not understand organization relationships.

5   Control of performance

Degree to which managers are involved in establishing controls, not as restraints, but management tools for measuring and improving business and individual results:

(1)   All senior managers are involved in establishing and implementing controls to assist in problem-solving and improved planning.
(2)   There is some downward delegation of control, but used for policing performance instead of guides to improve performance.
(3)   Controls are highly concentrated at the top and used primarily for policing and punishment.

6   Decision-making

This refers to who makes the decisions and where they are made, and how much latitude is given to the individual manager in making his own decisions. This is closely related to motivation:

(1)   Important decisions are evolved through participation, involvement and usually consensus, with clear mutual understanding of specific job relationships.
(2)   Decisions of major impact are highly concentrated at the top, but problems are usually discussed with subordinates.
(3)   All important decisions made by one or two people with little, if any, discussion with those who must implement.

Exhibit 11 (cont.)

7 Advancement and personnel development

Degree to which the individual feels he has opportunity for professional growth, advancement and development:

(1) Ample opportunity for career advancement based on faith and confidence in top management.
(2) Limited opportunity for development and promotion.
(3) No opportunity to demonstrate capabilities; underutilized by the boss; no chance to get ahead.

8 Performance review and appraisal

Degree to which the individual has clearly defined performance standards for his position, and a formal, annual discussion of his performance and how to improve same:

(1) Lets the individual know periodically how well he is doing and, annually, specifically, how his performance and contribution can be improved.
(2) Seldom discusses performance constructively; normally confines discussion to pointing out mistakes.
(3) Never lets the individual know where he stands or how to improve his performance.

9 Compensation

Degree to which the individual feels he is properly compensated for his contributions (includes total remuneration, including incentive compensation:

(1) Directly related to performance and improvement of business results.
(2) Little relationship to performance and position responsibility.
(3) No relationship to performance or position responsibility. Arbitrarily determined.

Comments

Any additional overall comments about manager's leadership style.

INTERNATIONAL MANPOWER INVENTORY
DIVISION PERSONNEL RECORDS

DATE

PERSONAL DATA

Address	Place of birth	Date
	Citizenship	
	By birth	Date of employment with
		1.
Tel. no.	By naturalization	2.
	Valid passport held	3.
		Date of leaving
		1.
		2.
		3.

Change of address

1.	Medical history	Date of retirement
	Physical limitations/handicaps	**For completion by ID office**
	Last medical exam date	Code status no.
Tel. no.	Height ft ins Weight lbs	Transfer function
2.	**MARITAL STATUS**	Transfer country
	Divorced Single	Sex
	Married Widowed	Please affix photo
	Separated No. of dependents	
Tel. no.		

COMPLETED BY	Date	APPROVED BY	Date
NAME	TITLE	REGION	LOCATION

Exhibit 12 (cont.)

ACADEMIC BACKGROUND AND QUALIFICATIONS

Institution and location	Degrees/Diplomas	Dates

CAREER INTERESTS

Indicate order of preference

1.
2.
3.
4.

WILLING TO RELOCATE

Indicate order of preference

1.
2.
3.
4.
5.

Anywhere   Yes   No

LANGUAGE PROFICIENCY

Language	Degree of proficiency
1.	
Read	
Write	
Speak	
2.	
Read	
Write	
Speak	
3.	
Read	
Write	
Speak	

A Limited
B Adequate for business
C Fluent

INTERNAL AND EXTERNAL TRAINING

Institution and location	Subject	Dates

JOB HISTORY

Company and location	Job title	Approx. salary $	Dates	Job code

Professional interests and affiliations

EVALUATION POINTS

Year	Position	Know-how	Problem-solving	Account-ability	Total	Profile	Grade	Position in grade

Company loans

Amount
Date

FRINGE BENEFITS US Home Assgn.

Pension
Medical
Life insurance
Stock purchase
Travel-accident insurance
Long-term disability

Year	Position	Perfor-mance	Potential	Salary increase	Salary	Salary and bonus	Foreign Service Allow-ance	Exec. incent. comp.	TOTAL

Code status no.
Exec. incent. comp.
'B' bonus
Proficiency level
Advancement potential
Grade
Transfer function
Transfer country
High potential
Foreign-service employee
Third-country national

NAME   TITLE   REGION   LOCATION

Exhibit 13

EXECUTIVE BACK-UP FORM

Name	Position	Code status no.	Perf. level	Advance potential	Replacement for (back-up) (Time perf. pot.)	Replacement by (back-up) (Time perf. pot.)	Altern. back-up opinion	Altern. career pattern	FSE/ TCN	Total salary and grade bonus	Training recommended		Specific action required
											Minor skills	Major skills	

DIVISION _____ REGION _____ COMPANY

Exhibit 14

ORIENTATION CHECKLIST FOR FOREIGN ASSIGNMENT

To be prepared in advance of individual's acceptance of the assignment by the host company

COMPANY .... COMPANY LOCATION ....

---

1   GENERAL INFORMATION

1.1   *Temperature* (Fahrenheit)   *Summer*   *Winter*   *Autumn/Spring*
       Day-time
       Night-time
       Hottest period of the year: Begins .... Ends ....

1.2   *Rainfall*
       Inches per year ....
       Rainy season: Begins .... Ends ....

1.3   *Company location is* .... feet above sea-level

1.4   *Population:*   Country .... Company location ....

1.5   *Language* ....
                 ....
                 ....
                 ....

1.6   *Government*
       Majority/ruling party   ....
       Political persuasion   ....

1.7   *Industry:*
       Major industry: 1 .... 2 .... 3 ....
       Percentage GNP   ....

1.8   *Comments*
       ....

2   HOUSING AND PUBLIC UTILITIES

2.1   *Cost of middle-income housing*   *Minimum*   *Average*   *Maximum*
       (month)
       2-room apartment
       3-room apartment

Exhibit 14 (cont.)

    4-room apartment
    5-room house
    6-room house
    Deposit payable
    Agency fees

2.2   *Availability of middle-income housing*
        Easy to find   ....
        Possible but difficult   ....
        Month's waiting list   ....

2.3   *Quality of middle-income housing*   *Minimum*   *Average*   *Maximum*
        Size of drawing-room
        Size of bedrooms
        Size of closets
        Size of garage

        Housing usually includes (yes/no)   *Furnished*   *Unfurnished*   *Import*
        (or should be imported)
        Gas/electric stove
        Refrigerator
        Running water
        Telephone
        Electrical fixtures
        Fitted carpets
        Air conditioning
        Central heating
        Hot-water heater
        Plumbing

2.4   *Availability of electricity and water*   *Electricity*   *Water*
        Dependable 24 hours daily
        During specific hours each day
        May be withdrawn at any time for
          undetermined period

2.5   *Electrical apparatus*   Cycle ....   Volts ....
        Foreign appliances adjustable   Yes ....   No ....
          locally   Yes ....   No ....
        Foreign appliances usable with   Type ....
          transformer

2.6   *Sanitation standards*
        Tap water safe to drink   Yes ....   No ....
        Bottled water readily available   Yes ....   No ....

2.7   *Comments:*

....

3 APPLIANCES, FURNITURE AND HOUSEHOLD EQUIPMENT

3.1 *Availability and average cost* ($)   *Quality*   *Availability*   *Imported*   *Local*

Washing-machine
Clothes-dryer
Refrigerator
Cooking-stove
Freezer
Air conditioning
Spare parts
Transformers
Conversions
Plugs
Adapters
Sockets
Service
Furniture
....
....
....
....
Steam-iron
Electric frying-pan
Toaster
Vacuum-cleaner
Mixer
Blender
Hair-dryer
Radio
TV
Record-player
Kitchen equipment
....
....
....
China
....
....
Glassware
....
....

Where items are not available locally, expatriates should import their own
possessions.

3.2 *Comments:*
....

Exhibit 14 (cont.)

4 FOOD AND SUNDRIES

4.1 *Type of stores usually used by expatriates:*
Supermarkets   ....
Small grocery stores   ....
Open street-markets   ....
Discount stores   ....

....

4.2 *Availability/cost*   *Quality   Availability   Cost*
US food brands
Frozen foods
Canned foods
Fresh meat
Fresh vegetables
Fresh dairy products

Note. Cost as x times more or less expensive than similar class of food in US

4.3 *Local average prices* (\$)	*Unit*	*Cost*
Bread	large loaf	
Milk	pint	
Butter	1 lb	
Eggs	1 doz	
Rice	1 lb	
Coffee	1 lb	
Tea	1 lb	
Beef steak	1 lb	
Pork chops	1 lb	
Shoulder of lamb	1 lb	
Veal scallops	1 lb	
Carrots	1 lb	
Onions	1 lb	
Cabbage	1 lb	
Cauliflower	1 lb	
Bananas	1 lb	
Apples	1 lb	
Oranges	1 lb	
Grapes	1 lb	
Whisky	large bottle	
Gin	large bottle	
Soda drinks	small bottle	
Cigarettes	20	
Tobacco	8 oz	
Paper tissues	4 oz	
Talcum powder	250 g	
Soap	bath-size	
Toothpaste	large	
Washing-up liquid	250 g	

Exhibit 14 (cont.)

Furniture polish	250 g
Washing powder	500 g
Scouring powder	250 g

....

....

....

....

Newspapers, local
Newspapers, foreign

4.4 *Popular local foods*

....

....

....

....

4.5 *Comments:*

....

5 TRANSPORT

5.1 *Quality of transportation*	*Yes*	*No*
Railroads connect major cities		
Highways connect major cities		
Highways passable all year		
Bus, subway or taxi system is good		
European/US cars available locally		

5.2 *Necessity of transport*

Car is luxury	....
Necessary for business/pleasure	....
Absolutely necessary	....

5.3 *Availability of automobiles locally*	*Size*	*Price*	*Insurance*
....			
....			
....			

5.4 *Home-country automobiles,*

Shipping costs	....
Import duties	....
Licensing	....
Insurance	....
Required adaptations	....
Cost and quality of gasoline	....
Service cost and availability	....

Resale value	....
Home-country tax rebates on new cars	....
Minimum driving age	....
Driver's licence (local/international)	....

5.5 *Comments:*

....

6 DOMESTIC HELP

6.1 *Need and availability*   Yes   No

Luxury
Useful sometimes
Absolutely necessary
Readily available
Certain help available
Hard to find

6.2 *Cost* ($) *and conditions*   Number   Cost   *Live-in*   *Part-time*

Occasional cleaner
Maid
Cook
Gardener
Driver

6.3 *Comments:*

....

7 COMMUNITY SERVICES

7.1 *Availability and cost*   Yes   No   Low   Medium   High   Quality

Laundry
Laundromat
Barber
Hairdresser/beautician
Shoemaker
Dressmaker
Tailor
Plumbers
Electricians
Furniture repairers
Decorators
Restaurants
French
Italian

Exhibit 14 (cont.)

German
Spanish
International
Chinese
Indian
....
....

7.2 *Services not available*
      1. ....
      2. ....
      3. ....
      4. ....

7.3 *Comments*
      ....

8 MEDICAL FACILITIES

8.1 *Availability and quality (by US standards)*   *Availability*   *Quality*
      Hospital
      Maternity hospital
      Specialist doctors
      General practitioners
      Dentists
      Oculists
      ....
      ....
      Prescription drugs
      Patent medicines
      Facility to fill US prescriptions

8.2 *Comments:*
      ....

9 RECREATIONAL AND SOCIAL ACTIVITIES

			Cost:	
9.1 *Public recreational activity* ·	*Availability*		*1 person*	*2 persons*
Golf				
Tennis				
Basketball				
Soccer/football				
Rugby				
Baseball				
Skiing				

Exhibit 14 (cont.)

Swimming
Fishing
Hunting
Boating
Camping
Bowling
Riding
English-language films
Foreign films

		Cost:	*Cost:*	
9.2	*Private recreational activity*	*Availability*	*1 person*	*2 persons Family*
	Club			
	(facilities ....)			
	Club			
	(facilities ....)			
	Club			
	(facilities ....)			

			Size of	*Type of*
9.3	*Radio and television*	*Availability*	*set*	*set*
	English-language radio programmes			
	Television			

9.4	*Nearby recreational areas*	*Place*	*Distance from location*
	Weekend		
	Longer vacations		

9.5 *Churches in company location*
   1. ....
   2. ....
   3. ....
   4. ....

9.6 *Comments:*
....

10   EDUCATIONAL SERVICES

				Curriculum	
10.1	*Availability and quality*	*Availability*	*Adequacy*	*accreditation*	*Costs*
	English-language schools				
	Local state schools				

Exhibit 14 (cont.)

       Tuition schools (local)
       Tuition schools
        (countrywide)
       Language tutors

10.2 *General information*
       School-term dates   ....
       Enrolment requirements   ....
       Uniforms   ....
       Local transport   ....
       Grading system (class, age) ....
       Extracurricular activities   ....

10.3 *Comments:*
....

11   CLOTHING

11.1 *Clothing needs*   *Number of months*
       Winter clothes necessary
       Summer clothes necessary
       Changes for night/day

Men	*Unnecessary*	*Quite necessary*	*Very necessary*	*Bring from home*	*Do not bring from home*
Winter business suit					
Summer business suit					
Overcoat					
Raincoat					
Black tuxedo					
White evening jacket					
Dress suit					
Sports coats					
Sport shirts					
Sweaters					
Dress slacks					
Casual slacks					
Shoes: white/two tone					
Shoes: black/brown					
Shoes: casual					
Women					
Summer suits					
Summer dresses					
Winter suits					
Winter dresses					

Summer coat
Winter coat: fur
Winter coat: wool
Raincoat
Formal gown: short
Formal gown: long
Slacks
Shorts
Blouses
Sweaters
Skirts
Shoes
Winter shoes
Summer shoes

11.2 *Comments:*
Children's clothes ....

12 BANKING SERVICES AND RESTRICTIONS

12.1 *Banking services*
Company's local bank   ....
Foreign banks   1. ....
                          2. ....
                          3. ....
                          4. ....
                          5. ....

12.2 *Currency transfers and conversions*
Restrictions   ....
Method   ....
Exchange costs   ....

12.3 *Comments:*
....

13 IMPORT REGULATIONS

13.1 *Pets*
Entry requirements   ....
Quarantine requirements   ....

Firearms
Entry duties   ....

Exhibit 15

FOREIGN ASSIGNMENT CHECKLIST PROCEDURES FOR TRANSFER

ASSIGNMENT COUNTRY..
                      COMPANY LOCATION ....

EMPLOYEE.............................

This list outlines common pretransfer procedures for completion on acceptance of
offer.

Check who is responsible for the completed action and the deadline.

Items for action	Responsibility (individual)	Responsibility (company)	Deadline
1 EMPLOYMENT LETTER			
Formalization			
Dispatch			
Acceptance			
2 LEGAL DOCUMENTS			
Passport			
Residence visa(s)			
Entry visa(s)			
Certificate of health			
Re-entry permit(s)			
Work permit(s)			
Police certificate			
Birth certificate			
Will			
Driver's licenses:			
Domestic			
International			
Translation (if necessary)			
Power of attorney			
Household inventory certificate			
3 REMOVALS AND SHIPPING			
Selection of packer			
Selection of mover			
Insurance:			
Inventory			
Appraisal			

Items for action	Responsibility (individual)	Responsibility (company)	Deadline

Removal
Packing
Shipping
Automobile:
    Purchase
    Shipping
    Foreign-insurance coverage
    Import documents

4   FOREIGN ASSIGNMENT ORIENTATION

Briefing on living conditions
Special courses:
    Enrolment
    Completion
Language training:
    Enrolment
    Completion
Interviews with other executives for:
    Broader assignment understanding
    Insight into different culture
Reading lists and materials:
    Provision
    Implementation and completion
Dependents' education:
    School enrolment
    Arrangements for payment

5   BRIEFING ON COMPENSATION ARRANGEMENTS

Assignment conditions and procedures:
    Base salary
    Position allowance
    Foreign-service premium
    Cost-of-living allowance
    Housing allowance
    Tax equalization
    Education allowance
Salary payment arrangements
Banking arrangements
Employee benefits:
    Automobile allowance

Exhibit 15 (cont.)

Items for action	Responsibility (individual)	Responsibility (company)	Deadline
Club membership			
Home leave			
Local vacations			
Employee loans			
Provision of forms:			
Social security			
Company benefits			
Company assistance:			
Provision of equipment abroad			
Purchase of additional equipment			
Disposal of house			
Termination of lease			
Signing of overseas lease			

6 MEDICAL REQUIREMENTS

Physical examination
Vaccination and immunisation:
    Smallpox
    Cholera
    Typhoid
    Typhus
    Yellow fever
    Tetanus
    Bubonic plague

7 NON-LEGAL DOCUMENTS

Letters of credit
Business cards
Letters of reference
Emergency identification procedures
Notices of changes of address

8 TRAVEL ARRANGEMENTS

Itinerary
Type of accommodation
Reservations
Instructions on:
    Stopovers
    Excess baggage

Exhibit 15 (cont.)

Items for action	Responsibility (individual)	Responsibility (company)	Deadline
Miscellaneous expenses			
Insurance claims on damages or losses			
Credit cards:			
Air travel			
Hertz			
Avis			
American Express			
Diner's Club			
Insurance cards			
Travel expenses			
Cash			
Travel cheques			

9 OTHER

Exhibit 16

SPECIMEN LETTER OF ASSIGNMENT TO THIRD-COUNTRY NATIONAL EMPLOYEE

2 January 1975

STRICTLY CONFIDENTIAL

TO: Mr J. L. David
Works manager, Omega France
FROM: J. F. Ortega

In regard to your future assignment in Colombia, as managing director reporting to me, I am pleased to confirm to you the terms and conditions of your transfer, effective 1 April 1975. The conditions of your transfer will be the following:

1 Status

Your status will be that of an international employee on indefinite transfer with France as your base country.

Exhibit 16 (cont.)

2   Base salary

Your annual base salary will be: 297 000 pesos, paid in Colombia, and
91 797 French francs, paid in France.

3   Incentive compensation

You will be eligible for participation in the subsidiary bonus plan, on the
basis of your overall performance in Colombia, and the profitability of the
subsidiary company.

4   Adaptation allowance

You will receive an adaptation allowance which will be paid in Colombia.
This allowance consists of:

A transfer allowance of 130 100 pesos. This allowance takes into
consideration the cost-of-living difference between Bogota and Paris, and
the required change in life style.

A housing allowance, calculated on the following basis: The company will
pay 90 per cent of the difference between 15 per cent of your present base
annual salary and whatever will be determined in accordance with your
regional manager as to what constitutes reasonable housing costs in the
Bogota area.

A tax equalization allowance if the net tax rate is higher in Colombia than
in France, including the impact of *allocation familiales.*

The company will reimburse the difference between taxes in Colombia,
computed on the basis of salary plus bonus, and the taxes you would pay
in France.
  The adaptation allowance will remain constant for a period of three
years. After the third year, it will decrease by 20 per cent each year, but
the annual reduction will not exceed the amount of your annual salary
increase.

5 Expenses

The company will pay you and reimburse the following items. All payments mentioned in this paragraph are subject to tax regulations when not substantiated by receipts:

Tuition expenses. Tuition costs will be paid by the company for each of your children attending primary or secondary schools in Colombia.

Moving expenses. The company will reimburse the cost of moving a reasonable amount of your furniture and personal belongings and travel expenses for you and your family.

Temporary living expenses. For up to a maximum of four weeks, the company will reimburse the cost of hotel accommodation and living expenses on a reasonable basis for you and your family, while you are locating a permanent residence.

Relocation expenses. The amount of 55 468 pesos will be paid to cover miscellaneous expenses related to your relocation (such as appliances, curtains, etc.).

Home leave. After 12 months, the company will reimburse you, once a year, the cost of round-trip tickets, economy class, from Colombia to France, for you and your family.

6 Social benefits

You will continue to maintain the Omega France fringe benefits with the employee's portion being paid directly by you.

7 Vacation

You are entitled to an annual vacation corresponding to 20 working days.

8 Individual tax liability

According to the company policy, it is the responsibility of the individual to declare his income to the tax authorities of all countries involved, in accordance with the applicable laws and regulations. The company assumes no responsibility for an individual's tax liability.

Please confirm your acceptance of this offer, in writing, by signing below, so that we may arrange for a smooth transition into the Colombian company; retain a copy of this agreement for your records.

J. F. Ortega

cc: International director of human resources
Vice-president European region

Accepted   ....

Date   ....

SPECIMEN LETTERS RE MEDICAL AND DISABILITY PLANS

Exhibit 17a

MEDICAL UMBRELLA PLAN

Date ....

To: Mr ....

During your assignment in .... starting ....
you will be entitled to the benefits of the Medical umbrella plan of Omega.

1   This plan gives you the right to the same reimbursements as those
    provided by the Omega US medical plan (see booklet attached).
2   Reimbursements will be made after deducting any amount that may
    be paid to you from social security or any other plan in any country
    (except from private insurance plans subscribed by you only).
3   Payments will usually be made in your assigned country and in that
    currency. In exceptional cases, the company may authorize payments
    in another country or currency.
4   The entire cost of this plan will be paid by the company and *no*
    contributions will be required from you.
5   To obtain reimbursement, you will have to send documentation to the
    compensation department in New York through your assigned country.
    Enrolment cards and detailed instructions will be sent to you directly
    by this department.
    The amount to be paid to you under this medical umbrella plan will
    be computed by New York and the instructions to pay you these
    amounts will be forwarded by New York to your assigned country
    company, with a copy to you.
6   Your participation in the medical umbrella plan will cease to apply
    upon the end of your assignment in ....

Exhibit 17a (cont.)

7   The plans will be administered by Omega and all disputes and
    differences involving this plan will be decided by the company in its
    sole discretion.

                              Signed by an officer of Omega ....

cc: Compensation dept., New York
      Omega International
      Regional headquarters
      Assigned-country company

Exhibit 17b

DISABILITY, DEATH AND RETIREMENT UMBRELLA PLAN

Date ....

To: Mr ....

As a consequence of your transfer, you will be entitled to the benefits of the disability, death and retirement umbrella plan of Omega as of .... In case of disability, death and retirement, you will be granted *plan benefits at least equal to those provided* in .... , referred to as your 'designated country'. The provisions of this plan are as follows:

1 *Omega promises to pay* any lump sum or periodic remittance equal to the difference between:
   (a) What you can or could reasonably collect from all mandatory and nonmandatory plans in any country in which you have worked during your career with Omega. This includes any indemnity you may have been paid at the time of transfers.
   and
   (b) What you or your beneficiaries would have received in your 'designated country' had you remained there during your entire career with Omega at the salary levels that you have actually been paid.

   The rights to indemnity or pension will be computed by applying the rules of your designated country to the basic salary earned during your Omega career, excluding all other remuneration.

2 Benefit payments will always be expressed in the currency of your designated country and will normally be paid in that country. If you or your beneficiaries desire to be paid in another country, Omega will investigate that possibility at the time payments are to be made.

3 You will not contribute to the disability, death and retirement umbrella plan unless the rate of your personal contributions actually made in both your designated country and your country of assignment is less than the rate you would have paid in the designated country had you not been transferred. If there is a difference, your adaptation allowance will be reduced by the corresponding amount.

Exhibit 17b (cont.)

4 In case employment is terminated prior to normal retirement, because
   of early retirement, resignation, dismissal, death or disability, the
   benefits will be calculated according to the provisions for disability,
   death and retirement benefits (excluding severance) of the designated
   country at the time of termination.

5 The plans will be administered by Omega and all disputed and
   differences involving this plan will be decided by the company in its
   sole discretion.

Signed by an officer of Omega ....

cc: Compensation Dept., New York
     Omega International
     Regional headquarters
     Assigned-country company

Index

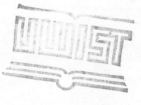